»Never Surrender
(Or Nearly Good Looking)«

An Autobiography
by Biff Byford and John Tucker

I.P. Verlag Jeske/Mader GbR
Haydnstr. 2
12203 Berlin
Germany

February 2014, second edition
ISBN 978-3-931624-44-6
Copyright © Biff Byford and John Tucker 2007

Photo Credits:
All Photos Saxon Archive, except page 90, 91 Rainer Krukenberg;
page 180, 181 Tobias Thiem; page 183 John Tucker
Cover Photo: ICS/Stefan Malzkorn
Cover Layout: Kai Swillus

Dedicated to Sue, Stephanie, Sebastian, Thomas and Alexander, for their love and support, and to the fans, who've kept the dream alive…

Contents

Part One:
Hungry Years

Chapter One

I can't remember now at what point I wanted to be a musician, to sacrifice everything for music. There was no defining moment, no epiphany, and no role model either. Where I came from you either worked in the coal mines or the textiles industry; being a musician was not an option, really. You left school, got a job, got married, had kids, retired and died. Life was pretty much pre-planned from conception to grave, if you let it.

My father worked in the coal mines when he was younger. He had an accident there, I think, and hurt his back, so he moved out of the coal mines into the textiles industry. Funnily enough, like him, I also ended up working in them both in the days before Saxon. Like father, like son, eh?

I was actually born in a place called Honley, which is in West Yorkshire. A lot of people think I was born around Barnsley but that's just one of those inaccuracies that take root over time. I was born in West Yorkshire, in the foothills of the Pennines – well, the Dales and the Pennines, where they meet. Just a small town really, and I think we moved from there when I was still very young as I can't remember much of the place at all, just vague memories, shadows, of people and places in that area. We Byfords moved to a place called Skelmanthorpe which is close to a place called Denby Dale which is close to a place called... And so on. It's all in that Home Firth area of Yorkshire. We moved there after my father got the job in textiles and so most of my childhood was spent in Skelmanthorpe. I had great times really. Countryside, school friends making tree camps or rafting on the river, just general country things that you did. I mean, in those days, it must have been 1955 or so, you made your own fun. We obviously didn't have a car; my uncle did, and that was considered to be extremely posh back then, and he'd take us out every Sunday for a drive. As we didn't have a car we had to go everywhere by bus or train. I suppose the nearest big city to where we lived would be Huddersfield.

I was a child of the Fifties: Peter Rodney Byford, the only child of Earnest Charles – two good traditional English names there – and Irene Byford. Am I a typical Capricorn? Ask Lemmy. If he is, then I am.

I have absolutely no idea how my mother and father met. He probably seduced her, or maybe it was the other way round! They'd both been married before and I think maybe my mum's husband died, although I can't remember exact details now. I never knew any of my grandparents, as they'd died before I was born. I saw pictures of them of course, the usual sort of 1900s photographs, all faded and sepia, but I must have been quite a late child for my parents. They'd already had children before; I have a half-sister who was my father's daughter, Enid, and a half-brother who was my mum's son called Michael. Me and Michael lived together with my mum and dad but Enid had already moved out years ago. I think they're all still alive – my sister Enid definitely is – and I presume Michael's alive as well. But he left fairly early on as well, from what I can recall. I don't think my dad was very nice to him so he left.

We lived in a big stone weaver's house, as they called them back then. There was an attic and that's where I used to play music and generally get it together in the Sixties, which is when I started to become aware of music. It was all The Beatles and pop music and stuff by that time as I was too young to be into the really early rock 'n' roll thing. My brother was a Teddy Boy but I was too young to be into that really; back in the Fifties and Sixties you really didn't start to be allowed to do anything on your own till you were sixteen or seventeen. That's kind of when you started to become a teenager then, at sixteen or seventeen, not twelve or thirteen as it is now.

I only have good memories of my early childhood really. Mostly playing on my own, with a model railway and soldiers and things; the sort of things you had back then. But mostly good times – up until my mother died when things obviously took a bit of a dive. It affected me quite badly, and I think in the longer term one of the effects is that I like to have a family around me; I like to have a stable relationship and although I haven't had many of them, to be honest, it's something I have always striven for. I think I always want security; I think that's one of the legacies of my mother dying. Virtually all of my friends on the road have actually been women. I have spent half my life touring and I can probably count on one hand the number of male friends that I've made over the years. They're almost all women. If someone asked me, 'who or what is the greatest love of your life?', the answer would probably be music and women, which may sound a bit flippant but I have spent most of my life with those two. When we were touring, as I've said, I often spent very little time with the band; most of it was spent with girls, actually. And given the choice, wouldn't you? So maybe that's connected in some way to my mother's death too, some kind of over-compensation for losing my mother at an early age. I think it did make me a survivor though. I have always been able to organise myself, and other people too. But that said, the sad parts of life, losing people who are close to you, is something I find very hard to deal with.

This was all still the post-war period, and although I can't re-member rationing and conscription to the army and stuff like that, it was still going on at that time. In fact I can't remember much of the Fifties at all. What I can remember is living in a very rural place with the steam trains running through the valley not far from the house and very nostalgic and romantic images of people working on hay bales in the fields, and my uncle's car. It was a Vauxhall Wyvern, and I thought it was the most fantastic car I'd ever seen in my life. It was based on the lines of the classic American car but smaller. And I remember staying with my auntie and uncle later on when my father had his arm torn off; my cousin was about the same age as me so we were absolute rogues together. These are the good memories really, and although there were some tragic times there were good times too.

I also remember we used to holiday in Teignmouth in Devon, when I was young, with my mum and dad. They used to do a mill trip. It was absolutely fantastic. The whole mill had their two weeks' holidays and we used to go to the train station where there were two huge steam trains with thousands of carriages and we'd jump on and they'd give us a bag with an orange and an apple and a bag of crisps and we'd all sit in our compartment and next stop, Devon. Back in the Fifties, don't forget, going from Yorkshire to Devon was almost like going to the Moon. And then we'd go to our digs. I had such great memories, the red cliffs, there was a model railway exhibition on the front, I think... I just remember so many happy, sunny summer days with my brother on the beach. That was our big holiday place, Devon.

All-in-all, I would say I had a pretty happy childhood, until my mother died. I must have been about eleven when it happened. It was basically a thrombosis, and it was all so sudden. I was talking to her one day and she was dead the next: it really was as quick as that. And that totally wrecked me for quite a long time. My family considered me to be in too much of a state to go to the funeral so I actually stayed with my auntie and uncle for quite a long time. Back in those days, no-one understood grief, and there was no such thing as counselling – certainly not in working-class Yorkshire. You were just meant to get on with it. No-one seemed to realise how I felt, or what I was going through. I can remember crying every night for a month, maybe more, and it still bothers me that I wasn't allowed to go to her funeral; it's a major bone of contention to this day.

Afterwards I was sent to live with my auntie and uncle for a while and they weren't particularly sympathetic. It was all very 'stiff upper lip' and keeping up appearances, and you certainly weren't allowed to be seen to cry. I was just a kid, and I was struggling. They were nice enough people; they were my uncle – my father's brother – and auntie, so obviously to me they were nice people; they were family after all. But they weren't very loving, a tendency they shared with my father (so this must have been something from my father's side of the family, from my grandfather on my father's side). They just weren't a family to show much affection. With my children, we're all very much sort of 'love you' and kissing and hugging. This is something I never had from my father when I was a kid, but I don't think boys should be treated any differently from girls when they're young; I think they should be shown as much love and affection in that way as you'd show to girls, if you see what I mean.

So I was sent to stay with my auntie and uncle. These were the ones who had the car, so they were fairly up-market compared to how we lived. Theirs was a detached house with a car and drive, and I had to have a bath every night at 8 o'clock which was a pain in the arse! An absolute pain in the arse! My cousin, their daughter, was to them the most perfect being on the planet and on the other hand there was me: the scum of the earth from down the road. Filthy, unwashed... And, well, on top of my mum's death it was a strange period in my life. They were nice people, don't get me wrong, but they didn't have any boys in their family and probably didn't understand boys, so I was the male urchin that needed to be scrubbed clean every night without exception.

I had been extremely close to my mother. She was a musician, she played piano, she played organ in the Methodist church, and she played piano accordion. I can remember travelling with my mum to see her side of the family and they all had pianos in their houses and wherever we were, it always seemed like she ended up playing piano all night. They're happy memories of my mum. I was only with her for a short time really so it was very sad, but from what I can remember of her she was fantastic, and we were very close, but she just... went. In those days, life expectancy wasn't that great anyway. Things like tuberculosis and pneumonia were quite common; there was no central heating and she worked in the textile mills where the conditions weren't that good at all. The thing about the 'good old days' is that they were actually shit, really.

About two years later my father had his arm ripped off in a factory accident, and so while he was in hospital – I have no idea how long he was in there, but to me it seemed like forever – I was back living with my auntie and uncle. My father wasn't very... Well, let's say I went from my mother who was very loving to my father who wasn't a very touchy-feely loving type at all. He was the archetypal solid Yorkshireman. He was a nice man, don't get me wrong. I loved my father dearly and he did buy me my first bass guitar (which set me either on the road to fame and fortune or into the downward cycle of heavy metal and debauchery, depending on your point of view), but, all of a sudden, I was a kid of thirteen or so and had to look after him.

Both Enid and Michael had gone by that time. They were that much older than me and had left home, and they didn't really help at all; in fact, I don't recall ever seeing them in that period. It was a quite traumatic time, but I just had to get on with it really. I remember my father coming out of the hospital and it wasn't a fantastic re-union. It was like 'have you been good?' rather than 'I missed you'. Quite strange really: I guess that summed up our relationship at that time. So my next few years were largely spent cooking, cleaning and tidying up for my dad until he learned to use his one arm more fully. And as I said, you have to remember that in the Fifties and the Sixties, things were very different to what they are today. Back then, twelve, thirteen years old was still very, very young. Kids today mature much quicker, but at twelve or thirteen I was still just a boy in those days. All my friends would be out playing and I would have to stay in and basically care for my dad. As I got older though I started going to discos and listened to stuff like Ike and Tina Turner and was finally able to do the stuff that boys of my age did. I think I began to make up for lost time, as I turned into a bit of a rocker at an early age, getting into motorcycles, so my early teens were spent riding motorcycles around. My father bought me my first motorbike which was pretty cool, although in a vain attempt to impress some local girls I showed off on it, doing handstands: the front wheel flipped out and I fell face first onto the handlebars, smashing in my teeth and jaw and earning me a stay in hospital. That must have been pretty traumatic for my audience, and, unsurprisingly, it didn't do a lot for me, either.

At the turn of the Sixties, I do remember seeing The Beatles on TV doing "Please Please Me". The music I was into in my early teens though was The Kinks – not so much The Beatles because although I did like their melodies I couldn't stand their haircuts – the Rolling Stones, The Pretty Things; all the rebellious rock guitar-orientated stuff. I loved "You Really Got Me"; a classic song based on a classic guitar riff: that's the sort of stuff I was in to when I was a teenager. I remember we had an old Dansette record player at home, which I worked to death. Also, at that time if you went into Woolworths on the High Street, you could buy songs that were basically cover versions on their own Embassy label; you could buy a record by, say, The Kinks, but it wasn't The Kinks, it was Woolworths' house band who played it. A bit like the »Top Of The Pops« records that were popular in the early Seventies – cheap albums with the label's session musicians recording ten or twelve Top Ten hits. It was really odd to be honest, but it was a cheap way of getting records. Another thing at that time was that most of the shops had listening booths; I remember going into record shops in the Sixties and going into the listening booths to listen to the latest releases. And I absolutely loved it; it was great fun. Never bought jack shit of course. But Saturday afternoons were always made up of going into Huddersfield and sitting in these booths and listening to all the singles that had been released that week.

Aside from pop music, my first real musical awareness was my mother playing piano. That was all hymns like "Oh Come All Ye Faithful" and stuff like that. My mother was a Methodist and, consequently, I regularly attended Methodist Sunday School. They used to have guest preachers, evangelists and such like, who'd come in Sunday afternoon, and of course I had to be there because my mum played the organ. So they'd come in and say, 'Jesus lives in the light', and they'd draw big suns on the chalk board and ask, 'who's been saved this week?' My mate Mick would jump up every week – because it would invariably be a different preacher – and shout out, 'me, sir' and the preacher would ask where and Mick would reply, 'in the Co-op; I saw the light in the Co-op,' and then he'd get a sweet. Now I never did this because I was so shy; I was always thinking, 'OK, I'm going to say it this week' but of course I never did and so everybody else was saved apart from me. I never saw the light because I was too shy, whereas everybody else saw the light every week, and got a sweet as a result!

So that was my early indoctrination into both the Methodist church and also the Church of England. It was quite normal because most Yorkshire villages have a strong Methodist tradition; it's the same in Lincolnshire too, come to that. But the Methodist religion is not over-stuffy though and I suppose it's a bit middle-class really, although we were never middle class. Most of the people there were do-gooders. I didn't dislike it and, besides, when I went to school if you went to church for assembly it lasted thirty minutes longer than if you were atheist, which meant that if you went to church you got off some classes because it all took half-an-hour longer. So that's how I got the Church of England indoctrination as well. I'm not into organised religion, but I am quite religious in a sort of spiritual way. I'm not a Jesus freak, as a lot of Methodists turn into. And besides, when my mum died it all stopped anyway; there's nothing like losing a parent at an early age to make you question religion.

Chapter Two

A s a child I was very shy. Incredibly shy really. I mean really, absolutely, totally shy. At school I would never do anything to bring any attention to myself. A lot of people don't realise or understand what it's like to be painfully shy, but it is a really, really terrible thing. You blush as soon as anybody says anything to you. You don't want to be noticed. I was a really shy person as a young boy and I had to overcome it, basically. I think this happened when I was about fourteen years old or so when I was looking after my father because I had to sort of get my act together then and I finally came out of myself. When a teenager has to look after a parent it's quite a big responsibility and you can't be shy then; I mean, I just didn't have the time! And also I was surrounded by people that were confrontational. I mean, a school situation is highly volatile for a shy person, it really is, and I just think self-confidence is what I lacked really. If you have that thing about you where you colour up in a situation, you can't get rid of it and the more you try, the worse it becomes. There's nothing you can do about it; I just had to get over it.

In some instances I still can be shy now. I still don't like crowds, which I know sounds weird for the singer of a band. But if there's a room full of strangers, then I'll probably either not go in or get out as quickly as I can because that's one of those situations that I don't feel comfortable in. I can play in front of hundreds of thousands of people, but that's different. It's an introvert/extrovert 'two sides of a coin' thing. But I don't really like being with groups of strange people and, to be honest, I generally don't like strangers. I'm much happier being with whom or what I know. People often ask, 'why did you stay with that record company if they were so crap?' It's because I don't like change. I like things to stay the same. I like consistency. I like everything to work. Loyalty and friendship are very important to me. And when something works, or appears to work, I don't like changing it. It's almost like a fear of the unknown. This could come back to the loss of my mum, I think, this fact that I don't like change.

The school that I went to was literally just over our back garden. The school grounds backed on to our house so I could get up as late as I possibly could and just jump over the wall. It was great. Well, that much of it was. My school days were very strange. I was always somewhere else in my head and as a consequence in my primary school I was bottom of my class every year, I think. They were big on rugby, because in Yorkshire rugby, well, rugby and cricket are the only sports to be into. I guess really that's why I'm not so much of a football fan because where I lived the local team would probably be Huddersfield or maybe Leeds, so not overly local, and the indoctrination I had at school was rugby. I don't think we even played football at school; in the early years when most kids are kicking a ball around we were playing cricket and rugby because that's what our school was into. The headmaster was a total rugby freak and, being a big burly bloke, he just liked seeing us lads scrumming down, and getting covered in mud, filthy and sweaty. The playing field was about a mile away and we used to have to trudge up there in winter in the snow in our shorts and in our boots – big leather boots; no lightweight plastic then – freezing our bollocks off, walking up this country lane to the rugby field, playing rugby in the mud and the squalor and then walking all the way back again. It was absolutely freezing; torture, really, but you had to do it. I wasn't any good as a player, though. I was too tall, and kids would go through my legs all the time. I know there are tall rugby players, but also, I never had the muscles, never really had the physique for it when I was younger.

That was Skelmanthorpe Primary School I went to, then I went to a secondary school at Scissett which is quite close to Denby Dale. My brother had been to that secondary school and he was known as a bit of a lad; he was also like six-foot-seven or so, so as soon as I got there I was known as his younger brother. But unfortunately when I got there he had just left so I got all the aggro arising from the 'family reputation' without any physical assistance. 'Oh, you're Mick's younger brother, are you?' – bang! Just across the road was a Borstal, a young offenders' institute full of hard cases, so we used to get all those kids coming over as well so it could be a fairly dodgy place at times. In general though, it wasn't that bad; it was a nice school actually, so long as you were careful. Like any school there were some pretty nasty characters there, and one wrong word or glance and you'd get thrown into the hawthorn hedge or the pond. It's where I really got turned on to music though because the music teacher was fantastic, and the funny thing is that at the end of the first year I was top of the class; so either it was a very good school or I made some kind of connection. I certainly made an impact on the first day. I was all young and happy and running down the corridor and some evil bastard tripped me up and I went skidding down this highly polished floor, knocking this woman off her feet. Unfortunately she turned out to be the deputy headmistress, and sent me for the cane. And this is my first day! 'Go to the headmaster's office and tell him you want the cane.'

So on the first day I was famous; I got three on each hand. It was just like all the stories I'd heard. There was something like a gun rack in the Headmaster's office with fourteen or so canes, each of different twanginess. As it was my first day and because I was a young lad he picked one out for me rather than asking me to choose one for myself. And boy, did it hurt! The next lesson was English, and I kept dropping my pen; I couldn't hold it properly because my hands hurt so much. (And of course it was a real ink pen in those days with an ink well and a proper nib.) So it's fair to say that I'm never likely to forget my first day at senior school in a hurry. Aside from that though, I began to do quite well. I really excelled at History and Geography; Music and Science I liked, and Engineering too – there was an Engineering class and I was good at that. I was crap at Maths, but overall I was pretty good actually. I figured that there was nothing else to do, so I might as well take notice of what the teachers were saying.

The big thing in those days was who got the first pubic hairs, and who got the first moustache. That was the standard by which everything else was measured. Of course, there was some big strapping kid with jet black hair who had the first moustache and a dick with masses of pubic hair all over it. Talk about making the rest of us feel inferior: we all looked to be about twelve – which I guess we were – and he looked about thirty-six. There's always one in every class that comes on really young. If you misbehaved during lessons, they used to make you stand on a chair, and as it was a mixed school his big party trick was to have a stiffy on when he was told to stand on his chair.

There was a lot of kissing and fondling in the bike sheds, but I was a bit late in that respect. I was still quite shy when I started at that school. This was the Sixties though and things were beginning to hot up a bit. I was still quite shy but not as shy as I had been; things were getting better in that respect. I was also getting much better at avoiding the sorts of situations that I feared. Besides, I wasn't too shy with other children; if somebody came up of my own age I was pretty much all right. (Like most boys of my age I was shy with girls obviously at that time, but that's different.) My problem mainly arose in situations of authority where somebody was singling me out; that sort of shyness. I was OK with other children and I had a lot of friends there; it wasn't as if I was stuck in a bubble or something. As a first-year everyone older than you pushed you around – you know, having snowballs flung at you with stones in them, and other stuff like that – but that's just part of being at school.

As I mentioned, the music teacher at that school was pretty cool. What he used to bring in was mostly classical music, but he would also bring in electric guitars and things, probably Vox guitars, and in that way he really inspired his pupils to love music. Actually, to love melody; that was his thing. He would bring in pianists and tenors for us to listen to, and I found it truly inspirational. Around that time I made friends with a family called the O'Melias whom my brother knew. I became friends with Robert, I think his name was, and his brother Chris was a guitarist. I used to go to their house and he'd always pick up his guitar. My brother was there too, although he wasn't musical at all; wasn't into music at all really, as far as I was aware. But Chris was though; very much so. For the first time, I heard a Fender Stratocaster being played through a Vox AC30 and I was fascinated by the sound.

Right about the same time, somebody moved into the house across the street from us and he played banjo; he was quite a good banjo player, in fact, and he taught me how to play bass guitar because they're the same tuning. So between the O'Melias and this guy across the road I learned to play something called "Hang On Sloopy" by The McCoys. It's just a three-chord thing but it was their first single and made the UK Top 5 in 1965, and that was the first thing I ever learned to play: another early favourite was "You Really Got Me" because it's so easy. Later on, I joined a band with this O'Melia guy, the first band I was ever in. I wasn't allowed to join unless I learned to play the flute, because the Jethro Tull thing was happening then. So I learned to play the flute, not to any classical standard, but I did learn to play the thing. It took me absolutely bloody ages though. When you learn to play the flute you have to learn to play the mouthpiece first without the barrel so you have to learn to play a note – the low note, middle note and high note – just by blowing across the hole in the mouthpiece. It's really hard, believe me! Only when you've done that are you allowed to put the other end on. I was self-taught and I was quite good actually playing blues, because everything was blues then. The band used to play generally American stuff like Otis Reading and the Beach

Boys (because the Beach Boys played Chuck Berry covers and Chris was that kind of guitarist, the sort of Chuck Berry kind). I thought he was like God on two legs. He'd got a nice blue Stratocaster, 1956, it would be worth an absolute fortune now if he's still got it. But I joined that band playing flute and we did a few shows together and I guess that's when I began to realise just how much music meant to me.

My dad bought me my first bass. It was a Vox Stroller bass. It's a bit of a haze looking back now, but it must have been in my early secondary school years, so I was about thirteen, fourteen years old, something like that. I must have been about fifteen, sixteen, when I joined this first band. So although I could already play a bit of bass guitar and a bit of guitar they wanted a flute player, and I was desperate to get into a band because I thought it must be the coolest thing on the planet. I have no idea what they were called now; they must have had a name but I have no idea what it was. But as I said, it was the coolest thing on the planet, because I got to play three or four shows with them. But more importantly, I got to rehearse with them in the village hall. And more importantly than that, I learned the importance of rehearsing, of learning your craft. They picked some daft American nickname for me, Long John or something equally stupid like that, but my brother was called Biff at school, you see, and so was I, and so the name stuck really from there.

Outside in the real world, work beckoned. The first job I had was as a carpenter, and I was on an apprenticeship, earmarked to be a carpenter for life. I only lasted about a year and I packed it in. It was like £3 per week which in theory was a lot of money back then but you couldn't afford to live on it. Or I couldn't anyway. So I packed in being an apprentice carpenter and went to work in the weaving sheds in Skelmanthorpe.

After my father lost his arm we'd lived on sickness benefit and the compensation they'd given him (which wasn't much, maybe about £4,000 or something). More importantly, they gave him a job again and he went back to the same factory, and he got me a job there. I was in the factory for quite a while and that's where I learned to sing, in the weaving sheds. It's a funny thing really, but these machines are going all day. I don't know if you've ever been in a weaving shed but it's a fantastic place. You've got about forty of these things all in rows – clickety-clack, clickety-clack, clickety-clack – with shuttles going across and when the weft runs out you change the shuttle. The weavers used to lip-read each other, talking from room to room because it's so fucking noisy; the only other thing you can do is sing to yourself.

So I used to sing and make up all these rhythms and melodies, singing away to myself all day long. It soon became apparent that although the weaving sheds are fantastic places, I was crap at it; I was just so dreamy, somewhere else all the time. If one of the threads snaps, it can be quite expensive. You've got like about 2,000 of these warp threads coming through and they go up and down and the shuttle goes through and it makes the pattern. They do two at once and the blade cuts the carpet or whatever it is you're making – we were making rugs – and if anything goes wrong, they lose a lot of money.

So they soon took me off that job and put me on a machine with a couple of hundred blades flying round which, because the original cut can be uneven, just crops the carpet. It also cropped the top of my finger off. You used to have to spike these carpets together and they went through the machine and when the spike got to the blades you would lift the blade up with a foot lever. One day it lifted the blade and my hand got caught on the spike so I stopped the machine and it went up, cutting my finger end off.

It was pissing blood everywhere. They took me to the doctors – this is how they used to be in the Sixties – they took me to the doctors with my finger pissing blood everywhere, and the doctor popped a bandage on it and sent me to hospital on a bus! By this time I was playing the guitar and I was paranoid that I'd never be able to play again. So I was going 'I play guitar' all the time to anyone who'd listen. There were two doctors there, an Asian guy and a White guy. And the White guy is saying, 'no, we'll take it off at the first knuckle,' and the Asian guy is going, 'oh no, we can skin graft it' and the White guy is going 'no, let's cut it off at the knuckle' and so on. Thankfully, the Asian guy won; either he was the senior doctor or maybe the White guy just thought, 'aw, let him do what he wants.' So they took a graft and skin grafted it. And that's fucking painful, I can tell you. But that's how it was back then. They didn't really bother much and you had to be tough. Can you imagine what would happen today if they told you to get a bus to hospital or walk there?

The best paying jobs though were at the coal mines; at the time they really were the highest paying job that you could get. So I did my training and went down the pit. I'm six-foot-one and in the coal mine where I worked, the seam was only three foot high so they said I was much too tall. It was mostly worked by Polish guys anyway; four-foot Polish guys – they were four-foot tall and three-foot wide! And they're all down there digging coal by hand; it wasn't a mechanised pit at all, it was fully manual. The first day I went down (and it was a big pit, something like a mile deep) they were bringing a guy out who'd had his arm ripped off. That was a bit nasty, and I couldn't help thinking of my father. We'd already had that once in the family, thank you very much.

But the coal mine was a good place to be. My first job was a button pusher. If you've never been down a coal mine I can tell you they are at one and the same time the most fantastic and the most frightening place on the planet. You're down below everything; a long way down. And so it's a long way back up too. I used to have to sit at this junction of two conveyor belts. These conveyor belts are long; they run for miles, and where they come to a corner the coal drops onto another lower belt, because of course conveyor belts can't actually go around corners. When the buzzer sounded I had to stop it as it meant there was an obstruction somewhere or somebody was working on it. So there I'd sit. It's completely pitch black; just a little light on my helmet for illumination. I'd be sitting there for hours, waiting for the buzzer to sound. Eight hours the shift was – an hour to get to the place, six hours there and an hour to get back – and I'd sit there by myself, and sometimes I'd see this light bobbling away in the distance about a mile away; this would be the deputy walking back up to see if you were all right. All you could see was light coming towards you – di-dah, di-dah, di-dah – swaying from side to side as he walked, and because you could see him from so far off, it was like one of those films where you just see the light getting closer and closer and closer. Of course the guys down there, the old hands, would tell you all the stories of the ghost deputy who'd come by and say 'you all right, son' and you'd say 'yeah, fine, thanks'; then the real deputy would come along and ask again if you were OK and you'd say 'I've just seen the deputy' and they'd tell you, 'no you haven't, son; I'm the only deputy here tonight.' So they used to fill your head with all these ghost stories and I'd be sat there, petrified, as this light would be coming towards me, thinking, 'is this the real deputy or a fucking ghost deputy?'

I wasn't strong enough to be down the pit, they said; I was too tall and too spindly; I only weighed about seven stone or something, I was nothing more than muscle and bone basically. So they gave me the job of boiler-firer which meant all I had to do was shovel coal into this fire to feed the steam engine which brought the cage up and down the mine shaft. It was the ideal job for me. I could sit there all night with my bass guitar, just practicing, because it was only a two-shift pit so at night nobody else was there. It was a really nice job for me, steaming up the boilers. It was great: it wasn't that hard a job, I could practice all I liked, and I got paid for it too.

I'd have been about sixteen when I was a carpenter and when I was down the coal mine I would probably have been about seventeen or eighteen. It was roundabout this time when I first got married.

21

Chapter Three

My first sexual encounter was a strange one. When I was about fifteen or so, I used to baby-sit for a couple who had a baby – I mean, they must have done or I wouldn't have been babysitting for them! (It's funny, I can remember the experience vividly even now, but I can't remember the baby at all.) There were these two couples who went out together; the women went out somewhere and the guys went out somewhere else; they'd come back home where I'd be sat on the sofa watching TV and they'd make some chips or something and I'd go home. And I got paid for it too, so it seemed like a pretty good deal to me.

This particular night the women came in pissed and were larking about with each other. I can't remember exactly what they said but it was something like, 'have you ever seen two women kiss?' and of course I'm going, 'er, no,' sitting on the sofa, bright red and terrified. So anyway, they started turning each other on and I was sat there watching them thinking, 'OK, this is pretty wacky.' There I am, shy and self-conscious as I am, watching them with a huge boner while they were touching each other and putting their hands down each other's pants – pissed out of their brains, mind you – and I suppose they both must have got off, had orgasms, and I'm still sat there. Then one of them asked me, 'have you ever had sex?' and by this time I'm just fucking petrified! There's two older women, quite nice as well, thin, blonde, beautiful women coming on to me. The upshot was, if you'll excuse the pun, that one of them gave me a hand job there and then. That was first real actual sexual encounter, and it was quite an experience for a lad my age; most young guys aspire to that sort of situation and I started with it. I guess the women were probably quite embarrassed, or worried, as I could have told their husbands, or the police, or all my mates, but – unsurprisingly! – I fully enjoyed the experience and kept it to myself. They still paid me as well, two shillings and sixpence, something ridiculous like that, so I got a wank and got paid at the same time. Unfortunately, they never asked me to baby-sit again…

Probably not much longer after that, I had a serious girlfriend and she became pregnant, so we got married which is what you did back in those days. I'd left school at fifteen (they increased the school leaving age to sixteen the year after I left) and that's when I moved onto carpentry for a short period. But by that time the music thing was burning in me so strongly that I just couldn't actually keep a job. I had seemingly hundreds of jobs, looking back now, but basically I was just a bum with this passion to play, to perform, music. And this passion totally ruined my family life back then. For a short time I was married with two young children, but eventually she took the children and left because she couldn't handle it. And nor could I. We were just much too young for that sort of responsibility.

Her name was Linda, and she was probably my second serious girlfriend. The first was a girl called Imogen whom I met at the youth club. Her mum and dad must have been stinking rich because they lived in a really big house, and she was a really nice girl; I was very taken with her. I used to walk her home which was about a mile through the woods, and although we never actually got to sexual intercourse, on a number of occasions I got my hands down her knickers in a vain attempt to find the elusive clitoris. I mean, it's not as if you can say, 'have I found it yet?' so I, like many of my sexually uneducated generation, used to have to fumble around and hope that I was playing with the right thing and not one of her kneecaps or something.

Unfortunately, all this came to an end when one night her brother caught us with my hand mid-way through yet another of its less-than-successful clitoral-hunting expeditions, and he beat the shit out of me. Funnily enough, I never saw her again after that! She was a really lovely girl though, and really wacky too. She used to make her own clothes and would turn up at the youth club in all these silver things – for some reason she had a thing about silver. I guess, as befits her status as my first real girlfriend, I can remember her quite vividly; my first real walk-you-home, try-to-have-sex-with girlfriend.

So my next girlfriend was Linda, the girl I married. It was quite sad actually because I think she just wanted – and would have been content with – a husband who worked and brought home a wage for her and the children. I think she would have been very happy with a very ordinary husband-wife-and-two-kids marriage, and I just couldn't do it. I was a total dead loss really. I was in one of my early bands at that time and trying to play in this band and be married at the same time was totally impossible. I couldn't hold a job down so eventually she left. She took our two babies and walked out, and I was totally gutted. Part of me still wanted a family but the other part really wanted to make it as a musician and I felt like I was being torn apart. Back then, you have to remember that being a musician then wasn't a real job; for quite a long time it wasn't seen as a profession as such and even now my sister still says to me, 'what are you going to do when it finishes? When are you going to get a real job!' So this view of being a musician still permeates through, even now. But Linda's parents thought I was the scum of the earth because of my inability to settle down, maintain a job and earn a decent living to keep the family. My family. She moved back to her parents' house with the children. I went there to ask her to come back but she said no; well, actually it was her mother who told me she wasn't coming back. I wasn't even allowed to see her, so my first attempt to beg her to come home with me resulted in me being told, in no uncertain terms, to go. I went down again and her father got me against a wall with a knife and said, 'if you come down again I'll slit your fucking throat.' I did try it one final time but he had me again and this time I knew he meant it. He was a big bloke, and angry too. I didn't go back there ever again.

I can't actually remember now where I met Linda; it was probably at a youth club or something like that, I guess, because youth clubs then had become quite big. You know, the youth were rebelling quite a bit so they had to be put in places and kept off the streets. I remember playing in the local youth club band, playing guitar very badly. Like most youth clubs, we had our own band and we used to principally play "Paint It Black", because it's nice and easy to play. One day a 'real' band came to play at our youth club party and, unfortunately, somebody asked if we could play too. So we got up to play "Paint It Black" and the equipment was so loud it was just a complete and total disaster, and we had to leave the stage in disgrace and abject humiliation. As a result, our fantastic youth club band dissolved within minutes as we became the laughing stock: 'hey, I thought you guys said you could fucking play!' It had been good fun while it lasted, though. I was with Imogen at the time and I think she would have probably packed me in anyway – her brother's clitoral intervention notwithstanding – once I was no longer the youth club band guitarist any more. The dissolution of the band was a great shame really, because I was now starting to sing a little bit by this time. It seemed I'd got rid of my shyness; I had conquered it.

So I probably met Linda at the youth club about that time and began a passionate affair, as you do at that age. I seem to remember a couple more girls between Imogen and her, but nothing serious. I remember me and my best mate, a guy called Michael Cooke, had a couple of girls in my house and again we were trying to find the clitoris generally and trying to turn them on to the heights of pleasure with no demonstrable outcome whatsoever. At that time the girls never fondled you; it was always you fondling the girls, which is a bit strange really; I guess girls weren't into finding the penis, they were more into you finding the clitoris. All of a sudden my dad came home. We were in the throes of passion (or as close as we were likely to get) on the floor, laid in front of the door, and he couldn't open it. We were frantically trying to put our clothes on and get on the sofa as if nothing had happened and I banged my toe on one of the castors and broke it – the toe, not the castor. So not only did I have to look innocent, I had to look as if I hadn't broken my fucking toe! The girls were disgusted with us so they left. I can't remember who they were now, just another one of those dark nights in the house in front of the fire. The early Sixties were a great time, but sexually I never appeared to be old enough to be a full participant.

Linda and I must have got married about 1967 or 1968, and as I said, that's what you had to do back then, even though it was very young to get married. Too young for the both of us, really. Later on, I had to pay maintenance and all through my early years of being in bands I was always in trouble with the police for non-payment of maintenance, and then for non-payment of fines. The penalty for not paying maintenance was to be fined, so they used to fine you for not paying the maintenance and then you'd get in trouble for not paying the fine. Now, if you haven't got any money to pay the maintenance, you end up owing twice as much money which you never had in the first place: a warped logic which I could never get my head around. Later on, my father moved into sheltered accommodation, and he gave me his house: I had no money, no family and, face it, no prospects, but at least I had somewhere to live. Before then, Linda and I had bought a house. I was working and earning a steady wage for a short time so we got a mortgage and we bought a very nice house. Because of my passion for music and my inability to keep a job down for any length of time though we lost it; I didn't keep the payments up and so it was re-possessed.

Looking back, it must have been an absolutely terrible time for her; for me too, because it wasn't what I wanted, but for her and the children it must have been horrendous. I have to hold my hands up and say I was an absolute bastard really, but I'd just got this thing somewhere inside me telling me that I didn't want to work a factory job all my life and that I wanted to, had to, make music. And, as I said, it wasn't considered a job back then. It was one step up from being a layabout; in fact, it might not even have been one step up. Maybe because I didn't have a mother, and my auntie and sister weren't particularly close – neither really bothered much because I was the black sheep of the family – and my father was basically getting on with his life, I was pretty much on my own. The decisions I made were obviously the wrong ones; or maybe they were right, depending on how you look at it. But the decisions I made I made on my own at a very young age. I had to stand or fall by those decisions, and Linda must have had a shitty life because of it. But there was nothing I could do. The dice were rolling and I went through doors and down alleyways and trod different paths to her. The children were quite young when she left, one was just a baby and the other one just one or two years old, but obviously they have no memory of me. Now I just regard my first marriage and all my mistakes from that time as a thing of my past that I've had to put behind me really. Because I had a lot of grief in my early life I've found myself able to shut off things like that; I put it in a compartment and lock it away and there it stays. That's how you have to deal with things like that.

At roughly the same time, all kinds of things started happening around me. Meeting people who were like-minded who were absolute nutters, running into a drummer who was a complete maniac in the Keith Moon mould. We used to practice in the village hall, just me and him, me on bass guitar and him on drums, for hours, just jamming. Our favourite band at that time was Cream. I like Jack Bruce and he was a Ginger Baker fan and so it was things like "I'm So Glad" and that sort of stuff that we used to jam: I'd say that Cream was my musical basis for rock music. And there were always festivals to go to; I remember going to Lincoln Festival, and the Bath Festival to see Led Zeppelin. It was fantastic, because I was just a young guy with a burning passion for music and meanwhile back home there was a young girl with babies too early in her life.

Me and this drummer did some work with various people like the O'Melia guy, doing clubs and playing covers like "Under The Boardwalk" and all the ballads and maybe some James Brown stuff; mostly black soul and blues music. And then at the end of the night we'd do the rock stuff like Cream; Zeppelin wouldn't have been around then, but Cream, some Rolling Stones, and that was always great. So I had an early introduction to improvisation as we'd jam a lot of stuff which is where we (and many other bands) were at, at that time. I wasn't really singing much then, but I did sing a couple of songs.

It just snowballed from there really. Once the marriage had gone pear-shaped obviously it gave me much more freedom to be a bum and a musical gypsy. After Linda's father's second throat-cutting threat I never went back; I took his threat very seriously. So I shoved it all to one side and really began to do what I'd always wanted to do, which was play music; and that became my sole focus in life – to play music (and hopefully get laid in the process). No different from the teenagers of today really. I didn't have any money, so regrettably I sold the house my father had given me. I needed money and I needed equipment so a friend and I got a flat together for a pound a week: even back then, that kind of rent was ridiculously cheap, so you can probably imagine what the place was like! We survived on dole money and bits and pieces here and there; odd cash-in-hand jobs, a bit of shoplifting, anything to survive really. My flatmate wasn't a musician but he was into music though, and ended up being a roadie.

So basically during the time of my marriage my musical outlet was jamming with this drummer John (I can't remember his surname; I've had a real difficulty with drummer's names over the years, for some odd reason). He was a good drummer though. By the time my marriage had ended I'd formed a number of contacts around the Barnsley area. I don't now why I went there, I can't remember, but for some reason I'd started making contacts there. I might have met people in music shops there; in those days you could meet a lot of people in music shops and make a lot of contacts. I got together with an absolutely brilliant guitarist called Chris Morris and his friend – whose name again I've completely forgotten now – who lived with his grandma and used to let me bunk down in one of her spare bedrooms. And then me and Chris and another guy, a drummer called Alan Dodd started a band together called Coast.

Chapter Four

oast was basically the first real band I was in. We were playing mostly our own music and we entered a competition called the US contest and actually won it. And we got our names in all the local newspapers at the time so it was a really big deal to us. I think we won some equipment, some cabs and things. Chris was an outstanding guitarist but I think he got agoraphobia. He certainly couldn't handle crowds and I was worried that the band was in danger of fizzling out really.

Prior to Coast I'd been a member of the Iron Mad Wilkinson Band, where I was the bass player. They were from just outside Barnsley and used to rehearse above a pub. We used to do cover versions and our own music, but mostly cover versions. A lot of blues music, stuff like "Walk Me Out In The Morning Dew" and all that sort of stuff, with head-bands, velvet jackets and crushed velvet hipsters, the hippy look basically. We did quite a few shows supporting different people; Chicken Shack was one I remember, String Driven Thing, East Of Eden, quite a few bands locally. They were fairly big acts, and as we used to be the band of the town when they came through we used to pick up the support slot (although we didn't get paid, of course). I can't remember if the band disbanded or if I left, but I learned a lot more and was a better player by the time we formed Coast.

I can't remember how I found the Iron Mad Wilkinson Band, or how they found me. This would have been shortly after my marriage finished. It was quite a big band. As I said, I was the bass player (and I used to sing backing vocals as well), and there was a singer, guitarist, mouth-harp player, drummer; we might have had a percussionist, I don't remember now. We didn't have a keyboard player because they weren't cool for us. I've never played with a keyboard player for any great length of time, because I just didn't like the Hammond sound. The one guy I did play with had a Mellotron. It was so bloody heavy that we sacked him! We had to carry it up the stairs at every gig. I think this would have been just before or just after the Iron Mad Wilkinson Band. I formed a band with a local hero keyboard player. We were all pretty well known in that area. We were all sort of, well, not stars, but local celebrities. You know, the rock band who wrote their own songs – was that cool or what? But this Mellotron; we had to carry it up the stairs and it was so heavy because they've got these anchor plates and they have to be perfectly dry because otherwise they go out of tune, so we sacked the bastard after the fourth gig. Too heavy. Way too fucking heavy. The Moog was the big thing back then, but if you couldn't afford one you had to have either a Mellotron or a Hammond. And the reason we never used Hammonds – aside from their weight – is because they sounded too much like guitars. You listen to Deep Purple, and sometimes it's very difficult to distinguish between the Hammond organ sound and the guitar in, say, "Smoke On The Water". I think it was Blackmore who wrote that riff but it does sound more like an organ riff to me. So as a band, and me personally, we were just never pulled towards keyboards. Now, if I was starting a band I'd definitely have a keyboard player, because keyboards open up so many different sounds. And they're lighter these days.

But the Iron Mad Wilkinson Band was the first band where I got real stage experience. I liked that band. They used to drop LSD regularly, but I didn't know they were on drugs – I just thought they played solos for four hours continuously for the sake of it! I just carried on, dum-de-dum-de-dum-de-dum, on the bass while they soloed endlessly. But it was good fun, rehearsing above the pub until 9 o'clock and then getting pissed, twice a week. That was how it was. It all sounds boring now but that's where it all comes from – playing in pubs, rehearsing solidly, talking to friends about music and having a circle of friends who become your fanbase. You play locally and they all come to see you. That's what it's all about really.

So by the time we'd formed Coast I was pretty clued in. As a band we began to make quite a name for ourselves in the Barnsley area. It was a three-piece jamming band, quite progressive in its way. Wishbone Ash were one of our big influences; we all liked Wishbone Ash. And then I met Paul Quinn.

Paul reckons he joined Coast in about 1974 or thereabouts. Before that he was in a 'Top Twenty' or 'Jukebox' band doing covers but with a slant towards songs that would suit a brass section because they were a seven-piece. I suppose they were what you might call a cabaret band really but were playing stuff you wouldn't expect a cabaret band to play. They touched on lots of stuff, including Chicago and Elvis because the singer was a bit of an Elvis impersonator, and were really a professional working-men's club band. Coast was a four-piece for a short time, but Chris Morris's demons got the better of him and he quit.

Coast did get a lot of gigs. The local gig in Barnsley was the Changes nightclub and we used to pack that place out regularly. We did quite a lot of gigs travelling around up and down the country. We had a Transit van and a friend of mine whom I was bunking down with was the roadie who drove the van, was the sound guy, lighting guy, and with a broom stuck up his arse swept the floor on the way out. (This was not the guy I shared a grotty flat with, by the way; this was another guy, and his mum and dad had a pub so they had shitloads of rooms and were happy for me to bunk down in one of them. They were really nice people, actually. He was with us right from the early days, right through the Eighties.) Anyway, we'd play anywhere and everywhere. We'd played quite a lot of shows with different people; we did a few shows with Barclay James Harvest and Argent, bands who in those days were quite 'up there', but we weren't really having a lot of success with Coast. We'd send off demos but for some reason we just weren't happening at that time. Record companies weren't that interested in what we were doing. We were playing some strange stuff really. If you listen to the first Saxon album, we were playing songs along the lines of "Frozen Rainbow", "Judgement Day", "Militia Guard", songs that were in a way quite progressive but quite unique in the way they were structured. I was writing what I thought – or hoped – was quite 'different' material. "Judgement Day" is about Jehovahs' Witnesses really, banging on your door and pestering you; "Militia Guard" is, conceptually, a little based on the French Revolution or the Russian Revolution, although, to be honest, I just thought the word 'militia' was a fantastic word and wanted to write a song around it. And "Frozen Rainbow" I thought was just a fantastic concept really; finding a rainbow frozen in the ice.

But no matter what I thought of it, it wasn't what the record companies were really looking for at that time. What they were looking for was either university students, you know, musical geniuses, or throwaway pop music; they weren't really looking for anything else. A lot of the 'real' music at the time was very highbrow, university music dropouts, not quite classical standard but something like that. And we weren't as good as that technically, and our music was more blues-based. I do think it was quite unique at the time, but whatever, we were sending demos off and getting told, 'the song's good, but you need to change the lyrics,' so we'd change the lyrics to a love song and then they'd write back and say, 'oh, yes, right... Don't like the song much.' So it just seemed like an endless stream of making demos at a four-track studio at Wakefield (it had a four-track Teac; it was like, 'whoa, dude; four-track Teac, state of the art!'), and scraping coal down windows to make seagull noises, slapping water around and all that shit, just to experiment really with atmosphere and try to create a physical picture with music. To paint a picture with our music; that's where we were at, and still are: to this day I still write what they call picture lyrics.

At this point the drummer was still Alan Dodd. I was bass and vocals, with very high leather boots, and a Rickenbacker bass, with Paul on guitar. We were extremely loud for our time; two Carlsberg two-eighteen cabs, and Paul had a Fender Strat with two Marshall stacks so we were up there, we were really going for it. We were young and managed to survive on £1 a day or pinching food or living off girlfriends. Basically it was mostly girls that fed us really, and I think girlfriends kept us alive back then. It was a bit soul-destroying sending off demo after demo but we tried, and kept trying. We were sending tapes off all the time to each and every record company. Wankers, the lot of them; I mean one guy – it wasn't this band, it was later in Son Of A Bitch days but it gives you an idea of what things were like – one guy came all the way from London to the church hall to hear us practice and we played about eight songs for him one after another. Bang! Bang! Bang! When we stopped playing to ask his opinion he said, 'you're too loud – I can't hear a fucking thing!' Why he didn't stop us after the first song I have no idea, but you have to go through these pathetic ordeals.

Our main aim in life in Coast was to get a record deal, writing our own songs and not playing cover versions like the rest of the bands in Yorkshire that we considered to be pub groups who earned good money but who had basically sold their souls. I think that Paul's friends who were with him in Pagan's Chorus are still jealous today because he's a songwriter and has moved on from that cover version mentality. They still take the piss out of him. It seemed that in Yorkshire in those days there were two mentalities: there was the club mentality whereby if you could headline a club and get £500 per night to play cover versions you'd made it, and people there still do think that. But we had the other mentality. We wanted to be more like Cream or the Stones and write songs; good songs. Songs that would make people stop and take notice. And that was what was inside me, to write those sorts of songs. So that's what we did. We stuck to our guns and to be fair we did reasonably well; we weren't making thousands but we were making £50 a night after a while which was all right, and we spent most days hanging round music stores playing guitars and chatting, drinking coffee and talking music. The next big album would come out and we'd listen to it, discuss it, analyse it; it was fantastic. Good days, really. A lot of the "Denim And Leather" lyrics are connected to that period of my life. 'Did you queue through the ice and snow? Did you hang around your local record store?' That's all from my musical background. I mean, although we were singing about our fans then – "denim and leather will set the spirit free", which is a very unlikely concept and certainly not the greatest lyrics I've ever written, it must be said – it goes back to those days when we used to hang around the record store, and queue for tickets for Alex Harvey or whoever was in town. It just brings back memories from those days and basically that's where the thoughts behind the lyrics originally came from. It was like a merging of past and present, and also showed just how we could identify with our fans because we had done exactly the same things in days gone by.

Coming from a village in rural Yorkshire, I never really came across any drugs when I was younger and I didn't come across any as a teenage either, although they were obviously there. By the time I was playing in bands, a lot of people that I played with were on LSD but I was very naïve; I was basically a village boy who knew nothing whatsoever about drugs. I'd play bass with people on LSD like in the Iron Mad Wilkinson Band and think 'what's the matter with them?; what the hell are they playing?' It wasn't until later that I took a tab of LSD and went a bit wacky – saw some beautiful colours and things, probably wrote some inane lyrics – that I realised what had been going on. I wasn't really on the drugs much at all. I'd never been approached as a teenager so I never developed a habit of liking, or needing, drugs. We basically used to drink vodka to get shit-faced and that's what we did. So I was never into drugs. I remember the first time I ever smoked dope in a band/gig environment and that was in Blackpool. Me, Paul and Alan the drummer were playing a gig in this cellar bar and we played the first of two sets and it went fine. In the interval we met a couple of guys who offered us some grass and we smoked it. Paul had smoked before, I think he was a big smoker in Pagan's Chorus, but I'd never smoked dope before. Neat Thai grass, it was. I just got back on stage and was tripping, completely out of my head. The microphone was the size of a melon, the lights were like searchlights. After a while, I took off my bass, wandered off stage and went up onto the beach, leaving them playing. I could hear the music, seemingly miles away in the distance, and I eventually wandered back down, picked up my bass and started playing again. I came down later, got severely depressed like you do, and probably started crying. I asked Paul how long I was gone and he reckoned about three minutes. Seemed to me that I'd been gone an hour or so.

Anyway, that was the first time. The second time was when we were playing at the Barnsley Civic, which was the Big Gig in town – the place you've got to play. There was another band on before us, our local rivals, a bit of a biker band, and they went on first and did quite a good set. Meanwhile we were round the back on the Thai grass and then went on and played a fantastic set.

Or so we thought. The audience was slow-hand clapping and we thought, 'yeah – they're getting into us big time!' but I hadn't even turned my amp on. We thought we were shit-hot and they couldn't actually hear us! After that, I said to myself that there's no way I'm ever going to smoke dope again before I go onstage; I must have some kind of chemical imbalance or something, the way it just screws me up totally, so I never did it again ever. This experience really turned me off drugs. I was totally out of control, I couldn't handle it: I was playing with no sound on, and thought I was playing fantastically. It was the other band that orchestrated the slow hand clapping; I mean, they probably loved it. They got to do their set again because we only did about fifteen minutes, although we were so out of it we thought we'd done a full set. We must have had about five joints one after another of this Thai grass but it stopped me dead ever having it again. In all the parties I've been to in America with jars of cocaine and dope on display, I've never touched it. I've had cocaine a couple of times, but to me it's no big deal actually. It certainly didn't have much effect on me: a bit wired maybe, but I certainly didn't feel any more alive. That said, I can understand why, when you've done six months of touring and you've done one gig after another and you're not sleeping, people take stuff like cocaine to keep themselves going. I don't have a problem with that. I don't criticise people for doing it because touring can be so fucking difficult without some kind of support.

Saxon had this 'squeaky clean' image, but, in reality, as a band we weren't like that at all. The other guys all did their thing, whatever it might be. Their paths in their teenage years were not the same as mine: they were from a big town, so things were different for them. So I can only really talk from my point of view, and that is that drugs totally messed me up. Jimi Hendrix might have been stunning on drugs; Angus Young's good on dope – a lot of people are, but for me it just whacked me out completely. As a musician I was terrible on drugs of any kind. I could not play full-stop. I just couldn't do it. So I stopped there and then and it probably did me a big favour really – you know, shocking me into stopping before I'd developed a habit or dependency.

But that was Coast. When Paul first played in the band he was an absolute madman. He used to hurl his guitar around, play it with the tremolo arm; an absolute fucking madman. I always remember playing a gig with Paul – might have been Son Of A Bitch, might have been Coast, I can't remember – and he used to be pissed off all the time. He was an angry, angry, angry man; very gentle, but when he was onstage he was a complete nutter. Typical guitarist too – never happy with his sound: 'amp's fucked' or 'guitar's fucked.' This particular day we played this quite big gig in Wales and Paul gave his guitar a terrible time on stage, throwing it about and everything, and afterwards I was collecting the money in the corridor and the guy is counting it out in his hand, £150 or something, quite a well paid gig, and Paul came hurtling down the corridor from the stage, pulled a fluorescent light fitting straight off the ceiling and hurled it down the corridor. It passed between the two of us, me and the club owner, still lit, and hit the floor and smashed into a million pieces. I just ignored it and the owner kind of looked at the light, looked at Paul, looked at me and said, 'he's going to have to pay for that.' I said something like, 'it's OK, he's just in a bad mood', as I watched the guy count the notes back. It was so funny; or it would have been, if it hadn't cost us so much. Afterwards I said to Paul, 'what was all that about?'

'Ah, I was a bit mad.'

No further explanation. He was always on the edge, and in certain respects he still is on the edge now. The thing is with Paul, he is a very gifted guy. Paul can be a genius, actually, a complete genius on the guitar sometimes. And sometimes he can be the worst guitarist on the planet. I think truly gifted musicians are like that – they have certain blasts of brilliance. And Paul's like that. We used to say that Paul lived on another planet, and we called it Planet Vortex. We used to call him a Vortexian and thought he only visited us occasionally. You see, when you talk to Paul he used to stare into space a lot, and then answer the question you asked him four days ago. And those were the times we'd say he was actually on this planet. I think we actually wrote a song called "Vortex" at one point. I often used to think it was a totally different life where your brain is four million times bigger than it should be. I still sometimes say to him, 'where the hell are you, on Vortex?' But he is an exceptional artist and still plays fantastic guitar, right on the edge. He's a really innovative blues player, which is really where he comes from. And he still surprises me sometimes, even now. Some of the playing on the thirteen shows' worth of tapes we waded through to put together »The Eagle Has Landed III« is so precise, so crystal clear, so innovative, that it really is true genius. And some of it is shit. But that's how it is.

Paul was always the main guitarist in Saxon, and Graham was pretty much the rhythm guitarist actually. Graham was the more 'showy' of the pair though. He used to hit his guitar, set fire to it, make love to it, do all the showy stuff: that was his contribution to the Saxon show, while Paul was the mainstay of the guitar work. Paul was the truly innovative one: "20,000 Feet", "Princess Of The

Night", they're all stunning guitar riffs when you actually listen to them. "Princess Of The Night" is a song we play all over the world and he's not once started that riff without everybody in the venue knowing what song was coming and going crazy. It's a great song, a real metal anthem. It's up there with some of the best and it is very innovative. With Paul, when it flows, it flows; I suppose I'm the same in some ways. I can write brilliant lyrics and sometimes I write absolute shit. That's just the way it goes. It's the same with any other artist. An actor can be in one play and can be brilliant, and the next day in another play he's totally crap. Your best days are like being in a state of grace and you have to wait for that state of grace to come upon you. At that point the ideas flow and the inspiration is at your fingertips, and as you become more experienced you learn how to milk that and keep it with you as long as you possibly can. And that's what I am good at. I do write music, but what I am really good at is really collating the band's ideas and putting them into order and then putting melodies and lyrics on top. That's what I like to do, and that's what I think I excel at.

If you listen to the early tapes of Saxon in the Eighties we were really cooking. You can't take it away from Graham and Steve and Pete, it was a great band. We were going for it, playing brilliantly, writing bloody good songs. It always seemed to me though that Graham and Steve felt that they were lucky to be doing what they were doing and were happy with that, whereas Paul and I were always striving to be better – better songwriters and better musicians doing innovative things, and not relying on the past all the time. To me, they appeared to be more rooted in the past, in Free and bands like that, so as Saxon progressed, Graham sank more into a Hendrix, well, I can only say fantasyland, really. He went more and more into the past with Hendrix; as he got more money he delved more and more into it, and it went from a hobby to an obsession. Pictures all over his house, little shrines everywhere, picking up the most obscure bootlegs and out-takes; it was just strange to see someone doing this. I believe if Hendrix had wanted to release albums of himself splashing around in the bath, he'd have released them when he was alive. The song "We Will Remember" is all about that; if I want to remember Phil Lynott, I'm not going to put on some tape of him jerking around in the studio with a bass guitar. I want to remember him in Thin Lizzy at his greatest. I'm not interested in what he did in his bad moments, I'm only interested in what he did in his great moments. I'm not a fanatic of his life. I knew him, and when he died it was terribly sad; I met him a couple of days before he died, but that's beside the point. It was still a tragedy. It's like Bon Scott. I turned the whole band onto AC/DC but I don't want to hear Bon Scott singing Christmas carols that someone once taped in the studio. It's just silly. I think that if people are hungry to hear every Saxon mistake and out-take, well, they can't! Just because somebody somewhere wants to hear it is not a good enough reason in my opinion to release it. I feel the same about songs we've written that we haven't put out. The reason we didn't put them out is that I didn't think they were good enough. If you can't mess around and try ideas without someone in the future thinking 'that's shit' then you wouldn't do it, would you? As an artist, you have to be safe in the knowledge that all your failures are never going to be heard. There is some sanctity in that and every person who dies in a band now is going to worry that 'one day the bass guitarist is going to release all that crap when I was singing Benjamin Britten or something.' You shouldn't do that. I believe strongly about that. If somebody gets into Hendrix because of any one of his classics, or hearing "Crosstown Traffic" on a TV advert, that's great. But churning out demo tapes and bits from »Electric Ladyland« that some engineer stuck in his pocket... I just don't get it. I don't get any joy from it, and I think it shouldn't be allowed.

Chapter Five

With Coast, nothing was happening. We used to play in and around Bradford a lot and there we met John Verity, who'd had his own album out and who'd got quite a thing going for himself. He was involved with the guys in Smokie who were quite successful for a time. They too were from Bradford, so it was quite a hotbed there on the more melodic rock front with Smokie, a couple of other acts and John Verity himself. We were going nowhere and he needed a backing band so we joined together with him. Coast is dead, long live the John Verity Band – me on bass and backing vocals, Alan the drummer, Paul on guitar and John Verity singing and also playing guitar. It was all right for us; in fact, it was quite good fun because we would have quite big gigs around the Bradford area.

Almost out of the blue John was asked to join Argent and he did, obviously, and that was that basically. We went to see them a couple of times when they were doing this really wacky tour called »The Circus« or something which was the name of their 1975 album. They had tightrope walkers and stuff to go with the circus theme and, to be honest, it was a disaster really. I had nothing against the band but that music was definitely on the way out; the university music, or 'trained' music, this impresario keyboard player with his band. I think the only one that survived was Manfred Mann; he went on and is still around, playing to quite big audiences, but obviously he moved with the times. The progressive rock thing was really in decline, and people weren't really into it any more. It still had its following but Argent had really lost it by then. I mean, their big hits were quite poppy – the stuff Russ Ballard wrote – "Hold Your Head Up", that sort of thing, which reminds me of a story that John Verity once told me. They auditioned loads of singers, and that was the audition song – 'hold your head up, woman', and one of the guys was singing 'hold your head up, Norman'; now that really is putting a personal interpretation on the lyrics!

So after a short while we were back to being Coast again with no ill-will towards John. He's a nice guy, and he supported us (alongside Battleaxe) on the Crusader tour. But with him in Argent, playing dire shows at massive gigs to almost nobody, Coast began gigging once more until it became apparent that Alan didn't want to be a professional drummer. He wanted to drive a truck or something so he quit the band, leaving Paul and I to look for a replacement. Meanwhile, another Yorkshire band, Sob, was in the process of looking for a singer.

To tell you the truth, I didn't really like Sob. I knew of them, it was only a small local scene after all so most of us knew each other or at least had heard of each other, but I wasn't that keen on Sob because they used to play Free covers and although I liked Free I wasn't fanatical on them. Steve was a total Free fanatic, used to go to the concerts and scream at them, and so a lot of their stuff was very Free-based, not in the guitar sense because the lead guitarist certainly wasn't Paul Kossoff but he was a blues-based guitarist. Graham was their rhythm guitarist. The lead guitarist was also Sob's main singer. Neither Steve nor Graham can sing particularly well, and Graham used to sing "The Hunter" – 'they call me the 'unter' – badly! We used to go and see them when they used to play this club Changes; they were quite good but it was all very much single-stringed riffing. 'Freeway Mad' is a Sob riff. I don't think it was called 'Freeway Mad' at the time, but it's very twelve bar-y and riffy if you listen to it. Paul and I were much more experimental, more progressive, more blues-progressive stuff; maybe something like Rush in their early days, that sort of thing. And Sob were much more influenced by the likes of Free.

So, I was staying at the pub and somebody called up and asked if we were looking for a drummer. I said we were, and he introduced himself as John Walker. I assumed he was ringing me for a try out but he said, 'no, I'm from a band called Sob, we're looking for a singer.' I just told him that I was a bass guitarist and that was that, nothing more happened, until a little later on, they 'phoned again. I can't remember who 'phoned the second time and again I wasn't that interested, but they suggested trying to work with two bass players. Well, that's a concept – two bass players: very progressive. 'But the thing is,' I added, 'I'm not joining anything without Paul, my mate.' So we went down to see them and it was all right but we weren't really that enamoured because their stuff was a bit, well, old-fashioned, actually. It wasn't really experimental enough for me. Playing below our standard, perhaps; we could play their songs standing on our heads. There was nothing wrong with it, it's just that we were more into creating different chord patterns and odd notes on the bass. We were experimenting with all sorts of weird shit. However, after we talked about it, we decided we'd have a couple of gigs together and although from the off I didn't like the name Sob – you know, crying, sobbing tears; they took it from the Free album »Tons Of Sobs« – we did a couple of gigs together and I quite liked it actually. So we decided to go for it. We didn't want to call ourselves Coast, and we didn't want to call ourselves Sob, so we came up with Son Of A Bitch, which is more or less Sob anyway. And that stuck, purely and simply because we couldn't think of anything else at the time really.

Me and Paul used to do this "Bap Shoo Ap" thing in our set which we took on to Son Of A Bitch, and we basically wrote our own stuff from there. And that's how it all started, the Son Of A Bitch/Saxon thing. Paul didn't mind working with another guitarist; to be honest, I think we were all willing to give almost anything a go. When Chris Morris left Coast, rather than ditch the guitar harmonies, Paul worked out how to do them on one guitar; after that, joining forces with another guitarist must have been a piece of cake. We amalgamated all our gear, with the two respective massive PAs making one really massive PA. And we could pool other resources as well, like they had a better van than us for a start although we seemed to spend most of our time putting new engines in it and continually changing the wheels. We used to paint everything matt black because it looked so heavy. We bought this van from an auction, painted it matt black and when we painted it the sign from the previous owner came through the paint. It said 'Sid Cummings – Tripe Dealer'! (Tripe is an offal meal – the stomach or entrails of a cow or something like it. It was a cheap working class meal years ago. But it's also slang for rubbish.) So we used to travel around the country and call ourselves the tripe band; hence the saying, 'that band's full of fucking tripe.' Later on, in-between the first and second albums we got pretty posh because we actually bought an American school bus off an air base and put bunks and a kitchen in it to make it our first tour bus. We'd read about these tour buses and we wanted one so we made one ourselves. It was highly dangerous with gas bottles inside of it and all sorts of shit. And bunks at the back with a special bed in the front if anyone pulled a girl. It was horrendous. And, to make things worse, the back door kept falling off. We'd set off from a traffic light and someone would shout, 'Whoa – back door's off again!' and someone would have to get out and go and fetch it and strap it back in. But we liked it. It did about three miles to the gallon – must have had something like a seven-litre engine. We painted it yellow – it was already yellow anyway being an American school bus, but we painted it even brighter yellow so it really stood out. It was the first thing we had that wasn't matt black so it was a big deal for us. But it didn't last long because the engine blew up.

When we weren't fixing our transport the rest of the time was spent on the road really. Our big stomping grounds were South Wales and the North-East. We didn't really play much in Yorkshire at all really, just Barnsley, and we had this circuit we played constantly once every month. We played our own songs, and our stage act was really wacky – we were like absolute bastards really. The guitar tech/main roadie was our guy, and the sound guy was Sob's old crew. We had another guy with us called Buxton who did the lights, and that was the basic unit that was the Son Of A Bitch touring band. We used to have a routine; we'd get to the gig and steal everything in sight. We used to have a long pole with a six-inch nail taped on the end; all the bars in the clubs had these grills on them to prevent you getting behind the bar so we would poke the pole through the grill, stick it into packets of cigarettes and pull them out. All of our packets of cigarettes had holes right down the middle. Then into the cellars, steal all the Newcastle Brown, cases and cases of it, fill the van and sell it outside the gig. The lighting guy would always have a bag of blown bulbs; and he'd climb up into the club's lighting rig and take out some good bulbs and replace them with the blown ones. A couple of times he got trapped in there; he'd be up in the rafters when they kicked us out and we'd be outside, shouting instructions through the letter box for him to get out; and then he'd just let himself out and leave the place completely open. Another time, we played at an art college and pinched six screen-printing screens to make our own t-shirts and posters. We were like a total craft fair really. I'm not saying I'm proud of what we did; but the point is that we would do almost anything to make enough money to survive.

We would play up to three sets in a night, maybe with bingo in the middle, in some really rough clubs. Fights broke out all the time – it was like the Wild West some nights. By this time, I was wearing an SS camouflage jacket with the eagle on the arm, and a chain, and braces and a white shirt. We must have looked a right bunch of hard bastards! Part of the deal was that if the sound guy got any feedback I'd jump off stage and whip him with the chain. That was all part of the act, to go with the Son Of A Bitch name. So I'd regularly chase him round the gig, and the audience loved it. I used to nail Steve's Doc Martens to the stage, and he'd lean right over, securely pinned to the floor. I'd pour water into the monitors and tell the audience we'd got fish in there... It was a crazy show really. There was always a stripper on with us, and we'd play the backing music on stage. Then after a while we wised up and made a tape which we could stick in the PA while we settled down in the front row to watch the show. I've seen a lot of dirty things done with teddy bears' legs, believe me!

It was a great time really, but it was hard work though. We kept making demos all the time and sending them off to various record companies and to hear nothing back, until sometime in 1978 (it must have been) when we got some positive news. Our old mate John Verity 'phoned us and said a tape we'd given him, he'd passed on to Queen's management, Trident, and they liked it enough to offer us a management contract. Shortly after, a guy called Pete Hinton from EMI came to see one of our gigs; I think it was the Talk Of The North, some wildly cabaret place that just so happened to be putting rock on that night. He thought we were pretty radical. And we were; we were going down very well, the band was cooking, and the crowd loved it.

'I thought you were great, got your demo tape, will get back to you,' he said. And off he went.

We didn't hear anything for ages, although Hinton had said something else encouraging like, 'I can tell you've got a good following' before he left that night. In the meantime, he and another guy, Freddie Cannon, who also worked at EMI, were headhunted to lead the UK division of what seemed to be at that time an obscure French record company called Carrere. They had had some success with Sheila B Devotion, a disco singer, and a Number 1 hit with a song called "Substitute" by an Australian girl band (can't remember their name now). So they'd had a couple of big single successes, but I don't think they'd had any hit albums. But they offered a deal: £30,000 advance for two albums and an option on further records. We were stuck in a 'fucking-hell-shall-we-shan't-we?' quandary. Obviously Pete Hinton was from EMI originally, and to be truthful we were disappointed because we thought at first that the approach was from EMI, but it wasn't; it was this Carrere Records, whom I don't think we'd even heard of at the time. So we did a lot of soul-searching: 'it's a French company. Should we wait for EMI or some big British company to sign us, or some big American label? What should we do?' But at the end of the day, we thought we had nothing to lose, so let's do it. At that point in time we could have waited another six months and lost all chances of getting a deal. So we took the decision to sign. And it was the right decision at that time; I am convinced of that. Some people in the band who were always right in retrospect, Graham in particular, would say that we should have waited and gone with EMI because Iron Maiden are much bigger, but that doesn't mean to say that we would have been, does it? Especially when you consider that at that label we would have been in direct competition with Iron Maiden. And when we did sign with EMI later on that's exactly what happened; we were in direct competition with them, and it wasn't good. It wasn't good for us at all.

But back then there was a great buzz. We were all very excited. I mean, we'd got a record deal, and we'd got a big management company in Trident (although unbeknown to us, Queen were suing the shit out of them and had written a song called "Death On Two Legs" about them). The guy that handled us was a guy called Dave Thomas (as you will notice, the name 'Thomas' and management keeps recurring throughout our career although I have no idea why) but I don't think he was involved with Queen at all. Trident had a huge studio in London, in the West End behind the old Marquee called (naturally) Trident Studios, and although we never used it we went there a lot to lig.

Everything was tied up for us though. With a £30,000 advance we were given £40.00 each to go and buy some clothes from the Kings Road (and for me to get a decent haircut). It was fantastic actually. I bought some white boots, some denims and a leather jacket. We then flew to Paris; the first time I'd been on a plane; first time I'd been out of the country in fact, and we signed a contract with Claude Carrere, a slightly weird guy who was obviously a midget with really high boots. He was obviously the bees' knees in the French record business. I can't help but laugh really, thinking back on it now; we'd flown to Paris with Pete Hinton, a man who possessed the sweatiest top lip in the world. We did the business and signed the contract, and when Claude Carrere left the room, Pete walked over and said, 'well, that's it then: you've got your recording contract,' and he leant on Carrere's desk in this sort of superior pose. Now I'd never seen anything like this desk; it was huge, glass, and must have cost a fortune. As Pete Hinton leant on it, the desk split right down the middle and crashed onto the floor. Carrere came back in and had Pete thrown out, and as far as I am aware, he never went to the Paris office ever again. He didn't sack him, but he had him unceremoniously bundled out of the office. We were absolutely cracking up, laughing our fucking heads off; Carrere obviously then had us thrown out as well!

Signing that contract was a fantastic feeling: a great buzz and butterflies in the stomach at the same time. I'd tried a long, long time to get a recording deal and that was my one thing in life, the one thing I really wanted. It's not just the contract though; it's the support that comes with it. The support from the label, and the distribution company they were with was very powerful – it was Warner Brothers – so everything was in place. And John Verity was chosen to produce our first album.

As I said, we had an advance of £30,000 but despite this we were booked into some dingy bed and breakfast place. The owners had this huge green parrot that never, ever shut up from morning till night. We fed it all sorts of shit but it just wouldn't die! Anyway, we were staying there while we worked at Livingstone Studios to record the album with John Verity. After a day's work we'd go back to this dump every night and while we weren't around he'd put on all these backing vocals – 'oohs' and 'ahhs' everywhere – so in the end to us it became the 'eee-ouu-ahh' album. It sounded good, you know, but it was a bit dated for us, and it wasn't really us because we didn't have a backing vocalist in the band. He didn't mess with the heavy tracks like "Stallions Of The Highway and "Backs To The Wall" fortunately, he just beefed up "Frozen Rainbow" and a few of the more melodic things. Russ Ballard also came down, did a bit of twiddling around, and Rod Argent played keyboards, so it was almost like having all his friends and relations in the studio. We quite liked the end result and they paid for everything – you could have anything you wanted but no cash! – so we wanted for nothing and we were happy. We'd got a rental car and when we were done we'd just go into London. I saw Van Halen at the Rainbow – my first sight of the iconic band – and I was gobsmacked: Eddie Van Halen was brilliant.

Coast and Sob must have joined forces about 1976 or 1977 or so. I really can't remember now. It was a bit difficult for me getting used to not playing bass, but I soon grew into it. The first shows were with the two basses, but it didn't really work; it was pretty soon after we hooked up that I became solely the singer. I was more into the Rickenbacker Chris Squire sort of sound – I quite liked Yes – and Steve Dawson was more into staying with the A and giving a good bass run. Besides, I pretty soon found that I was a better singer than I was a bass player anyway. I had a tambourine for a while, but you can't hide behind a tambourine the way you can hide behind a guitar – unless it's a fucking big tambourine! – so that didn't last for long. Pretty soon I learned to use the mikestand as a symbol (not a phallic symbol, just a symbol) and honed my craft in the clubs, making the transition from being in a three-piece band with a bass guitar to leading a five-piece band as the frontman. I soon found that just singing wasn't enough really; you had to be more of a storyteller and comedian, especially in the clubs where you get a lot of shit thrown at you. After a while you start to get used to the one-liners from the crowd and it's quite good fun really; you get some wit in the crowd shouting some stupid things so you shout something back. It sharpens your skills – you have to be 'there'. It's considered kosher in Yorkshire and the North-East and South Wales to barrack the singer and to expected to be heckled back and put down. It's all part of the game. In a way it's a bit like being a stand-up comedian really, doing a routine; even today if we play in Yorkshire, people will shout things like 'where's your cucumber?' and I'll come back with, 'it's still up your girlfriend, mate!' This is how it goes, and you learn to expect things like that. 'I shagged your girlfriend last night and she didn't have half as much to say as you'; it's all that kind of thing going backwards and forwards. I don't think a lot of other bands had that. I don't think Def Leppard did much of the club circuit like we did and I don't think Iron Maiden did much of it either.

The first album was quite pleasurable to do. We had some girls from Yorkshire we'd brought down who were into gang-banging so a lot of the evenings were spent shagging really, and experimenting, and just having a good time. We were living in a dormitory in the attic – it was like theatrical digs – so there were all these actors, jobbing, and we were upstairs creating debauchery on the top floor. They left us alone though; no-one ever complained about screaming and running around despite the fact that it must have been horrendous for the other guests. But I liked the album when I first heard it. I wasn't experienced enough to have a really focussed idea of how we should sound. It was just a total helter-skelter of happenings; one moment we were nothing, we had no prospects and were just a club band (albeit one that refused to play covers), and the next all that was swept aside – or so we thought – when we made the first album. We were going to be massive, we were all going to be millionaires and our music would be worshipped across the world. Some friends did all the artwork, I think modelling the warrior on the cover on me. I like the cover, but I think it was more in keeping to how we were to be later on. But we liked it, the record company liked it; it was a strong image, and the logo was good too.

We'd stayed in a hotel in London before we flew to Paris and Pete Hinton told us that we couldn't be called Son Of A Bitch – 'the record company wouldn't have it and you won't get anywhere with that name' – and I didn't particularly like the name either. It was a vehicle for the clubs really, it was a bit like swearing back then, a bit rebellious, and it was a bit different. We had a lot of comments about the name and we liked that because it was controversial. But it had served its purpose and it was time to move on. So we came up with hundreds and hundreds of names like Spitfire; Singe And Crackle was one name that was horrendous; I mean you can't think of a band name in three seconds. We couldn't think of anything so just thought, 'fuck it! Let's go and sign the contract anyway'. When we came back we went into Freddie Cannon's office the next day and he came up with Anglo Saxon. I thought about it for a bit.

'I don't like the 'Anglo', but the 'Saxon' bit is good.'

So that's what we went with – Saxon. The name's been great and it's been crap at the same time. It's good, but sometimes it might have been better to have been called something else because you get tied down to certain things. But overall I like Saxon as a name; it's certainly as good as anything. And once a band is popular, the name doesn't matter any more anyway. We could have been called 'Spectacles' – if you write a big song you'll find it doesn't actually matter.

»Saxon« came out in a blaze of, well, nothing really. It sold quite well for a band's debut. We must have had an immediate following of about 12,000 people around the UK, and the record company put adverts out saying 'Saxon – formerly Son Of A Bitch' so that every-body knew who we were. It must have sold about 2,000 in Barnsley, and then went on to sell to our 12,000 fanbase. Trident, the super management company dropped us immediately, saying that on those sales figures we couldn't afford their services, and Carrere reminded us that we only had one more album on the deal. So we did what we knew best. We went back into the clubs. But this time it was different, because now we were back in the clubs with an album behind us. It's a very different thing, being in a band that doesn't have an album compared to being in a band that does; the record's out there in the shops so you can promote it and the record company can advertise your concerts.

And it was around that time that I think things started to change in the UK and we started to see a big difference in the gigs we were doing. The working men's clubs were still there and we did well in them, but we were getting a lot of university gigs and we noticed that the general mentality of people was changing towards heavy metal music – this was 1979 going towards 1980 – and we started to see a big influx of schoolkids, young kids, getting into the music.

But I haven't told you about Pete Gill, have I?

I never actually knew what happened with John Walker, the old Sob drummer. He fell out of the van one night. I mean, he was a pretty good drummer and a really nice guy. But he did actually fall out the van one night and we didn't see him again. I guess in that respect we were pretty ruthless actually. There wasn't a lot of compassion especially from Steve Dawson and Graham Oliver's side of things; they were perhaps a little hard that way, to be honest. Anyway, we were without a drummer, so we put an advert in Melody Maker, and amongst the responses – of which there were quite a few – was one from a guy called Pete Gill. I think we must have asked Alan Dodd or someone to play with us for a while because we had a gig at a school, a grammar school, and Pete Gill came to see us, and said something like, 'fucking great, I'll join.' And we were like, 'whoa' because he'd been in Gary Glitter's band and he'd been around the world, so compared to us he was a real musician.

We had quite a lot of respect for Pete and he was a great guy actually. As I said, I liked him a lot, and have no bad feelings for him whatsoever. He was a great drummer, really into John Bonham and that's the style he drummed which was great for us. He was a good-looking guy as well, so he brought a lot to the band. I don't think people really related to the Gary Glitter thing, I don't think that was as much of a negative connection as the Toyah thing was for Nigel. I don't think people really knew Pete's Gary Glitter past anyway because there were two drummers in his band and more importantly, I don't think anyone focussed on any of the band, everyone focussed on Gary Glitter himself. Pete brought a lot of power to us and was really refreshing after the other guys we'd played drums with. He was more 'worldly' too; he'd been to Africa and India and knew a lot about the important things in life. He was a total debauchery fucker too; he'd shag himself to pieces given half the chance.

Pete was the missing piece and we were now a great band. He was a great drummer and we could write great songs that he could play. I think John Walker was a great drummer too; but he wasn't as powerful as Pete, either as a drummer or as a personality. He was quite charismatic, Pete, and he brought a lot of girls to the band too because he was a bit of a babe-magnet. The important thing though was that the band was now complete. We were a unit and we were able to go onwards and upwards from there. Yes, when we flew to Paris it was nothing to him because he'd done it all before, but on the other hand he was just as excited as we were because he hadn't been in a band such as us before where he could contribute to the songs.

And so we were off. We took no prisoners, we didn't give a flying fuck. As far as we were concerned that first album could have sold two copies – you know, two people liked us and that was it. We didn't care. It didn't diminish our resolve or our determination.

This was it, as far as we were concerned; we were going all the way to the top.

Chapter Six

By this point in my career, don't forget, I had sacrificed a lot: my family, my father's house which I'd sold, my life, really. I'd given up a lot, and put a lot of effort and time into this. And I never had a second thought. This was the only path I was treading. I could have got a job as a carpenter or a miner or a factory worker or anything really: I'm a hard worker so I didn't really have a problem finding work – it's staying there that was my problem. But the only path I wanted to tread was the music path. I have – always have had – a passion for rock music; in fact, a passion for music full-stop. I like all types of music; I'm not really, deep down, a heavy metal singer. I'm a singer who sings heavy metal. I like Judy Garland, Ozzy Osbourne, Frank Sinatra, Rob Halford; I like all music and I like countless hundreds of singers.

Really though, I wanted to be a guitarist. I really love guitars, and I love playing the guitar. People like Leslie West, Joe Walsh, Michael Schenker... All these people were so influential and mean so much to me. But having said that, I'm a singer. I can't be a guitarist, could never be a guitarist, because I didn't sacrifice enough to be a guitarist, and, well, my talents obviously lay elsewhere. Guitarists do sing though: they sing with their guitar; they sing with their strings and the fluidity of their playing. Think about it. A lot of people might not realise that, but they do.

I was also drawn to the whole improvisational side of playing an instrument. I think it's the improvisational side of the music that hooks people, and it is a talent in itself. A lot of musicians who sing in choirs or play in orchestras are extremely talented, but couldn't improvise to save their lives; couldn't write a melody if you stuck a gun to their heads. They've trained to read music and to interpret and play what's on the page in front of them. Improvisation is a talent in itself. If you have it, you have to follow it. You can't do anything else, it's just a driving force and you are drawn to it. And that's how I've felt almost all my life,

We were riding the wave, and it was a fantastic time for us. Pete had made the band complete. As we were, I really don't think we would have made it without him, and I think Pete was a major force in the band at that time. He was a fantastic drummer and he had the power – he could play double bass drums all day, he was that strong. So we were able to write and play the music that we so desperately wanted to write and play. Each person in the band had almost completely different influences. Steve was into Free, and obviously his favourite bass player was Andy Fraser. Paul was more into soul music and R 'n' B, and his guitar hero was Ollie Halsall from Patto, a band who kind of mixed rock, jazz and bizarre time changes with a wacky sense of humour; fantastic guitarist though. Graham had this Hendrix vibe going on. Pete was more AC/DC, Judas Priest, Rush and Led Zeppelin, with, as I've said, the John Bonham approach to playing drums. As for me, I was into, well, everything really because I was a total musical rag-bag. I was into anything from Cream to The Kinks to Yes; all sorts of different things, but all linked by anything with a really good hook. So our song-writing was a bit of a mish-mash really, with the five of us locked in a room hammering out different riffs and ideas. Being the only singer, most of the time I'd be in control of the arrangements. I don't remember anyone in Saxon or Son Of A Bitch ever writing a complete song from start to finish on their own in the early days. I remember a lot of the songs we wrote that were on the first album were mine and Paul's: "Frozen Rainbow", "Militia Guard", "Judgement Day", all originated from Coast. "Freeway

Mad" on »Wheels Of Steel«, was definitely a Sob song, as were a couple of other things. "Backs To The Wall" was co-written, "Stallions Of The Highway" was co-written, so in that respect it was all a bit of a mixture really. As with most bands, the second album, »Wheels Of Steel« was the first real band album, the first album written in total by the band as a complete unit.

The period between the first album and »Wheels Of Steel« was a big learning curve for us because we fully understood that if we didn't get our shit together we'd be back to the clubs – where we'd already ended up again – although this time it would be (a) without a record deal and (b) probably forever. So it wasn't a fantastic period for us, but the audiences were getting bigger and there was this hugely apparent growing interest in rock music in general: punk had been very big, very big, and had taken most music journalists completely off guard ("Big Teaser" on the first album incidentally is our sort of nearly-punk thing) and what was happening now, with what became known as the New Wave Of British Heavy Metal, could be as big as punk, if not bigger.

In that period between »Saxon« and »Wheels Of Steel« we did quite a lot of shows with the Heavy Metal Kids who were a big influence. In particular, their singer Gary Holton inspired me personally, because he was an extrovert frontman. One time he told me, 'you're a good band; but stop doing the "Bap Shoo Ap" thing because it sucks. If you get your shit together you'll be a great band.' I thought that was pretty cool. I liked him because when he went on stage he took complete control immediately. A lot of people probably knew him better from his TV days in »Auf Wiedersehen Pet« than from the Heavy Metal Kids, but he was a fantastic frontman. I wouldn't say he was a fantastic singer, but he was a great frontman and in their day they were a great band to see live.

Another band we got into and who were highly influential was AC/DC. I got into them on the »Dirty Deeds Done Dirt Cheap« album and then turned the rest of the band onto them. The other guys thought they were quite simplistic, and in some ways they were, but I liked their power, and also I really liked the fact that once they started a riff they stuck to it; they didn't deviate, they just hammered it home to you until you liked it. And I respected that type of approach. I persuaded everyone to see AC/DC at Sheffield University on the »Dirty Deeds…« tour (I'm pretty sure it was that tour; whatever, it was obviously long before they broke big over here with »Highway To Hell«) and won them over. I loved AC/DC's style, and I loved watching Angus going nuts. It was a show, and I like shows. Alex Harvey was another band we'd go and see a lot; another charismatic frontman and so another big influence on me. Again I liked the way he controlled the audience. I saw Uriah Heep with their original singer 'Lord' Byron and he was a character. I guess I tended to like the frontmen who told stories, who really got their music across. I mean, I saw Ian Gillan and to me, he's the reverse. He's a great singer, no doubt about that, but I wouldn't say he's a fantastic frontman though; not in the sense that after the gig's over, you feel like you know him. For persona, Alex Harvey, Gary Holton, these were probably the most influential in my make-up. People like that, and cutting our teeth on the club scene are what's made me the frontman I am. I just can't resist talking to the audience, and trying to get to know them for the ninety minutes we're on stage. Whether it's in Moscow or in Barnsley, I just feel that there should be a connection between audience and band. The only other singer whom I thought had a bit of a rapport going with the audience was Paul Di'Anno when he was in Iron Maiden, with what Geoff Barton called his 'roughly hewn stable boy charm'. He always seemed to be quite 'honest' with his audience.

I must have had something in me from the off to be a frontman though, to be able to take both the glory and the crap because the guy up front takes them both in equal measure and not a lot of people realise that. Yes, if the band is great, the frontman does bask in a lot of glory. But if the band screws up, the crowd turns on the singer, and when the band fails, it's virtually always the singer that cops the blame. I came to singing late so I didn't really have the early 'wanna-be-a-singer' megastar bullshit. Of the bands that I liked, the people who sang were the likes of Jack Bruce or

Mountain's Felix Pappalardi, so not exactly what you'd call super-duper singers; good singers, but not exactly unique or great. The singer of the Iron Mad Wilkinson Band turned me on to a band called Trapeze, and their young singer/bass player Glenn Hughes. We used to go and see Trapeze quite a lot, particularly at the Black Swan in Sheffield. We saw loads of bands from the Seventies there; but used to have to walk home too, twelve miles, because we'd always miss the last bus. Totally pissed on eighteen pints of whatever it was, stop off at the fish-and-chip shop, eat fish and chips and puke it back up straight away; carry on walking, stop someplace else and get cockles and mussels and puke them up too. All this time we'd be trying to thumb lifts from passing cars but – unsurprisingly – nobody in the world ever stopped to pick us up. At that time, I was just the bass player so, and I know this will sound like heresy, I didn't take much notice of Hughes as a singer, although I did realise that he had a fantastic voice and that some of those Trapeze songs feature his finest singing really. Later, we even named Coast after the Trapeze song "Coast To Coast" (although we obviously knew the word 'coast' existed!). I'd become a big Trapeze fan, although I did lose interest in Glenn Hughes a bit when he went off to join Deep Purple. I wasn't really a big Purple fan actually while he was in the band as I didn't really like the direction of »Stormbringer«; too soul or R 'n' B for me. You've got to admit though that he still has a fantastic voice and he did influence me quite a lot in the early days; not that I sing anything like him, but his choice of octaves when he lets go is fantastic. Another singer I heard and really liked in the early days was Ronnie James Dio; I'd got the »Butterfly Ball« album, and when we played it we couldn't make our minds up whether it was Glenn Hughes or Dio singing certain parts. I'd never heard of Dio before then; what a voice, though! It was people like that, people who were really innovative with their vocals, that did it for me. Up to that point people were mostly just singers, but Hughes, Dio, and people like them, these were the singers who really did something with their vocals and they were hugely influential on me.

Patto, whose guitarist Ollie Halsall was one of Paul's influences, were another band from back them. They had a stage act, and they were funny: they were entertainers. I remember they used to have a microphone in the dressing room and pretend they didn't know it was there and talk about the audience, saying stuff like, 'there's a girl in the front row with massive tits; have you seen her out there?' or, 'how much they paying us tonight?'

'Dunno; 'bout ten quid, I think.'

'Ten quid? Stingy bastards, here, aren't they.'

All this was coming over the PA before they came on. It was highly theatrical, but the audience would be in hysterics. And they'd come on with their shoes on their knees and do a song about the seven dwarves. It was all great stuff. They were a fantastic band but it seemed they almost refused to be big.

Being born in the Fifties, one of the things that comes from my childhood is a fascination with steam because that was the main power in those days, despite the fact that the diesel engine and diesel locomotives were beginning to take hold. I mean, the diesel had obviously been around for a long time, but it wasn't until the late Fifties or early Sixties that they started taking over from steam on the railways. "Princess Of The Night" originally sprang from the fact that there's a big viaduct in Denby Dale that goes across the valley and we'd sit in the field and watch the trains go across at night. It was a fantastic sight in the night, you know. There was always something majestic about steam locomotives, but at night, with all the steam, the firebox dropping ash onto the track, it was almost magical. When the steam era ended, with Son Of A Bitch we used to play in South Wales a lot and we used to park the van up in Barry Island where all the scrapped steam locomotives used to be stored in one big elephants' graveyard. 'The writing on the wall' is all about the inevitability of the end of the steam period and actually seeing it happen. It's very nostalgic for me because when I was a boy one of our biggest games was to put pennies on the railway lines so that the train would flatten them and imprint the King's head or whatever onto the track. We used to sit and watch the trains for hours, you know, watching this heavy machinery moving. Another game... Well, it wasn't really a game, actually; it was real life. In town there was a coal depot where the lorries used to tip – the truck part would actually tip sideways – to empty out their load and we used to go down there as kids and collect coal. Our fathers used to send us down with a wheelbarrow and a sack and as the trucks used to negotiate the entrance of the coal yard they'd tip slightly and spill coal onto the road which we'd promptly shovel up and wheel home. I can remember many happy hours waiting for the coal trucks to arrive because for us it was all a game.

But going back to "Princess Of The Night", it must be one of our most misunderstood songs: a lot of people just didn't get the lyrics at all. I don't have a problem with people not getting it; I mean, every Japanese girl you meet always says 'I am the princess of the night.' It's a fantastic concept, and I reckon Udo Dirkschneider must have liked it for Accept to come up with their "Princess Of The Dawn". But "Princess Of The Night" has so many connotations and I don't know of any other band that's used it before us. So I don't mind if people don't get it. A lot of people don't listen to the verse anyway; most people just hum along to verses and then pick up on the chorus. Listen to yourself in the car someday! I don't mind if people don't understand what I am singing about. Does it really matter? That said, I thought it was fairly bloody obvious – the single bag had a steam train on it, and I thought "ninety tons of thunder steaming down the track" was a bit of a giveaway. But if you're Japanese, then you probably wouldn't get that.

It just goes to show how people can perceive things in different ways, and that's what it's all about really; that's what songwriting is to us. The chorus is everything for some people, both audience and songwriters; for others, well, some songs don't even have a chorus, just a hook on the end of the verse. That's a different way of writing and we have done that as well. Generally though, our songwriting is based around three verses – verse, chorus, verse, chorus, middle-8, verse, chorus, finish. A lot of our songs are written that way because that's the basic way of structuring a strong song. We do deviate from that, because it can get a bit, well, static, if you keep working to a formula. So we do move away from it a lot of the time but we are still songwriters with a classic sense of writing a good song with a strong hook and that's where our foundation comes from. If people mis-interpret the song lyrics, I don't think that's a bad thing; I don't come down on people who do that and I wouldn't make fun of them either. At the end of the day it's all about what that song means to an individual. When you write a song and it moves somebody with a vivid lyric or a really good melody, then you can't take that away from a person. People write to us all the time about the way that certain songs have changed their lives in a certain way. And I'm sure that's the same with a lot of bands. With us, we have a lot of people who say, for example, 'I've listened to "Dallas 1pm" and cried and cried.' It's just the way people are, really; women in particular. Certain songs move them. Obviously not songs like "Wheels Of Steel" or "Crusader", but more things like "Suzie Hold On" or "Do It All For You"; the more sort of intimate songs we do. And it's quite a compliment as a songwriter.

A lot of people tell us, 'you're a kick-ass band who never sold out' which is great, because that's the accusation that is levelled at so many bands, whatever it actually means. So if we are popular, in inverted commas, then our music must be moving people in one way or another, or they'd just buy the one album or so. "Motorcycle Man" meant a lot to people. No-one had sung about motorcycles much before, only Chris Spedding and the guy who was in the film »That'll Be The Day« with Ringo Starr – David Essex – that's about it really. A lot of people thought, 'yeah, "Motorcycle Man" – that's me.' Lyrically though, there's almost nothing to it. I didn't spend much time on the lyrics at all. There was a riff and I sang some words over it and they stuck and that was that really. There's only about twelve words to the entire bloody song. But it worked because people could relate to it; it's a concrete example of how the sentiment of a song can be as important to people as the lyrics. "To Hell And Back Again" is a song we played a lot on the 2005 25th Anniversary Of The New Wave Of British Heavy Metal tour. I didn't actually think it was that popular but I've been amazed: it's hugely popular, that song. I wrote it about some guy on Death Row who they said would be executed on Thursday and then they didn't do it, and they set another date and that came and went as well, and so on, and I thought, 'that must be fucking awful – just get it over with'. And that's where the song originally came from. 'Will I make the morning, to see another day, the guards may come at midnight, they're taking me away...' A lot of people won't twig that, and just like the sentiment behind the title. But it doesn't really matter, does it; people like the song, and that's what counts.

Like most writers, I worry about writers' block all the time. I jot down ideas all the time, but generally I usually wait until we have a nice guitar riff and then I'll pop my title in it, if it fits. I'll leave a lot of the lyric writing for later; maybe rough out a verse and chorus and then I'll move on to the next song. I feel you can get bogged down with the second, third, fourth verse so I'll move on and I'll change things as the album progresses. When you listen back you suddenly think, 'no, I'm going to change that lyric to the other song because I think it fits better.' "Wheels Of Steel" is a prime example. I swap ideas around quite a lot, because I don't think the book's closed until the studio door slams shut. I've learned in the past that to finalise something before you actually finish the whole album, if you see what I mean, results in you possibly missing so many more opportunities lyrically. You write lyrics to a song and rush to lay them down, and then realise that if you'd spent maybe another day on them, they might have turned into something completely different.

Fairly obviously though, if you are going to write a song called "Lionheart" it has to be a really moving piece of music. On the other hand, if you're writing a song about a fast car, it can be almost a throwaway fast riff, as the speed of the song almost nails the image. But "Lionheart" requires a lot of work, a lot of magic almost. 'Light the beacons, ring the bells, sing you minstrels, there's tales to tell...' It all has to be there in order to conjure up that period of time and a picture in your head. And that's quite hard; conjuring up the imagery for something like that doesn't come easy. You could easily knock up a song that goes something like, 'I went to the Crusades and I came back again,' but that doesn't inspire the imagination to create the image of what I'm trying to say. To our perception, Richard the Lionheart is a heavy historical figure, and if you are going to write a song about him it has to be a song that's moving, almost like a hymn or a psalm; an anthemic kind of song certainly, a call to arms even.

I think I have an advantage in that at my age I can look back with lots of memories that aren't just about rock 'n' roll and shagging; all the tragic and great things that happened in the Sixties and Seventies, I can write and sing about them because I witnessed them; maybe not first-hand, but I was alive and kicking and can remember how I felt when say, Neil Armstrong stepped on the Moon, or Donald Campbell was killed trying to break the speed record. And I tell you, it's a great position to be in. When I started in the 1960s there wasn't much in the way of bands writing historic songs. A few of the progressive bands maybe, but not many; much of what they did was more day-to-day stuff.

There's a fine line between entertainment and education, and things were taken very seriously in the Eighties. There were some good times, but some horrendous times too. We did a show on BBC Radio One called »B15«. Kid Jensen hosted it, with Tommy Vance, Anne Nightingale and us. We did some live in the studio songs and also did an interview which absolutely sums up the spirit of the Eighties under Margaret Thatcher. A guy died at one of our concerts: he had a weak blood vessel in his brain and was headbanging and he died, and as a result they were having this discussion about this craze of headbanging on the radio, and should it be banned, shit like that. And it was so formal. They've got a bloody professor on there, saying, in this really serious voice, 'well actually, the tribal people of Africa have been doing this for thousands of years and there's nothing really wrong with it. It's like everything – just don't do it too much.' And Kid Jensen is pushing it, saying, 'well, did this guy die because he went to a Saxon concert?' as if going to a Saxon concert is a guaranteed death sentence. And the prof. says, 'no, he could have done it playing rugby or football or anything like that.' But it was so 'establishment', still almost class-orientated, as though we and so many bands like us were a danger to the established order. (Well, maybe we were.) Immediately afterwards came a news bulletin that opens with something like, 'helicopters have just attacked an Argentinean vessel' or something like that; really heavy stuff in the midst of the Falklands War to follow a completely pointless discussion on the perceived dangers of headbanging. Pretty scary stuff, eh?

I have to say that I hated the Thatcher years. I think Margaret Thatcher and her cabinet of yes-men totally destroyed the country. She certainly completely wiped out whole communities. I feel really sad about it, actually. I hated her for it. I thought she was an absolutely evil bitch. The whole thing around the Miners' Strike, and her determination to crush it and the people who worked the pits... I was involved in the first miners' strikes when I was at the mines – back in the late Sixties, I think – and it was horrendous. I mean, I wasn't a fan of Arthur Scargill either, I thought he was a Communist stooge, but even so a lot of my friends were still coal miners, and a lot of people died in the mines, and their memory, their contribution to the country, was just being discarded by Thatcher and her Government. I don't think you can overstate it: Thatcher destroyed the country. The coal mining industry, the steel industry too, all over South Wales and the North East. She had this stupid advisor who told her to let it all go, with a mantra that the free-market economy will look after itself. Madness really; absolute fucking madness. Everybody was encouraged to set up their own businesses, and then they failed. And it's in this period of economic doom-and-gloom that Saxon became popular.

All the "Stand Up And Be Counted" songs, "See The Light Shining", all those early songs, the lyrics I wrote were about standing up for your rights and being strong, never giving up, never surrendering... All of that was based on the early Thatcher years when she destroyed the North of England and South Wales. But they are all songs of hope – stand up, stick together, be strong, get through it – they're all based on that mentality really. And we were having massive success in the early Eighties when all this was happening so we were very lucky really. To my mind, the country was going down the pan and all we – the people – had was music, and I think a lot of people got into Motörhead and Saxon and Iron Maiden and Def Leppard because it was a release from real life.

I think back then that people did think that music was a way to get off the dole queue. A lot of music came out of the industrial Midlands and North, a lot of the New Wave Of British Heavy Metal came from those regions. But I don't think it's the 'industrial towns' thing; I just think that a lot of young people were into music and rebelled – rebelled against everything through music because there was nothing else for them. And some of our popularity stems from that because we too were rebels in those days, rebellious against the police and every form of authority. We were just 'fuck you' basically. Going to the Dole Office to sign on for unemployment benefit used to be horrendous. They'd have a concert poster or flyer there and when we went to sign on they'd say, 'oh, I see you played last night. How much did you make?'

'About a quid each.'

'No, you didn't. You're lying. How much did you get paid?'

So we'd go, 'OK, stick your money up your arse then' and walk out. People thought we were sponging off the state but we weren't actually – we did try but they wouldn't give us anything! So it was quite a sacrifice. Now it's much easier; in the digital world it's easier to access music and to record, and there are more outlets at school and college for music. It's also seen as a massive export too and a legitimate profession to be a musician. But in those days it was horrendous. You were considered to be an absolute bum and a drop-out hippy, which was awful because we hated hippies. When punk came along we liked it because it was aggressive rock music against the system, and we were against the system as well, we just weren't fashionable at the time (and didn't like being spat at). We hated the police because we saw them as an extension of Thatcher.

And that was the environment we were in and the backdrop we became successful against. We were lucky; for many people it was a horrendous time.

I was already politicised by then through being a member of a Trades Union. When I was a teenager the unions were very strong and there were strikes all over the place. I have to admit that it seemed to me that the Communists ruled the unions, but whether you liked it or not you had to be in the union where I worked because it was a closed shop; union membership was compulsory. I'm not saying the closed shop is right; in fact I think that situation wasn't great either, but the unions did fight for workers' rights. The coal mines have an horrendous history – no health and safety rules, underage kids employed, people dying all over the place. So the unions did do a lot for working conditions. But they were run by a lot of far-Left people – I don't understand why they had so much control but they did – and between them and successive governments things swung from bad to worse. The big car strikes of the Sixties and Seventies were terrible. There were the power cuts and the three-day week. I remember having candles in the house for four days a week during those power cuts. It was really, really close to revolution back then. The students in America were rioting all the time, and I thought it was getting close to anarchy at times in England. And we loved it. Of course, almost immediately we were targeted by the police for going out with long hair. You know: we were obvious political agitators and non-conformists because we didn't have short hair and a job. We used to get stopped and searched all the time. And they'd plant stuff on us all the time just to get a bust. Bastards!

Is it any wonder we wrote "Strong Arm Of The Law"?

Chapter Seven

So we were back playing the clubs and lacking management after Trident had dropped us like the proverbial hot potato. To be fair though, there wasn't a lot of time between the first album coming out and 'failing' in May 1979 and the moment when things began to start hotting up for us. After a while without management we ended up signing with Blechner-Poxon: Ron Blechner and Dave Poxon, who sound like a couple of rogues and who probably were! We must have toured on that first album for a month or so before we even decided to get Blechner-Poxon on board. They were interested in managing the band and had an office in London, so we went with them and that gave us a bit of a base down south. I always remember that Hans Zimmer rented the room downstairs in the same building, where he stashed his keyboards. These days he's better know for winning Oscars for music for films like »Gladiator« and »The Lion King« but Poxon had played in a band with him called Krakatoa. Poxon was the bassist, and Zimmer obviously the keyboard player, Roger Adams was the guitarist, Terry Bennett from Sassafras was the singer and the drummer was one Nigel Glockler.

With Blechner-Poxon taking over the management, we started to get more work. (In the early period, by the way, we didn't used to have any manager, just an agent called Birchinall who used to book us in all these working men's clubs in Sunderland, giving rise to the catchphrase 'Birchinall gets fuck all'; but that's another story.) Poxon looked after us day to day, and Blechner did the office work. They were agents for a guy named Malcolm Hill who designed a fantastic PA, and they worked quite closely with a company called Light and Sound Design (L.S.D.) out of Birmingham. I'm not 100% sure of the time-line here, but Malcolm Hill supplied this PA to AC/DC, and I think people might have known people and as such we ended up signing an agency deal with Rod McSween from ITB, one of the biggest agencies, and I think from that point things started to move. Rod took an interest in us straight away and was a nice guy as well – always in the 'papers, always going out with Page 3 girls; as a guy, I personally could never understand their attraction, so obviously he must have a huge knob or something.

Because we were with ITB, we started getting good tours before »Wheels Of Steel« came out. We did a Slade tour which was not terribly massive but again, Noddy Holder is a fantastic frontman and I was watching and listening to him every night; we don't have a dissimilar voice when I go for it, actually. And they were nice to us. I mean, they took the piss all the time, but they were OK. It was mostly universities and discos but a lot of people, a couple of thousand people a night. We did half the tour and Def Leppard did the other half. Noddy Holder told me that everyone they'd toured with had become big – 'and if it works, it'll be great.' And it did, because both bands went on to be massive. So he was right.

Then at the end of 1979 we did Motörhead's »Bomber« tour. I think we were doing some of the »Wheels Of Steel« songs on the Motörhead tour; I'm pretty sure we did. Certainly by the time we did the BBC Session in January 1980 we had two »Wheels Of Steel« songs in "747", and "Motorcycle Man". But people were getting really interested in us. We had a couple of big interviews with Sounds about that time, and Melody Maker too; NME were never that bothered; they were still on the punk thing, writing about Generation X and the Sex Pistols.

We paid to get on the »Bomber« tour; I can't remember how much but it was well worth it and besides, Motörhead were really nice blokes. I think it was Lemmy who said, 'if they're buying on, they may as well use the same bus as us' which was like 'whoa!' So we travelled on their tourbus the whole time. No bunks, just really big armchairs as we stayed in hotels and just used the bus to travel from gig to gig (and to shag). We obviously knew of Motörhead because they were huge at that point. They were so big it took your breath away, but they were a bit like cartoon characters actually. It was great of them to let us use their bus though, and we got to see all their incredible model groupies. I don't know if they shagged them or if they were just for show, but they certainly impressed us!

We did a long tour with them because they kept adding more dates. It kicked off in November at Bracknell Sports Centre and culminated in three shows at Hammersmith Odeon just before Christmas. Two shows in Birmingham, three in Newcastle, all sold out. But the band appeared to be imploding really, even back then. Fast Eddie is, or at least appeared to be, a manic depressive. We'd be sat there in a hotel in Newcastle or somewhere and Eddie would say, 'you don't need me.'

And Philthy would go, 'fuck off. Don't talk so stupid.'

'Nah, you don't need me. You could get anybody and be fucking massive.'

'Look, Eddie; fucking pack it in.'

'Yeah, whatever; I may as well not fucking bother.'

'If you say one more thing, I'm going to smack you.'

And there'd be one of those thirty-minute three-second pauses, and Eddie would say, 'well, it's fucking true.'

Up jumps Phil, bang!, smacks Eddie, and the next thing you know, they're rolling around on the floor fighting for real. Throughout all this, Lemmy's reading a book. I'm like, 'Lemmy. Lemmy! LEMMY! Phil and Eddie, they're fighting!' And Lemmy would look over his book at them and go, 'yeah, they'll be all right,' and carry on reading. And that's how it was with them. But yes; it was a great tour. At that stage in our career, we couldn't have asked for a better tour. Lemmy would say during their set: 'Saxon are going to be huge, go out and buy their album tomorrow.' What better authentication do you need than Lemmy telling people to buy your album? It was a very mixed audience too, from young kids to Hells Angels, and all told, created a lot of buzz about us.

After we'd come off the road, we did a BBC session for the »The Friday Rock Show« with Tony Wilson at the BBC's Maida Vale studios. This was in January 1980. We were really hot by now and the BBC were really interested in us. Strange though it sounds now, at that time Radio One were actually the leaders in putting rock on the radio. They were really innovative and although John Peel had gone on to punk things and indie stuff, he was a great champion of bands in the Seventies like Wishbone Ash. We never had much to do with him because he'd moved on, and I don't think he was that involved much with the New Wave Of British Heavy Metal except for a passion for Def Leppard's "Getcha Rocks Off" EP. At this time the two big things on the scene were the explosion of interest in heavy metal and the new romantics thing with Duran Duran and bands like that, and in a way those two were pretty much the opposite ends of the spectrum. On »Top Of The Pops« for instance, you could have Saxon on there, Spandau Ballet, Motörhead and Duran Duran; almost like the rockers and mods all over again. You either liked heavy metal or you liked the new romantic thing; it was impossible to like both at the same time. It was all to do with what you wore, how long your hair was and whether you liked guitar-orientated music or a more fashion-orientated faddy thing. Our music was more male-orientated, without a doubt; we would have liked it the other way round but we didn't have a choice. And that's how it was. That said, the girls we did get at our shows were seriously into the metal music.

Tommy Vance went on to be one of our main supporters and we had some great chats and some great times with him. He was a leading light in the early days. That original 1980 studio session for Tommy Vance's show, the »Studio B15« session from 1982 and the edited version of our Reading 1986 show was released on CD by the BBC in 1998. We were consulted on that; I think Pete Hinton was involved. I think it was him who 'phoned me and said, 'they want to release the BBC tapes, and they'll pay you this royalty and that royalty' so I said, 'yeah, no problem.' Never got any royalties of course; I must look into that one day. The thing is though, I don't relate to those sessions much. Although they were important to us at the time, they're not really important to me now. I can understand fans wanting to hear a snapshot of that period, but what you have to remember is that, and I only found this out recently, if you listen to our early albums and you listen to the recordings from the BBC you'll hear there's no real difference whatsoever. It's really bizarre. On »Wheels Of Steel« and »Strong Arm Of The Law«, there's hardly any production on those albums at all, they're basically just us playing together in one room, with a bit of guitar overdub and a quick mix. So if you listen to us playing on the radio, it sounds the same. I recently found the tape of »B15« that went out prime-time – the one with us and Professor Headbanger – with us playing live in the studio, and it's really hard to tell the difference between the songs there, played live, and the album versions. It's near enough the same. It's almost uncanny. It was live in the studio, but the songs sound almost exactly the same as the album cuts. The point for me is that I don't relate to those BBC versions because they're no different; there's nothing new. The only thing – and this isn't on the CD – is I think I stopped the song on one of them. There was a show which Hendrix did and which Graham obviously loved, where Hendrix stopped a song, 'wait a minute, wait a minute, I'm going to stop playing this shit' and he went into "Sunshine Of Your Love" instead. I think Cream had just spilt up, so Hendrix did it as a tribute and they were trying to take him off air. So, I said to Graham, 'well, we'll do the same thing if you want. I'll stop "747" and we'll play "The Eagle Has Landed" so I did. I went, 'wait a minute, wait a minute; we're going to play a new song we've written,' and played "The Eagle Has Landed" live on air.

Another influential character of the time was Neal Kay, the semi-legendary DJ at The Bandwagon Heavy Metal Soundhouse who was quite responsible for getting us, Iron Maiden and Def Leppard into print. "Stallions Of The Highway" was Number 1 in his heavy metal chart in Sounds, which meant a lot to us as it was based on requests. He was really influential with the young kids and we played with him at his discos quite a few times. I mean it was a buzz to see "Stallions..." at the top of the chart when the album had, well, flopped really in financial terms, but people began to discover the songs off it and obviously the ones they came to like were the outrageously rock songs, the power songs like "Stallions...", so it was a pointer to future things. "747" and "Wheels Of Steel" are nothing like "Stallions Of The Highway" really, but even so, there is a certain aggression to them.

So Kay was very influential, and he pushed Iron Maiden a lot as well. We played some monumental shows with Maiden in the early days. We were good friends. We used to meet in motorway services all the time. We were highly competitive, not in an in-your-face way but both bands were competing for recording contracts. We played a fantastic show at Manchester University with Maiden on first, then us, then a band called Nutz. Although age-wise there probably wasn't much difference (they were probably a little bit older than we were), musically we were a century apart. They were based on long drawn out solos and singing obscure songs about some woman, and we went on stage to rip your head off, singing about motorbikes and wheels of steel and planes crashing and all kinds of shit. You know, nothing to do with love. Nothing romantic, you know. 'She's a prick teaser...' was the closest we got. Maiden and us totally blew the place to pieces, and I felt sorry for Nutz. I had seen them before this show and felt for them, the way the audience treated them. They're hard bastards in Manchester, and Nutz were used to pulling their own audiences and being cool, but the kids there that night wanted to rock, really rock out and go nuts (if you pardon the pun); they wanted music that rips your balls off. I remember the guitarist (who was the leader of the band and a very talented guy) coming into our dressing room and saying, 'I've never seen anybody go down so well and sound so fucking bad!' I guess that actually sums it up really because once we were up there, we didn't give a flying fuck what we sounded like. It's the same today;

once you start, that's it – it's set for the night. If it sounds pretty cool it's OK, but if it doesn't, go for it anyway! The more established Seventies bands were so into how they sounded, so precious about the nuances, whereas we didn't give a shit – all our songs were twice as fast live as they were on the album anyway. But it must have been like an assault on your senses! I mean, the crowd had Maiden and us, and then Nutz; it was like they were from the Georgian period or something compared to what we and Steve Harris's boys had just played. It was like a totally different concept and it really brought it home to me how different we were to the established bands of the time. Our attitude was just like, 'this is us; this is us and we're here – take it or leave it'; and that's how we were. And if they didn't like it, too bad – we'd just move on to the next place. It must have been like the Blitz really. Maiden were going for it as well, of course; that first album is fantastic.

I can really remember that time. It's hard to describe though; I don't think we set out to be different as such, but there was definitely a huge difference between us and the Seventies bands, the established bands of the time. They were definitely more musically-orientated and we were more entertainment-orientated. Punk focussed a lot of people onto what was important, and what was important to punk bands and punk audiences apart from the way they looked, was snappy riffs and straight to the point aggression. We and the bands that came up with us learned a lot from that. We loved the Sex Pistols' album. The guitars were so in-your-face, "Pretty Vacant" and "God Save The Queen" – that's how a guitar should sound. And if you listen to "Princess Of The Night or "20,000 Feet", the guitars are quite similar in that they're right in your face. The bands of the Seventies didn't have that kind of eye-opener. They were still doodling away and doing their thing, influenced heavily by the blues, whereas we had one eye on the punk past and one eye firmly on the future. Some of the great punk bands, the guitar playing is brilliant. We just didn't like their fashion; there's no way I was going to stick a safety pin through my lip just to get someone to notice me. But we were just as against the system as they were, just as radical as they were. It's just that we'd got long hair and our influences came from rock music rather than pop music.

The punk thing meant we found it hard to get work when it was at its height, which is why we concentrated on South Wales and the North East because punk wasn't massive there, punk was more of a big city thing – Manchester, London, places like that. It wasn't that big in what became our stamping ground. If people went out on a Friday or Saturday night they wanted to listen to rock music, not to some twat screaming on about police brutality in London. And although there were some genuine punk bands, a lot of them were crap bandwagon jumpers: poor pop disguised as radical punk. The people we were playing to weren't into it and couldn't relate to it; it could have been a million miles away as far as they were concerned, so these people literally kept us alive in those places. Besides, for all punk's posturing, I don't remember any lyric in any song ever changing anything. I don't think any one song is ever going to change the world. Politically, punk changed nothing at the end of the day, but it was very entertaining, which, when it all comes down to it, is what it's all about.

But as I said, although we had one eye on what punk had achieved and how it had achieved it, we had the other eye on the future. We had one more album to make on our contract, and then Carrere would either exercise their option to extend it for further albums or show us the door. Dave Poxon had this great idea of booking us into a studio in Wales, which sounded pretty stupid to me in the height of winter; but we were keen to get on with the second album, and besides, I had this great idea for a song about a steam train called "Wheels Of Steel".

Part Two:

Power And
The Glory

Chapter Eight

excuse me, but I've just finished listening to Saxon's »Wheels Of Steel« and I'm reeling shellshocked in the aftermath. My brain's scrambled, my mind's minced, my 'critical faculties' are in confusion and all I want to do is go – 'WOOAAAARGHH!'

Yeah, one more time – 'WOOAAAARGHH!!'

(Gasp) That's better. Now give me time to wind down, to catch my breath, for my heart to slow from its triphammer beat and I'll explain.

(Wheeze) Well, OK. Apologies for the lack of level-headedness at the beginning of this review, but »Wheels Of Steel« got to me in no uncertain terms. The album's nothing less than a powerful Kong-type chest-beating, throat-bursting, high-pitched hollering triumph and the initial ringing in my ears caused me to succumb to the call of the wild. Badly.

But now that I've cooled off a little it's time for the facts. After years in the wilderness labouring under the unfortunate monicker of Son Of A Bitch, Saxon suddenly burst forth in big teasing style from Barnsley last year with a debut album issued on little-known

Carrere Records, a label better known for French disco releases than for daubs of South Yorkshire warpaint.

Although spoilt by a couple of turgid Rushish epic tracks, the premier platter »Saxon« nonetheless showed considerable promise with songs of the footstomping calibre of "Still Fit To Boogie", "Backs To The Wall" and the blistering bikers' anthem "Stallions Of The Highway".

Since the release of the LP the five Saxons have toured solidly, both as headliners and as support to such bands as Rainbow and Nazareth, finding time between gigs to record a follow-up disc, and »Wheels Of Steel« is it.

And it's quite simply the best heavy metal album of the year so far. Unlike another recent rock release, »Wheels Of Steel« isn't streamlined and sterilised for Stateside consumption; rather, it's loud, proud, as British as bangers and mash and a towering testimony to the revitalisation of UK raunch 'n' roll.

Track count is one over the eight, each more riotous than a gang of soccer hooligans trashing a train carriage and none less than stupendous.

You get "Motorcycle Man" with engine revs running from speaker to speaker and a skull-splitting riff that necessitates the wearing of a crash helmet. You get companion cuts "Wheels Of Steel" and "Freeway Mad", Saxon 'burning solid rubber' and reaching 60 from zero quicker than any dragster in an airstrip speed meet. You get "747 (Strangers In The Night)" which is less to do with a UFO live double album and more about flight Scandinavian 101 losing power and overshooting a runway, its turbines whistling eerily in the midst of a fiercely bubbling HM melting pot.

And best of all you get "Machine Gun", a rabble-rousing rat-tat-tale of POW escape ('Over the top/Into the wire/Running like a madman/In the fire') with a grinding, churning, wild and wailing climax that has to be heard to be believed and is likely to lay you flatter than a tap on the cranium with a Giant Canadian Redwood.

Naturally there's much more besides all this but, aw, I'd rather just whet your appetites than blow the gaff completely.

So let me just say that if you like your singers to have more vocal power than the whole of the Kop Choir, if you like your guitar playing more raw than a sabre slash across the stomach, if you like your rhythm section to pound like the Incredible Hulk's footsteps... in other words, if you like your music more than a little on the heavy side, then »Wheels Of Steel« is for you.

It's out April 4. If I were you I'd take the camping equipment and pitch tent outside your local record store now. 'WOOAAAARGHH!' and out.

Geoff Barton, Sounds, 29/03/80

The five-star Sounds review of »Wheels Of Steel« was, for many people, their introduction to Saxon. To get such a great review from someone as well regarded as Geoff Barton was an unexpected thumbs-up at a time when we really needed one. As a band, we knew we'd recorded a good album; we just didn't know it was *that* good.

After »Saxon« we had one more album on our contract – one more chance really – and Dave Poxon was quite passionate about it. So we were stuck in the Welsh mountains, during the winter of 1979/1980, and it was absolutely freezing. The people that owned it lived in tepees and were total people of the land, vegans. Apparently they were quite famous in the Seventies; they were on TV and everything.

Basically we were working in one big room. We had a four-track Teac and I would fiddle with it and record anything and everything. It was a nice Welsh cottage but it was very cold, it snowed like a bitch and we all got snowed in. Every day they'd ask us what we wanted to eat and like complete bastards we'd ask for leg of pork, leg of lamb, beef steaks, and they would have to buy the stuff from the butchers and cook it for us. And their kids were slavering away at all these smells because they'd only eaten nuts all their lives. I can't help but laugh thinking about it; it was a terrible thing to do to them really. But anyway, we'd hack into these chunks of meat and give the left-overs to their dogs. The dogs got the lot, while the kids got fuck-all! Meanwhile, it was so cold we used to put these oil-filled radiators in the beds before we went to sleep to warm them up. And then one day Steve Howe, the guitarist from Yes walked in, wanting to buy the place. It was pretty bizarre, all-in-all; really surreal.

So we were in the Welsh mountains in the snow with nothing else to do but work, and we worked hard at what could be our last shot. One day, I said I'd got an idea about a steam train called "Wheels Of Steel". So we started writing riffs and putting things together and pulling them apart. I had turned the rest of the band on to AC/DC, and I think between me and Graham Oliver we wrote the "Wheels Of Steel" riff which is basically an AC/DC riff but different – sort of 'not-really-but-it-is', if you know what I mean – but instead of writing about a stream train I eventually wrote it about an American car we used to have. We had American cars quite a lot in the early years because they fitted a lot of people in, they were fast, cheap, and besides we liked them. So that's what the song's about. It's basically about street cruising and drag racing.

And we had "747" which is about two completely different things really. A lot of our songs are a bit ambiguous when it comes to verses and choruses. I must have a fascination with night, because it keeps cropping up in our songs all over the place. (Tommy Vance once asked me, 'what is it with night and you – you know, "Princess Of The Night", "Strangers in The Night" and so on?' The honest answer is that I don't actually know; I've just got this thing with pictures in my head of the night.) Anyway, "747" is a story about people, strangers, meeting in airports and generally people having romances, affairs, one-night stands and going off again, like ships in the night.

But then I saw a documentary about a power cut in New York where everything went off and there was an absolute baby-boom nine months later because everyone had just gone to bed and had sex. And those that weren't shagging were nicking things; when the lights went back on people were caught half-way down the stairs with their neighbour's television set. It's like people reverted to their basic instincts – sex and stealing everything in sight. It's like in Yorkshire, when it was foggy, you had to tie things down because that's when the thieves came out, and the thing is, everybody was a thief in the fog, so you'd be tying your stuff down and nicking your neighbour's shit at the same time. In the Seventies and Eighties, the fog used to be really thick. It's not so bad now. People in France where I live now and America still think we have perpetual fog, the old pea-soupers, but that's because they spend too much time watching »Sherlock Holmes« films. But I remember the fog and smog being really thick in those days though, and not being able to see a thing. I remember going to see a gig in Leeds and on the way there I walked straight into a lamppost – just didn't see it; bang! I was with this American girl and we got there, there was about 6,000 people in this car park. I thought, 'how did they manage to drive here when I couldn't even walk it?' Mind you, they'd been knocking over bollards all over the place though!

So "747" is a song about the power cut in New York, and there was this plane landing. But the runway lights went off, which I thought was fascinating, and the pilot managed to pull her up and flew on to somewhere else because he couldn't see to land. I just thought it was a fascinating concept, I was completely intrigued by the thought of this plane being unable to land. So that's basically what it is, two separate ideas linked in the one song: the plane and the power cut in the verse, and ships in the night in the chorus. On those early albums, I was just experimenting with words and stories, and that one just seemed to touch people really. And the 'Strangers In The Night' theme was something Frank Sinatra had made familiar to millions of people all over the world. No-one has ever accused me of ripping him off, but sometimes working with familiar themes can really help. I didn't think that at the time but, in retrospect, I'm sure it does actually work like that.

Elsewhere on the album, "Suzie Hold On" was loosely about a friend who had a brain tumour which killed her. And "Machine Gun", which I thought made a great album closer, wasn't actually about a POW escape but was just a World War One story about Ypres or The Somme, or any of those 'over-the-top' battles where young men were slaughtered in their thousands for a few miserable feet of ground.

So there we were in Wales, knowing we'd written a good album. We didn't know it would be as big as it was, but we knew we'd written a good album. Maybe the whole »Wheels Of Steel« album, the whole thing about being in the Welsh mountains in the snow amongst the tepee people was a state of grace. It just focused our minds somehow. Maybe being atop a mountain meant that something celestial could break through from above! But I knew "Wheels Of Steel" was a good song with a great hook and I knew "747" was a great song because I know what makes a great song; if the music is great and the riff and the melody are strong and the lyrics are catchy then I think you're on with a bit of a run. We just never expected it to do what it did; but Dave Poxon knew it was a big album, and people around us were starting to get excited.

The album was produced by Pete Hinton – one of the guys who'd signed us – with us assisting. He just turned up and took charge but we were all right with that because we knew what we wanted anyway. I think we were surprised that the finished album didn't sound much different from the demos, because that wasn't really what we wanted: we wanted to sound like a real band! When you start out, you see, you never feel like you sound like a real band; you compare yourself to the bands you like but you never sound like them – you always just sound like yourself. And that can be a bit disheartening at first.

But we knew we needed some guidance anyway because some of us wanted the album to sound like Led Zeppelin, some of us wanted it to sound like AC/DC. Everybody had different ideas so somebody had to take control and that's what Pete Hinton did. We recorded it at Ramport Studios – The Who's place – in London in February 1980.

The house where I was born; looking a bit worse for wear now

Weaver House where I lived from the age of about two to eighteen

My first school in Skelmanthorpe

The Methodist chapel where my mother used to play the organ, and where I
went to Sunday School but never saw the light

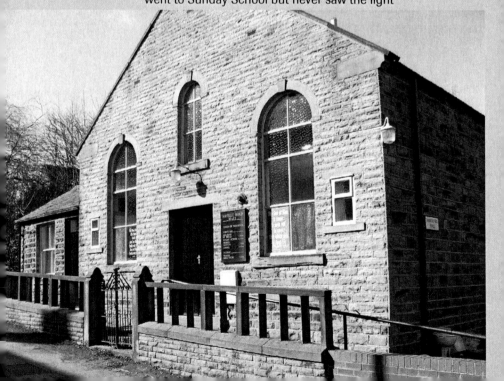

The factory where I worked and lost my finger end

Barnsley Civic Hall Centenary Room

SON OF A BITCH

SON OF A BITCH FAN CLUB
50 IVANHOE ROAD
CONISBROUGH
·· DONCASTER· ··

Spew from the gutter that's me
Spawned from the State Penni~~tentiary~~
Momma died there, Pappy too

...at's the truth

...to rock
~~~~ my stack
first
~~order~~
~~il term~~

...the city I feel small
...slouch to City Hall
...gutter on the

Dragged from th...
~~Stole from t...~~
Slapped down,
I w...

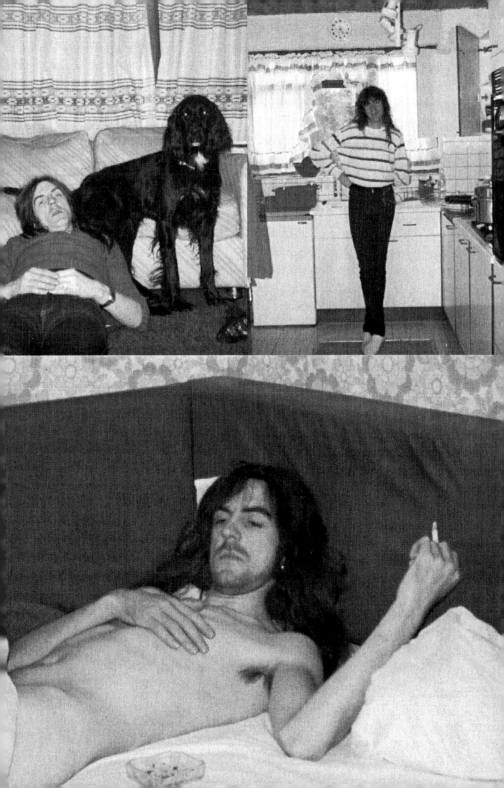

Live Cologne 1981

DURAN DURAN ■ SANDINISTAS ■ POSITIVE NOISE ■ PETER CRISS
THOMPSON TWINS ■ M ■ RITA MARLEY ■ GIRLS AT OUR BEST

so_nds_

ONE LUMP OR TWO?

Saxon, p.28

VOTE   IN   THE   POLL, p.37

STRONG ARM
METAL

STRONG ARM
METAL

CARRERE

PRINCESS OF THE NIGHT

The viaduct, and the field from where I used to sit
and watch steam trains at night

The guy who engineered it was Will Reid Dick – a nice enough guy with an odd name but quite a famous producer now.

We made the album very quickly. The studio was haunted, so they said, by a priest – because it was an old chapel – and there were a few funny feelings I had while we were there. I used to sing in a vocal booth on my own and later, during the »Strong Arm Of The Law« sessions, I actually passed out on while singing "To Hell And Back Again" because I was singing so hard. I sang so hard I starved my brain of oxygen. In those days I thought you had to sing loud – very heavy metal. I had a very loud voice back then; well, I still do, but since then I've learned to control it, and I've also learned that having a loud voice has got nothing to do with the recording process.

But »Wheels Of Steel« was a good album. We really didn't know that we'd written an album of epic proportions, but we had come out with an album that was very well received immediately; we really needed to deliver the goods or we'd be dropped, and against all odds we did just that. You can't get much more British than that, can you!

The title track was chosen as the first single from the album. Back then they used to do everything in mono as well as stereo, and there was a version without vocals as well. Carrere were very worried about getting heavy guitars played on the radio. The company was very singles-orientated and its whole ethos revolved around the hit single, so we were encouraged to have singles on our albums. We actually couldn't give a shit; we just wanted to have albums like real bands did. But back then there was a mid-week chart position (might be the same today, I don't know) and if you were about Number 36 and rising you were booked to play on »Top Of The Pops«. "Wheels Of Steel" made the cut and so off we trouped. I think Def Leppard must have been around with one of their singles – "Hello America", perhaps? – because I think that charted at the same time. But because the single could go either way the BBC recorded you without an audience, which is why the »Top Of The Pops« "Wheels Of Steel" performance has no audience – we were shot in an empty studio. On the Thursday, it had gone up to Number 26 or so and so they showed it on the programme. I think Def Leppard went down so they didn't appear; Joe Elliott might call me a lying bastard but I'm pretty sure that's what happened, and that's how close it was in those days. So we didn't meet any other bands on the "Wheels Of Steel" performance, as they kept repeating that one film. It wasn't until we did "747" that we did »Top Of The Pops« for real. It charted quite well at first, and the BBC went on strike the very week that the single went Top Twenty. They were on strike for two weeks, the two weeks that we felt we should have been on, so the single peaked at Number 13. As a singles company, Carrere were pretty switched on about the singles chart, and they always said that it would have gone Top Five; apparently, the day after a »Top Of The Pops« performance you could guarantee an extra 30,000 sales. But we were happy with Number 13 because almost from nowhere we had a massive album and two hit singles. And "747" was a good package too – picture sleeve, 12", live track on the B-side. They were fairly innovative at Carrere; they were into doing these neat packages and picture discs and things like that with their singles.

As it turned out, we started to get heavy rotation on BBC Radio One, so their fears about nasty, loud guitars on the radio didn't come to much. We must have been on almost once every half-an-hour or so at one point: "747" seemed to be on all the time. Pulling a third single off the album was pushing it a bit, and despite the fact that "Suzie Hold On" was a bit more commercial, it made a lot less headway in the charts. Maybe the radio stations didn't like it; maybe people had bought two singles and the album and thought, 'enough's enough'. It just shows that you never can tell. There was a good live version of 'Judgement Day' on the B-side though, even if Carrere printed the cover photo on the picture sleeve back-to-front and mis-spelled the title 'Suzy Hold On' rather than 'Suzie…' Wankers!

We were touring with Nazareth when it started to go nuts for us. Because people generally sat down to listen to music then, our sole aim in life was to get people to stand up and come to the front. That was a massive thing with me, to get people up and down the front, near to us, not sat down far away. I used to jump off stage and go and fetch people. The ushers with their torches would be like trying to make them sit down and I would be lifting them up from their seats. So it was quite radical; we were quite 'in-your-face' because we always had a problem with 'the establishment'. We didn't feel that women showing rock fans to their seats with torches was on. We thought they should all just come in and have a good time. A lot of other bands thought that too, but we were passionate about it, that people should come down to the front and take over the space that was there. Rock music is not a music you can listen to sat down; maybe the Sixties Woodstock shit was, but not us. We demanded, demanded, that people rise up and come to the front! And I used to spend most of the gig trying to get that to happen, having constant battles with the bouncers.

The Nazareth tour was great for us, and they basically played sold-out shows because of us, and they knew it. They actually said that to us. Dan McCafferty came down with a bottle of champagne and said, 'we've been pretty shitty to you, haven't we'. And we agreed. We didn't have a dressing room most nights. No soundcheck either. An article in Sounds picked up on the fact that we played just twenty-five minutes at Wolverhampton Civic – this would have been late March 1980 – and that 'the lights are straight up even though people are going nuts for an encore'. Apparently, I told the journalist, Chris Collingwood, that 'when you're supporting, some bands help you and others don't. Motörhead did, Rainbow didn't, but Nazareth neither help or hinder us. But they're pretty good guys…'

But anyway, McCafferty continued: 'well, you're going to be fucking massive. Good luck!' And that was it. It was just business really: they had a hospitality room every night, and that should have been our dressing room. But that's all right, that's the way it goes. The main thing is that it was a successful tour for us and we could see that things were happening because, well, we were different. I don't know how we were different, but we were just different to the other bands of the Seventies. We didn't fall into that 'drinking at the Marquee' VIP lounge ligging set really. We didn't really do that; we were totally committed artists and that's what we wanted to do. The drug-induced Seventies thing passed us by – we didn't get involved with it so when we went on stage in those early days we were like wild animals basically, really going for it, and I think the passion and aggression of the music hooked people.

Almost immediately afterwards we went out on our own headline tour, supported firstly by Lautrec and then by Tygers Of Pan Tang. It was a great tour, although badly co-ordinated as more and more dates were tacked on so we went up and down the UK like a yo-yo. Too much travelling really – we wasted a lot of time and energy; that said, we did play some pretty obscure towns.

Geoff Barton showed up and reviewed us in Sounds playing at the Colwyn Bay Dixieland Showbar. It was a good feature and great publicity for the band. He made some comment about us playing in such a place (I can't remember what word he used but it wasn't very complimentary), until I pointed out that not only didn't it bother me, but that compared to some of the gigs we did as Son Of A Bitch, the Dixieland Showbar was like the Royal Festival Hall!

Chapter Nine

One of my big bugbears is the band's management, which I'll keep coming back to because I think they do have to take a lot of responsibility for the bad decisions that were taken. Let's face it, if you are managing a band, you're managing it: you can't then say, 'oh, they were unmanageable' ten years later. That's not fair, is it? That's them shirking their responsibilities. In the early days they were OK and got us some great gigs, although to be honest, it would have been Rod McSween at ITB – International Talent Booking – who was responsible for the big ones, the tours with Slade and Nazareth and Motörhead. As I said, the record company paid Motörhead for us to be there, but as Motörhead let us use their bus, that was OK by us.

But the decision to put us back into the studio to record »Strong Arm Of The Law« was basically based on money. We made a lot of money touring and the »Wheels Of Steel« tour can't have cost much to stage because the production wasn't that big. It was just one truck really, and we must have done at least 35,000 people, if not 40,000 or more on that tour, so the t-shirts and everything else must have yielded quite a high gross. So why we got brow-beaten back into the studio so quickly to write another album I've got no idea. I think it was a big mistake. We should have at least been given a fucking holiday!

We did the Judas Priest tour of Europe which was again another fantastic tour for us. »Wheels Of Steel« was out when we toured with Priest so we were really cooking then; and they had »British Steel« and we had »Wheels Of Steel« which is a fair co-incidence when you think about it. They used to say to us, 'fucking hell, man; you're album's still in the charts in England. What's going on?' and their album was a little bit under ours, then over ours, in the charts so there was a bit of a competition going on between »British Steel« and »Wheels Of Steel« for a while – and I think we beat them in the end!

They were nice guys, Judas Priest, and »British Steel« was a fantastic album with "Breaking The Law" and all that shit. We did »Top Of The Pops« with them as well, so we used to see each other all the time back then. We enjoyed that tour though as it broke us in Germany, in my opinion. Three shows and we were massive in Germany; the fans and the press loved us there.

As the UK leg of »Wheels Of Steel« tour went from clubs to city halls fairly quickly we needed a crew so we basically nicked Slade's crew and tour manager. When a band first makes it – in big inverted commas – the crew that were with them before they made it, well, it's a big deal for them too. So they've made it as well, and it's all a big 'onwards and upwards' camaraderie kind of thing. I can't remember much about the tour actually. I remember Glasgow Apollo was monumental and Hammersmith was really frightening. We had the bus company that Motörhead had; in fact, probably even had the same bus. But the tour was very long, it never ended. It was a great time though. All those big old cinema gigs – two nights at Birmingham Odeon – were fantastic. When a new band has a big album, it's like a whole new audience have discovered the band (although we might have pinched a lot of it from Motörhead). Most people thought »Wheels Of Steel« was our first album. It wasn't until later that people got into »Saxon«. Generally it was by-passed because as »Wheels Of Steel« was so big people saw that as the first album.

When a band goes so big, so quickly, right across the country, the feeling of those first gigs can never be repeated. Never. Everybody is so excited, and it's just a fantastic feeling. We used to drive through the town to the gig and it would be deserted. And we'd walk through the doors and there'd be two thousand people going nuts! It was a fantastic atmosphere, and one you can never re-create. The second tour is fantastic, because you're a bit bigger then, but I don't think you ever really get back to the euphoric feel that you have on your first major tour on the back of your first successful album. After that you're always comparing everything to that first tour. The »Strong Arm Of The Law« tour was probably a much bigger, much better organised, much better production tour, but for us as a band it wasn't as magical. 'Euphoric': that's the only word for it. We'd been striving to be there for so long, and then suddenly we *were* there. It was like, 'whoa; what do we do now?'

But then, in the height of all of that, we were taken off the road to start our third album. I think the management decisions were very dodgy and, knowing what I know now about the business, I think probably playing two nights at Birmingham Odeon made more money than one night at a bigger gig. We should have toured more on »Wheels Of Steel« and really expanded the fan base. Everywhere we played sold out, so we could have played bigger shows. But instead we came off the road to record »Strong Arm Of The Law«. It was a great album to write so quickly on the back of »Wheels Of Steel«, but we should have stayed on the road.

We broke off from recording »Strong Arm Of The Law« to play the Heavy Metal Barndance at Bingley Hall. We were really on the way up by then, we were still getting played on the radio quite a lot and I was doing things like the Saturday morning show »TISWAS« and »Pop Quiz« and talk shows on TV, and I was having a great time. But that Bingley Hall gig was a totally Eighties thing. It's a shame Iron Maiden didn't play it as well – that would have been fabulous – but it was Girlschool, then us and Motörhead, with several other bands – Mythra, Vardis, White Spirit and Angel Witch. It was a good gig for us though, although it was really hot – rainclouds-in-the-ceiling hot; there must have been 14,000 people there. But I liked the venue, it was a cowshed, obviously, a cattle market, but we played it again on the »Denim And Leather« tour and did pretty well actually – it was nearly full. But Bingley Hall was a great thing for us to do. Although…

You see, the thing is, the Motörhead/Saxon connection was quite strong and as Motörhead lived in London they'd turn up at every London gig we did because we were big pals. But Eddie and Phil were always coming on stage and would either chain me to the mikestand or try and get Paul's cap off so we basically had to put a stop to it and that did piss them off a bit. I think they did understand – eventually – that we had to stop them coming on stage all the time because we never went on their stage. We felt there was a little bit of disrespect there from Fast Eddie and Phil so we decided to ban people from the side of the stage for a couple of shows in London. I don't think we ever stopped Lemmy coming on though, but we had to stop them because it was more than a little bit annoying. We had to put our foot down; we wanted to be taken seriously and not seen as Motörhead's pet support band.

Not long after that came the first Monsters Of Rock show at Donington. That was a fantastic bill: had Deep Purple headlined it would have been in my opinion the ultimate gig. But it was Rainbow, although of course they were pretty big, bigger than sliced bread at that time. It was Cozy Powell's last gig with them, which explains the mass of pyrotechnics. It also turned out to be Graham Bonnet's last gig as well, which was probably a good thing in all honesty. We'd done three shows with Rainbow previously and they'd kicked us off. I used to like to watch Graham Bonnet – he was a fantastic singer but the worst frontman in the world. He said something like, 'I'm from the BBC' and it was like, 'what the fuck is he on about? There's sixty thousand people here; stop fucking around.' They started to do all these really wacky songs, and encored with "Will You Still Love Me Tomorrow". What the hell was all that about? I stood there listening to him… "Will You Still Love Me Tomorrow"?

'No, I won't as a matter of fact! Fuck off!' What sort of rock band were they, doing a song like that? 'Play "Smoke On The Water" you cunt!'

But Donington really was great for us because I really think we really stole the show. Most of the reviews said that we were the band of the day. The Sounds review said that 'Saxon, who are fast becoming equal to or even better than Motörhead, gave Donington a very necessary kick in the lobotomy… Saxon are entertaining because they really do enjoy themselves…' If you listen to the tape of that show – the famous Graham Oliver tape which we'll get to later on – it is a really happening gig. We were still doing things like "Bap Shoo Ap" (despite the fact that Gary Holton of the Heavy Metal Kids had told us to pack it in) but back then it was a good sing-back. But it was a great day and the sun shone and we loved it and I got to ride a Harley Davidson round the Donington track so my day was complete. A very nervous day though; we were awe-struck. There was a lot of people there and I remember walking on stage, and seeing about sixty thousand people in broad daylight is frightening, believe me. It's not so bad at night because you only see the bits of the crowd but in the light it was frightening. We'd sold way over 100,000 records by that point, nearly 200,000, so virtually everybody there knew us and knew the songs. It was fantastic really. We couldn't do any wrong. Judas Priest were great. Personally I think Rainbow struggled at that gig, but the fans were loyal and the songs were catchy… "Will You Still Love Me Tomorrow" – was that supposed to be a bit tongue-in-cheek? Was it a bit of an in-joke or something? Whatever, I didn't like it. I thought a band like Rainbow should be playing rock songs. There was a tenuous connection between us and Rainbow via Russ Ballard; he wrote some of their hits, and our old mate and early mentor John Verity was a good friend of Ballard's, and Ballard used to come down to Livingstone Studios quite a lot when we were doing the first album. Ballard gave "I Surrender" to John Verity and he recorded it. Verity probably transposed it and arranged it from Russ Ballard's original demo (which was probably just an acoustic guitar and him singing) and his version was exactly the same as Rainbow's. So I think whoever suggested "I Surrender" to Rainbow passed them Verity's version because Verity sang high, like Joe Lynn Turner, and it pissed Verity off big-time because he thought he was going to do that song.

Donington was a huge success overall for all the bands, and I really believed that Judas Priest, Scorpions, Saxon, Riot, Touch and April Wine – whatever happened to April Wine? – was a strong bill really. And Rainbow were pretty big at that time, "Since You Been Gone" and "All Night Long" were not only massive hits, but great songs as well. An official live album from the festival was issued later in the year, with each band contributing one or two songs (we had one on the LP – "Backs To The Wall" – and also "Freeway Mad" on the cassette version). 'A fiery performance of "Backs To The Wall" demonstrates just why Saxon are so popular – no holds barred riffing of power and precision' said Paul Suter in his album review in Sounds.

»Strong Arm Of The Law« came out in November 1980, and also received a five-star review in Sounds (it was almost unheard of for two consecutive albums by the same band to get top marks), again by Geoff Barton, although we weren't particularly concerned with how many stars we got. We saw ourselves as songwriters. Well, Paul Quinn and I did. Whether the whole band saw themselves as songwriters I've no idea because actually only two people wrote the bulk of the songs. Back then we shared everything, including song-writing credits, because we were friends; the trouble is, some friends worked harder than others. Some of us used to stay up all night writing music while others went to bed or sat there reading »Auto Trader«, the used car magazine. I used to walk past Graham Oliver when he was reading »Auto Trader« and say, 'any fucking songs in there?' And he'd miss the sarcasm completely, and reply, 'no, but there's a nice Ford Cortina.' That said, though, with my hand on my heart, I don't think that any one of us could have written any of those songs on our own, to be fair to the others. But I do remember that on »Wheels Of Steel« and »Strong Arm Of The Law« I was still playing a lot of guitar and many of the guitar riffs came from Paul, with me and Graham chipping in. Most of the great guitar playing was from Paul, but I think early on that Graham decided to not let Paul's star shine quite so bright and to steal a lot of the thunder by doing the guitar gymnastics and pyro things; face it, anybody can set fire to a guitar. It was just part of the show. But as a guitarist Paul's contribution to Saxon was – and still is – immense.

The band was really hot back then, and all the live tapes of those early shows that I've come across, the band does nothing wrong. Nothing at all. Graham does some great guitar and Steve Dawson's playing some great bass; there's nothing wrong with the band, it was cooking. But from a song-writing point of view... Well, since those people have left they have made comments about song-writing so let's get it clear once and for all. All the fast riffs like "Princess Of The Night" were Paul's riffs: you've only got to hear his playing to know they are. But there was a lot of shit going on actually between Graham and Paul in the band that nobody actually noticed; he'd sit around waiting for Paul to work out a riff then jump off the sofa and join in. There was a lot of that going on, but, even so, we let it go because we were in production and we were pretty much knocking out songs.

When you are new in a band situation, and it's working, you don't give a shit if the other guitarist is in bed with a headache or gone home. We were used to doing what had to be done; if only two people were there, then that's fine. And in the early Son Of A Bitch days Graham regularly used to leave a note on the sideboard that he'd gone home. You see, in the early days, I'd say on stage, 'we need somewhere to sleep tonight' and usually three of four fans would come forward and say we could sleep in their living room. We had a couple of mattresses in the van so we'd move all the furniture, hurl the mattresses into the middle of the room and sleep there. But we'd regularly wake up in the morning to find a note on the sideboard saying 'had to go home.' So we did some of those shows as a four-piece. It was a bit bizarre – he was having problems at home I suppose and just went. But he was one of those guys who never told you anything about what he was doing. So there was a lot of that going on and we were used to working as a three-piece, four-piece, or whatever. It didn't really matter – we were just writing songs, churning them out almost. Which brings me to the 'are there any songs that we wrote and didn't record' question which crops up quite regularly. The way we wrote then – and the way we still write now come to that – was that we'd all bring together all our ideas, bits and pieces of songs, odd riffs, and I'd pick and choose which ones excited me to put a melody and vocal to and the rest of them were just left in the ideas' bank. So really before anything poor got to a song stage somebody would say, 'that's fucking rubbish!' and it would have been ditched, whether it was me or Paul or anyone; and that's how it is now as well. If it wasn't good enough it was ditched and taped over. So we weren't a band that really wrote tons of crap, to put it bluntly; we tried to write great songs and we worked and worked and worked on each song until we finally got it right. Sometimes it took twenty minutes, sometimes it took a week. But as a result we didn't end up with tons of patchy songs. There might have been three or four songs that we didn't release, but there isn't a massive vault somewhere of all our outtakes. Three from the »Power And The Glory« sessions turned up on the »Diamonds And Nuggets« thing that Graham Oliver and Steve Dawson put out, but they're all songs that aren't any good, to be truthful. They're fillers really; otherwise they'd have been on the album in the first place.

We wrote »Strong Arm Of The Law« at Transam Trucking's place, we used to use one of their barns. It was a nice place in East Anglia, near Diss; a big manor house with massive barns. We definitely wrote some of »Denim And Leather« there too… They were very keen, the management, to get a follow-up album out and we wrote it in double-quick time; about two weeks, I think. I remember writing lyrics in a hotel room with Pete Hinton, "Hungry Years" and things like that. It was all a bit haphazard though and by this time Nigel Thomas was on board as our business manager so I was in London quite a lot meeting people and doing interviews; I wasn't with the band all the time so it's difficult for me to focus as I was all over the place – the band was big so we were really in demand and it all gets a bit mixed up in my memory now. We were using different studios, all over the place. I went to Abbey Road but I don't think I did any work there – just wanted to look around for future albums. We did the most of the recording at Ramport Studios again, where »Wheels Of Steel« was recorded and we used the same team – if it ain't broke, don't fix it.

The thing I remember the most about »Strong Arm Of The Law« was that I wanted to call the album »Heavy Metal Thunder« but the record company were going to release "Strong Arm Of The Law" as the first single and they always wanted to call the album the same as the first single. I thought it was a lunatic thing, but again it was the thinking of a single-orientated company; if you had a hit single, the album had to be called that. It wasn't even a hit single; "Strong Arm Of The Law" only made it to Number 63 in the UK charts or something, which isn't exactly a hit. But it came so quickly after »Wheels Of Steel« I don't think anybody noticed it. So we didn't have a hit single off it, which wasn't really surprising. It was a much heavier album, actually, and there weren't any 'commercial' tracks on it which is why the record company put "Suzie Hold On" on the American version of »Strong Arm Of The Law« because there was no real 'radio' track on the album. The title track was of course a very anti-establishment song. It's about the police being wankers really, so it was never going to get played on UK radio anyway, although for us it was a real anthem. But that album broke the band massive in France and Italy; we became huge there. Nobody played in Italy at that time and we used to do thirty shows.

But as I said, I wanted to call it »Heavy Metal Thunder« but the rest of the band went with the management to call it »Strong Arm Of The Law«. I didn't like it: I didn't like the title, I didn't like the album cover. It should have been »Heavy Metal Thunder«, balls to the wall, because that's what we were. I did finally get my way twenty years later when we did the »Heavy Metal Thunder« album, but I thought it would have been such a great title back then in 1980. But it was a big album, making it to Number 11 in the UK charts so it was good for us to have another Top Twenty album. Another big tour too. And "Strong Arm Of The Law" is a mega-catchy song; it's just not radio material. I was quite happy with that because it appealed to my rebellious side but the record company didn't like the fact that they didn't have a hit single. There was nothing special about the single – no bonus tracks or anything – and although it was catchy – 'stop, get out, we are the strong arm of the law' – easy to sing along to, they were French, they had no idea what it was about and probably didn't realise it was never going to get played on 'establishment' radio in a million fucking years!

The opening of the album, with the thunder, and the crashing seas and the wind, and "Heavy Metal Thunder" itself was like 'whoa!' And it shocked a lot of people, that song, because it was so fast. The funny thing is, we actually had to re-record it. Firstly, you need to know that everyone was totally paranoid about speed, and they used to come to the studio at night after we'd gone home and varispeed our songs up and down. I think "Wheels Of Steel" is actually faster on the album than we'd recorded it so my voice is much higher than it really should be on that track. Anyway, bearing this in mind, I remember Pete Gill 'phoned me up and said, '"Heavy Metal Thunder" is too slow.'

'What?'

'No, it's too slow. It's not fucking exciting enough, we need to re-record it.'

So we went back down and completely redid it. So there are actually two versions of "Heavy Metal Thunder"; a slow version – which obviously wasn't that slow in the first place – and a really fucking fast version! Even today when we do that song, the chorus is really fucking strong and when you get 20,000 people singing it, it's pretty cool, believe me. It's a really daft song, lyrically, and if you listen to the tempo it's almost a swingtime song. But it was just a vehicle I had in my head for a strong song – 'throw your heads back, hold your hands high...' The Japanese lyrics, by the way, are hysterical. In Japan this guy transposed all our songs into sheet music on the piano and had a go at translating the lyrics, but the transcription of the lyrics was so bad. I'm sure that's why we never went back to Japan because we disrespected people all over the place. Somebody gave us the lyric sheet and I was reading them and we were on the floor in hysterics. I'm sure it still exists somewhere. 'Throw your skirts up, hold your heads high, up your bottom, fill your heads with heavy metal thunder...' It was so fucking funny. And they're like, 'what? Is something the matter?' And this Japanese guy transposed everything down to three chords on the bottom of the neck for the finger charts. How the hell can you play "Heavy Metal Thunder" in A? Japanese kids must have been tying their fingers up in knots trying to play it.

It's a good album, »Strong Arm Of The Law«, a heavy album, and one I like a lot. It was on the strength of that album that we toured Japan, and I think we were the first ones of our genre to go there. It was good fun in Japan. We were followed around constantly by Japanese girls who'd pre-book seats in first class on the Bullet Train so there'd be a carriage full of girls going crazy. Really strange really. I was having a shower in the hotel room and I could hear something over the noise of the shower, this giggling, tittering noise, and when I opened the door, twelve girls literally fell in. They were up against the bathroom door, listening, which can't have been that interesting, to be honest. Paul actually married a Japanese girl. The way he tells it is that 'three Japanese girls used to follow us around, and they came to Britain as well. I was seeing one of them, Pete Gill was seeing another of them… I can't remember how it came to matters of love but we got married; and we got divorced!' Paul's not much of a story-teller, as you can probably tell.

When we went to Japan, the promoters said to us, 'if you go with any of the girls, see us first, because a lot of them have got gonorrhoea. So see us first and we'll tell you which ones are OK.' Bands have been going to Japan for years so obviously the groupies there must be pretty well-known. I was in a bar after a gig, because the gigs are pretty early in Japan – on at six o'clock, off at eight, no support bands. So then you get carted off to a club. I started talking to two Japanese girls, one was really stunning, the other one wasn't… The stunning one wanted nothing to do with me, but the other one was interested. She wasn't ugly, she was just plain. Not a stunner. And she was a lawyer. But I got my first case of gonorrhoea off her. She wasn't even a groupie, and I didn't know I'd got it till I was coming home on the plane. I didn't know what it was, but of course everyone else found it hysterical. 'As soon as you land, just go straight to the clinic,' was their advice. So I went to the clinic in Barnsley and they gave me an injection, a massive dose of penicillin. The doctor said, 'tell me when you can taste almonds.'

'What?'

'Tell me when you can taste almonds,' the doctor repeated.

Odd thing to say, I thought, but there you go. So he stuck this huge needle in my arse, put it in very slow, and all of a sudden I had a taste like almonds in my mouth.

'I can taste almonds!'

He stopped. 'Right, don't do anything tonight and you'll be clear by tomorrow.'

'That's it?'

'That's it.'

The funny thing is, a little while later we were playing Hammersmith, and I'm singing and I looked across and the really nice Japanese girl is standing at the side of the stage. She'd come all the way from Japan to see me, and became my girlfriend for quite a while. She was great, really pretty; beautiful actually. I used to take her everywhere on the back of my motorbike, which is quite rare. But I couldn't handle having a Japanese girlfriend because they've got no sense of humour. You couldn't really take the piss out of them at all; no banter whatsoever. They spend a fortune on clothes, too, Japanese women, and she'd come down in the morning and she'd go shopping and I'd see her in the afternoon before the gig and she'd be in a tartan outfit or something. I'd make fun of it a bit, say something like, 'are we going hunting stag?' and she'd just break down in tears and go and change it all and throw it in the bin. I just couldn't handle living with someone with absolutely no sense of humour at all. She liked stuff like Benny Hill, that's the sort of humour she'd appreciate – my humour is a lot more, well, dry; and I can be like that even when I'm not even trying to be, so it didn't work out. I just couldn't handle it and, nice as she was, I had to pack her in. It was just so odd though, turning on stage and thinking, 'fucking hell, I know her.'

Obviously I didn't tell her that her friend gave me a dose.

Chapter Ten

After »Strong Arm Of The Law« failed to yield any hit singles we were packed off and ended up writing two to order. Obviously the record company weren't taking any prisoners this time; they wanted some singles so they manipulated us to go in and write two. We thought we were just writing for the album, and they just said, 'right, we'll have those two songs; thank you!' and released them as singles. They were both written at the same time. They were quite big hits though – two Top Twenty singles – and we must have done »Top Of The Pops« with both of them as well. "And The Bands Played On" was April 1981 or so and reached Number 12 in the UK, "Never Surrender" in the July hit Number 18, and then »Denim And Leather« followed in September 1981. They were obviously keen to get us back in the charts as both singles had extras – "And The Bands Played On" coming out as a picture disc and "Never Surrender" with a bonus single – but that's how it was. Whitesnake, Judas Priest, everyone did the same to get in the charts. A hit single sold a lot of copies; I think we sold about 250,000 copies of "Wheels Of Steel" so "747", "And The Bands Played On" and "Never Surrender" which were much more popular must have sold even more.

Again, we wrote "And The Bands Played On" and "Never Surrender" in the Welsh Mountains. It was freezing cold there – again – and on reflection I think we might have written three songs there; I can't remember the third. But I remember "And The Bands Played On": the riff I think was one Paul and I wrote, but it was loosely based on Toto's "Hold The Line". The saying 'the bands played on' is from an old Forties film, I think; that's basically where I got the idea from, I used to get a lot of lyric ideas from films and books. "Denim And Leather" is from an old Alice Cooper lyric and Steve and I thought that was cool. But generally as a lyricist, things that happened to me came out in our lyrics. So we were very topical; "And The Bands Played On" was obviously about Donington. There was more to it; there were four or five verses originally, and if you listen to the original version of "747" that was much longer too, but they used to chop the tapes up, you see, which is horrendous really; they used to chop them up into three-four minute versions, so sometimes some of the verses had to go – half the choruses as well. But I don't think there was much more to "And The Bands Played On" because I just wanted to paint a picture of the festival: 'we sat in the sun, and the bands played on…' There was a big discussion as to whether we should sing the wo-oo-oos or not; it was like, 'what? Wo-oo-oo? Is that in the fucking song then?'

'Yeah, I like it,' I told the dissenters.

'It's crap, that is.'

'Well, it's fucking going on!'

There was a lot of that sort of stuff happening back then, but once the song was done everyone realised it was quite catchy. Sometimes when you're writing lyrics the exact words don't quite fit and need a bit of padding out. And when you talk about it – 'wo-oo-oo' – like that it does sound stupid. But as a song it works.

And "Never Surrender" was really a "Stand Up And Be Counted" type of thing; I wasn't 'born in the back streets on the rotten side of town.' It was a fictional song, but it was a good sentiment, and a lot of our songs had fantastic sentiments. "Never Surrender" and "And The Bands Played On" are still two of our most popular songs when we play in the UK. They're the ones that everybody waits for, more so than in other countries. I think "And The Bands Played On" is quite popular in Europe but "Never Surrender", well, in Europe it seems that they can take it or leave it.

Doing »Top Of The Pops« was funny. The thing is with Carrere, as they were basically a singles-orientated company, for them the promotion for the album was always the single. And in the Eighties that's how it was; it was a predominately singles-orientated market. The albums were OK but most people bought singles. So the important thing for Carrere was that there were singles on the album, whereas with Iron Maiden I don't think EMI thought too much about that. But Carrere were infatuated with singles: the single goes on to sell the album, true, but they were a singles company and although they used us to branch out into albums they were still really singles-orientated. Everything was three minutes. For me, it was like, 'how can I tell a story in three minutes? You're fucking nuts.' And of course there were different versions, a version without vocals, and with this, with that, and a mono version because there was very little stereo back then on some radio stations, and a stereo version. To me it appeared to be a right mugs game.

But to appear on »Top Of The Pops« the musicians union had decreed that music had to be live. You couldn't just mime to the original track, you had to re-record it – and then you could mime to that. So we used to have to go to this studio – and I couldn't believe it the first time we did it – we used to go to this studio where the engineer would start to record us. But as soon as the musicians union guy left the engineer would go, 'right, stop' and they'd swap the tapes back for the original song. This went on for years. So basically, you were going on »Top Of The Pops« and the musicians union thought you'd recorded the song in the studio and been paid the going rate. But in fact we'd been paid £150 for the session for playing our own music – which is a bit odd anyway – and then we just went on »Top Of The Pops« and used the original track. It was a total con, really; a complete fraud. So every time we went on »Top Of The Pops« we had to go to a studio and go through this routine of pretending to play it. It was a real pain in the arse, and at one point we suggested sending an entirely different band along – they wouldn't have known the difference. Besides, some of those songs, you couldn't record them in half-a-day, in a tin-pot studio. But that's what they used to do.

»Denim And Leather« is a strange album, because we made that album in Switzerland, in Geneva, and Nigel Thomas produced it with a new engineer he'd discovered, Andy Lydon. That was another of my bugbears; Nigel Thomas was always 'discovering' somebody, and we never worked with anyone who was established; we were always either giving people breaks at the start of their career or working with people at the end of their career. These people never really understood the dynamics of our music. Nice enough people and good engineers, but they really weren't state-of-the-art on-the-cutting-edge people. We really wanted someone who new what they were doing and had had some success. Iron Maiden had a great producer in Martin Birch (who had a massive track record with Deep Purple) and they stayed with him for a long, long time. We met the Marillion producer, the guy who did their early stuff, Nick Tauber, he was going to do either »Denim And Leather« or »Power And The Glory« but for some reason it didn't happen. I just think that up to »Denim And Leather« we were right on course, actually; we were making great albums and we felt we were unbeatable. Paul once told me that he couldn't 'relate to production values on »Denim And Leather« actually. I just know when I don't like something but I've never actually said, send that producer back, he's shit, although now I wish I had, quite a few times! But on »Denim And Leather« we were trying something new which was (a) being out of the country and (b) Nigel Thomas producing it. I'm not sure either were good moves.'

Anyway, we did the album in Geneva. I remember we stayed in some shitty place and Nigel Thomas stayed in the Hilton. But we were still a people's band, if you like, and having some fan club members in to sing on "Denim And Leather" was great. And on »Denim And Leather« we had two major anthems: "Denim And Leather", although I know it's not everybody's favourite song, and "Princess Of The Night" which is a killer track. That's probably our biggest song of all time, live. I would think that's probably our "Smoke On The Water" or "Breaking The Law" or "Here I Go Again". I think "Princess Of The Night" was quite radical for it's time. We worked hard on that guitar sound, double-tracking vocals and all sorts of wacky things.

I did the vocals for that album in Abba's studio in Stockholm, which was strange because in the summer people were partying twenty-four hours a day. It was good fun; a great studio too. But we moved around a lot; we did the basic tracks in Geneva, the "Denim And Leather" stuff with the fan club in England... The album made Number 9 in the UK, and I think those two singles helped. I don't know about the rest of the band but I didn't want those singles on the album and had a massive argument with the record company about it. I thought it was being a cheapskate repeating the singles on the LP. Don't forget, this is well before CDs so you were really governed by the cut, so there was only really room for, what, nine songs and my argument was that there were two songs that people had already bought, so either don't put them on, or we'd write two more and have eleven songs. 'Oh, you can't do that, not enough running time' was their stock response. I'm pretty sure Steve agreed with me. In my opinion, when people bought »Denim And Leather« the impact of the album was immediately diluted because you already had two songs released as singles that everyone knew. So I think that it didn't have the same impact because people already knew what it sounded like, having already heard "And The Bands Played On" and "Never Surrender".

The »Denim And Leather« tour kicked off in October 1981 at the Brighton Centre and featured the debut of the eagle: the real one

– not the homemade hardboard and mirror squares thing that we'd knocked up ourselves – with two tons of aluminum and steel and 150 truly blinding lights. It also featured the debut of Nigel Glockler; the first ever Saxon show without Pete Gill.

It was a very strange period for us. Amongst other things we'd toured Europe with Judas Priest and America with Rush, were really big in the UK…I think we were as big as we could be in the UK in fact and cracks were starting to appear. »Denim And Leather« was our biggest album in terms of sales without a doubt. I did ask Nigel Thomas when we were doing »Power And The Glory« which was our biggest selling album, and he said »Denim And Leather«, and if it got to Number 9 then obviously it was. It must have gone double-gold, definitely 100,000 on release and then, of course, substantially more over time.

It was at this point that Pete Gill dropped out. Pete's departure was very strange. He was a fantastic drummer, but used to complain of these numb feelings in his hands; he was forever doing a lot of exercises, rolling-up paper and things like that. I don't really know much about what happened, and in retrospect we shouldn't have done what we did, but we had a sell-out tour all across the UK and Europe to promote »Denim And Leather« (on which we recorded »The Eagle Has Landed«) and about a week before we were due to kick off Pete said he couldn't do it. He suggested that we get somebody to stand in for him and he'd come back later. That's what he said.

On reflection, we should really have said we'd wait. I don't know why he suggested that we get somebody else to stand in; I guess he knew how important this tour was to the band. He came to see us in Sheffield and he was really, well, strange. He hardly said a word to us, and then didn't bother coming back to us. In the meantime, I guess we were so busy that we didn't really have time to understand what was really happening. But that said, we were pretty ruthless. I think it was Steve who suggested we keep Nigel, but I was pretty sad to lose Pete because I liked him a lot. We got on quite well because he was a womanising bastard as well so we had a lot in common: we had a few gang-bangs together which is obviously a bit of a bonding experience! I quite missed Pete though because he was quite a character, and I had some good times with him. And besides, I like characters.

That said, it seemed he was starting to lose it a bit, because by this time we'd already had to work with a session drummer. It was while we were writing »Denim And Leather«: we'd already written "And The Bands Played On" and "Never Surrender" at the earlier session with him, but then he just didn't turn up to one of the album writing sessions. We figured he was just with some girl or had decided to stay in bed, so the management got this guy called Mark Pinder to come drum with us. He basically drummed through the writing of "Princess Of The Night" and "Denim And Leather" and then Pete came back. I remember him saying that he thought the bass drum part in "Princess Of The Night" was a bit pointless but apart from that he said he liked what we'd come up with. And then of course we went on to record the album with him, and we thought that was that. But it was just really strange. He just went and we never really heard from him ever again. I mean, we'd decided to keep Nigel but I don't think he ever came back to us to be told his services were no longer required. We just didn't hear from him. Whether the managers Ron Blechner and Dave Poxon had anything to do with it I don't know, but Pete certainly didn't talk to us, and he didn't leave with any bitterness as far as we were concerned. He was never really sacked; maybe he's still in the band and we don't even know! He just went off and did his thing. Maybe if we'd known earlier what was going on, and that he had a problem with his hands, we could have cancelled the tour and waited until he was ready because the band at that time was brilliant. I'm not taking anything away from Nigel, but at that time Pete Gill was a big thing for the band, really.

But that's the way it was. We were doing production rehearsals in a theatre somewhere when Pete said he couldn't do the tour, and we'd just had the Eagle made, so this was going to be a big deal. We auditioned three or four drummers, and Dave Poxon suggested or brought along Nigel Glockler who he already knew. He was drumming in Toyah's band at the time, but I think something had happened, maybe she was disbanding because I don't think she did much after Nigel left. Anyway, he auditioned and we had him in, but only on the understanding that he was just a stand-in for Pete. As the tour progressed we obviously bonded with him, but if Pete had walked in the room and said, 'hi, what's happening, guys?' then we'd have gone back with him. At the time Nigel knew it wasn't a permanent job, and for us as a band it was a bit difficult, at first, going on tour with a stranger who'd been in a girly punk band wearing dustbin lids in his ears and pyjamas. And we got a lot of flak too: 'he's a fucking punk from Toyah. He's not a heavy metal drummer.' So there was a lot of that in the press which didn't help our confidence levels.

With Pete not getting back to us, halfway through the tour Nigel was offered the full time job and, well, he couldn't really refuse, could he? We were doing four to five thousand people a night, a dream gig really. But he wasn't accepted immediately, it took him a while. As I said, Pete was a babe-magnet; he was a womanising fucker and when female reporters came to interview us, Pete was all over them like a rash. And like the rest of us, Pete would take the piss out of everything and everyone.

Kerrang! carried the story – no doubt fed to them by Nigel Thomas – as a news item in February 1982: 'Drummer Pete Gill has left Saxon. His replacement is 29-year-old Nigel Glockler who played with the band on their recent British and European tour. The tour had to go ahead without Gill after he injured his hand and was ordered to rest by the doctor. This enforced lay off led to a number of tempting offers which, coupled with the fact that Glockler had worked out well, caused a rethink between Gill and the band. Saxon are currently in the States supporting and co-headlining with bands like Triumph and Molly Hatchet.'

Pete joined Motörhead about two years later, but he must have had something seriously wrong with him at the time and I just wish he'd told us what it was. Nigel was public school and he took a lot of jibes – and still does – being a Southern boy amongst us Northerners, but that's what it's all about. But he did a great job actually, learned all the songs in about a day or something, the entire repertoire, and then he was off on tour with us. He did a staggering job, actually. I remember he had a book beside him with all the songs written out and about two weeks into the tour I stole it. I decided he didn't need a comfort blanket any longer. Of course, he went fucking hysterical!

'Where's my book! Where's my fucking book!'

'I burned it,' I told him, deadpan.

'No, you fucking didn't!'

'Yeah, I did. I burned it.'

'Why?'

'Well, it's about time you knew the fucking songs by now!'

Nigel was a great singer as well, so we had him singing fairly early on in his career, and he used to bounce a few lyrics around. He's a good guy, Nigel, but he wasn't Pete Gill and I think that was a change in the band that some fans didn't like or wouldn't accept. These days when people think of Saxon's drummer they think of Nigel because he's been in the band longer and he did the »Denim And Leather« tour which up to that point was our biggest ever tour; big venues, like the Queens Hall in Leeds and a return to the Bingley Hall in Stafford where just over a year before we'd played at Motörhead's Heavy Metal Barndance. The American band Riot supported us in the UK, and Ozzy Osbourne and a band called Revolver supported us in Europe. Sharon was Ozzy's manager (I can't remember if they were married at that time), and it was the Ozzy, Randy, Rudy Sarzo and (my favourite drummer) Tommy Aldridge line-up. Of course we were huge Ozzy fans anyway and that kid playing guitar was brilliant. Graham was straight in there. Randy Rhoads' guitar was far too big for him though: he used to look so small compared to that Flying V, but he was a great guitarist, quite innovative, and they were a great band. I was in a hotel bar in Germany, sat there talking to some groupies, as you do; there was a weird one I used to go with who had a jewel in her forehead like a third eye (there were some really fucked up people in those days!). She was a big Joe Lynn Turner fan and he gave it to her so she could see him wherever he was in the world.

Weird.

Anyway, Ozzy walked in wearing a woman's dress with a dead chicken in a handbag. He'll probably say I'm a lying bastard, but he did, and we were gobsmacked. We didn't know whether to laugh or what. I mean, it's Ozzy Osbourne. Is it a joke or is it his thing, what he does when he wants to unwind? We guessed it was a joke, but we were too amazed to say anything. He just went up to the bar, got some drinks and just went up to bed. As you do.

We played in this place in Strasbourg and at the back of the stage was like a spiral staircase and we used to creep up the staircase and watch them. Ozzy came dashing up the stairs, went straight past the stage level and carried on running up the staircase. Sharon ran up and said, 'have you seen Ozzy?'

'Yeah, he's still running up them stairs.'

He'd passed the stage and gone up as far as the roof by the time she caught up with him and brought him back down to the stage level. And the last show they did with us, the band were all soundchecking on stage and the tour manager went up to them and said, 'that was Ozzy on the 'phone.'

Randy said, 'where is he?'

'London. He's gone home.'

When he played with us, I didn't see him fucked up at all. I didn't see it once. Maybe he'd got it together because they were only playing a support set, no pressure, but he was singing brilliantly and I know because I watched him every night. And the Malcolm Hill PA that we had, it was like crystal clear and he loved it. He loved all the gear. And the band were cooking. We had to go on and really give it some because they were really the first support band that gave us a run for our money. Everybody before that was easy-peasy really, but it was hard going on after Ozzy because people had a lot of respect for him and it was a big album. That tour was great for him because he got in front of a lot of people with us, but they must have missed about half the tour. I think maybe he just got fed up. The band were really sheepish, and just left.

I think it was More who replaced them, they were pretty big actually. The trouble is, tours all merge into one after a while, and support bands do chop and change during tours so now it's hard to remember who did what. We had Limelight, friends from Yorkshire and a bit like a Yes covers band. Tygers Of Pan Tang on the »Wheels Of Steel« tour had the possibility to be huge but they imploded. They were great on that tour though. I remember I think I shagged Jess Cox's girlfriend; either that or we both had too much to drink and ... No; just kidding! But I remember Tygers Of Pan Tang very well. I mean, they were destined to be a great band but they imploded, as do some bands sometimes. Unfortunately the Jess Cox version of the band didn't last that long. Egos got the better of them, I think, and Jess Cox went and was replaced by Jon Deverill. We never toured with the later line-up though; in fact, I don't think we ever came across them again. I don't know if they were a small band with huge egos or huge band with small egos; I could never make up my mind about them. I think they could have been really big, but they weren't; they had one or two singles in the Top 40, but never really got very far, never got into the major league. "Don't Touch Me There" really wasn't a rock song; it wasn't a "Wheels Of Steel", it was just a nice song about, well, shagging or something. I never really found out what it was about. Adolescent sex, I presume. The »Wheels Of Steel« tour obviously shot them into massive venues and in front of thousands of people. But in the long run they didn't survive.

But as I said, tours and supports do blur into one, and it is hard to separate them out after a while. Pretty Maids did »Innocence Is No Excuse«, Loudness did »Rock The Nations« (they were a great band), »Crusader« was John Verity and Battleaxe. We didn't tour the UK with »Power And The Glory«; I think it was decided that we give the UK a rest. Maybe we should go back and tour the UK with it now because I think it's a great album.

Chapter Eleven

One support act I do remember is Cheetah, the Australian band fronted by the Hammond Sisters, Chrissie and Lyndsey, who supported us on the 1982 tour we did to promote »The Eagle Has Landed«. They were pretty good entertainers. I thought their music was shit but they pulled young blokes out of the audience and pretended to shag 'em like strippers do. They were a novelty act really though, one album and that was that. A bit like Nashville Pussy, that type of thing, although Nashville Pussy do actually play; the Hammond sisters just sang and looked raunchy. Five minutes of fame and that was that.

The 1981 »Denim And Leather« tour had been taped for our first live album, »The Eagle Has Landed« which was released in May 1982. It was a good stop-gap for us. We had spent a lot of early 1982 in the US, and although later in the year we headlined the Mildenhall Festival in East Anglia and were then the first band ever to play the Monsters Of Rock at Castle Donington twice before doing the September tour with Cheetah, we had been out of the public eye in the UK a bit, and it wasn't until March 1983 that our next studio album would be released. So a live album was a logical move. Both Sounds ('Saxon's greatest vinyl achievement to date') and Record Mirror ('a landmark in Saxon's history') gave it a healthy thumbs-up.

Kerrang!, though, was obsessed with the fact that it wasn't a 'glossy gatefold-sleeved extravaganza' and didn't like the production. 'It's hard to see why, beyond obvious commercial gain, the band have put it out in this form.' So basically the reviewer had a go at everything that was beyond our control. It was a huge hit for us in the UK, and was massive in Germany – a huge album there. Maybe we shouldn't have used a real audience, but an American-style one where it's dubbed on afterwards. As for knocking us for the sleeve – they should really be knocking the record company. These days, they'd say the band's great but the record company should spend some more money on the artwork.

»The Eagle Has Landed« should have been a double album though; half of it got thrown in the bin. We had about an hour-and-a-half's worth of material from those recordings, which was basically how long our set was. We intended to do a second one, and that might have been the thinking behind the record company's decision – 'do one album like this and the next album like that' – so the pair would go together. I think that was the original idea. But the tapes got destroyed – they ended up on the cutting room floor. When you edited live albums in those days either the two-inch tape or the quarter-inch tape was sliced and cut apart; it was very crude, really. The sheer number of two inch tapes – because we recorded three shows and with two inch tape running at 30 ips you can only get six, six-and-a-half minutes per tape – we had was huge. They had two machines running so when one stopped the other took over. You can imagine the amount of gear they had to carry around, there must have been at least twenty multi-track reels, if not more; maybe forty. And they no longer exist. When Carrere sold the rights to EMI no master tapes were transferred over. So those bonus tracks on the »Wheels Of Steel«/»Strong Arm Of The Law« CD re-issue can't have been outtakes from »The Eagle Has Landed« because nobody has ever mixed any other multi-track tapes, believe me. Maybe they were from bootleg sources. We recorded three gigs: Nottingham, Hammersmith, and Sheffield I think. Most of the material used on the album came from Hammersmith and Nottingham. But like I said, we didn't have much to do with it. The album came out and we weren't there, we were touring. So that was really the only album that was done with us having nothing to do with it. But to me it sounds pretty good; it's a good album, and a genuinely live one. In the Sounds Readers Poll for 1982 »The Eagle Has Landed« was Number Six in the Album Of The Year chart. (We were voted second best live gig, by the way, and I copped sixth best male singer and sixth best male pin-up!)

Another problem that was rearing its head at this time was the simple fact that we had no idea whatsoever as to how much we were worth, or how much we were making. We were musicians, not accountants, and although we had an accountant, as soon as he started asking difficult questions the management told us to fire him. But Ron Blechner and Dave Poxon, Nigel Thomas (I think he and Blechner were both at Oxford or Cambridge together or something like that) and Carrere Records, between them they were supposed to be in charge of our career in those early days.

I don't really think that they could have done anything wrong in the UK because the course was set and we were on a roll; it would have been hard for them to screw it up. The music was right, the band was right, the time was right and I don't think they had to work hard to get us work; in fact, I'm pretty sure they were turning work down. They had been fairly influential in the writing of »Wheels Of Steel« in booking us into that studio in the Welsh mountains, but even so you can't really give the decision to put a band in the middle of nowhere much credit in the writing of the songs. So, I think they did all right at first but that it all just got too big for them.

Our newly-installed business manager Nigel Thomas – this 'big-time manager' whom Blechner-Poxon brought in – hadn't really worked with anybody other than Joe Cocker and a band called

Boxer which was Mike Patto and Ollie Halsall from Patto, one of the bands we used to see in the early Seventies. His one real claim to fame was that he was big on making quite controversial album covers. He was responsible for the Boxer one which was a girl sat on a tube of toothpaste with the toothpaste oozing out. It sounds weak now but it was quite controversial for the time. Later, it was his idea for the »Innocence Is No Excuse« album cover, for the girl to bite the apple; and the original had all the cum – sorry; apple juice! – running down her chin. Fortunately the record company vetoed that. At that time though, it was basically Nigel Thomas's role to set up offshore companies and deal with all the money so that we didn't have to pay any tax. This didn't really affect me because I didn't have any money anyway. It was more so that the management could avoid paying as much tax as possible. But as time went by he became more and more involved with the day-to-day running of the band, leading to an eventual split with Blechner and Poxon.

As I said, after »Wheels Of Steel« we went straight back in within six or so months to write »Strong Arm Of The Law«, even though we thought we should have toured the world on »Wheels Of Steel« because there were lots of miles left on that album, a lot of countries we hadn't seen that were really switched on to it. The management told us though that we needed the next advance because we'd spent all the money; 'so you need to write the album or else you won't get paid.' It was almost like blackmail in the way it was done. I remember receiving a letter via our accountant – as I said, we had our own accountant, but he didn't seem to do much – from Blechner saying that it wasn't a God-given gift that we had a salary. We were gobsmacked. We were grossing a massive amount of money on the »Wheels Of Steel« and »Strong Arm Of The Law« tours.

When Nigel Thomas joined the organisation, we signed a publishing deal and the advance was £25,000 which he actually gave to us. We actually got four grand each, and the accountant kept four grand for expenses. It was the first real money I'd ever seen. I'd never seen £1,000 before, let alone £4,000, and to have £4,000 enabled us to get mortgages and buy our own houses. I thought, 'fuck it; I'm going to buy a Porsche.' So I bought a Porsche 928, a black one; I went down to the garage in my little Volvo estate, and said, 'will you trade in this car for that' and they said, 'you've got to be joking, mate!' It wasn't that dear, the 928, and I drove it back and as we were playing, I think, at Reading Leisure Centre, I drove it back and parked it outside the gig. Dave Poxon looked out and said, 'that's a nice car.'

'Yeah, it's mine.'

'I don't believe that.'

'Yeah, it's my car.'

And all night, for about six hours, he kept saying, 'I don't believe that's your car.'

'Yes, it's my car. It's my fucking car. I went out and bought it!'

That was probably the most extravagant thing I ever bought. I loved that car, and what happened? My American wife Christine sold it while I was on tour! So I came back and bought her a fucking Skoda, an orange one, and I made her drive that car for a fucking month.

Giving us that money, even though it was ours in the first place, was a highly manipulative move on Nigel Thomas's part, because when Blechner and Poxon found out they went nuts. They went fucking nuts that we'd got *our* money. One of them told us, 'if you don't send it back, that's it; we're not going to manage you any more. We'll sue you.' And we're thinking, 'wait a minute. We've just done 30,000 people or whatever on a sold-out tour, so where's that fucking money gone?' I'm not saying that it didn't cost anything to keep the band on the road and in the studio, but you only have to do figures in your head. I mean, »Wheels Of Steel« went gold and probably double-gold in the UK which is well over 100,000 copies at, what, four quid each so you're talking in the region of half a million quid in Britain alone.

On the Motörhead tour, we were quite good friends with the merchandising people and I remember going into one of the girls' rooms, looking for some cigarettes and the bed – a double bed –

was just covered in bundles of notes. There must have been forty grand there. I think Doug Smith was their manager then and I have no idea where that money went. These were massive amounts of money. I remember seeing people leaving the venues with two suitcases full of cash. We headlined Bingley Hall – about four-and-a-half thousand people? We did Leeds Queens Hall; again, about four-and-a-half thousand people. We must have been selling thousands of t-shirts and all that money must have gone somewhere, as we weren't spending anything as a band. I think we were getting about £400 a month each, that's what our salary was, and we must have been generating thousands of pounds as a band. We were just naïve though, and didn't really comprehend the amount of money massive sell-out tours generate. We weren't spending a lot on production back then, particularly before we had the Eagle. In fact, the guitar tech and I made the first ever eagle out of mirrored squares and a big piece of board. It was a work of art really, which the road crew hauled up on ropes. That kind of summed us up though really. We were so highly motivated to succeed that we'd build our own effects, our own PAs, go to the library and get books on acoustics… We were totally immersed in the whole concept of bands, rock music, everything really. We just wanted to make it, but we never stopped to think about the kind of money you generate when you do make it.

Because we'd had no success in the singles chart from the »Strong Arm Of The Law« album, Carrere wanted – demanded, almost – singles. We wrote and they released "And The Bands Played On" and "Never Surrender" one after the other and they were both massive hits. And that's how it was with Carrere. It didn't matter about the rest of the world; they were solely focused on selling massive numbers of units in the UK, and, to a lesser extent, in Europe. We were quite big in France too, obviously, but their main focus was Britain. I remember going into the office after »Strong Arm Of The Law« and Freddie Cannon (who alongside Pete Hinton had signed us and who was a nice enough guy) told me how pleased he was because he'd got his bonus. The label bought him a Porsche turbo, a John Player Special. As we were the only successful band on their label in the UK, basically we'd given him that bonus. 'What do we get then?' I asked him; 'where the fuck's our bonus?' So as a treat he took me for a drive in his new Porsche. The point is, if they bought him a Porsche turbo, what sort of money were they actually making from us? What sort of money were we actually making? They had their share, and it looked to us that they were having our share as well.

During the Nigel Thomas years we were all signed to an off-shore company, so we were all employed by that company. So basically, we were nothing more than employees of the company for whom we were making a lot of money. And who were the shareholders of the company? Mr and Mrs Nigel Thomas. So we were screwed basically; fucked over big time, and there wasn't a thing we could do about it because it was all perfectly legal and above-board. We couldn't even get our own money because it was off-shore, and EMI still account to that company, even though the guy is dead and it doesn't exist any more. We've told them to account to us, but of course as far as they are concerned their contract is with this company, not us. That'll change one day; that's a battle for the future.

It's a sad state of affairs really, and a lesson for any band to take note of. I mean, the amount of Saxon back catalogue stuff that you see around the world is amazing. We must be selling shedloads. And you can download all our albums off EMI so there must be hundreds of thousands of pounds somewhere. Another thing is all the compilations we've been on. We've been on at least three compilations that have sold over a million; »Soft Metal« was just one of the big sellers. We've been on loads of them, all around the world. TV adverts, films… All this creates revenue. When we finally finished with that publishing deal I did another, whereby each member of the band gets paid directly, based on who wrote what song, and that's the best way to do it. So the money no longer goes into a central pot any more, it goes direct to the artist; and that's the way it should be.

Much later, Steve Dawson sued Nigel Thomas's publishing company, and out of the blue there was £150,000 on the table, just like that. But he made the mistake of putting them into bankruptcy so the receivers took over and it ended up being about just thirty to forty grand. But it's amazing how you can go from no money to £150,000, when you start throwing some legal weight around.

It's so hard to get a direct answer as well in this business. When you ask questions, it's always, 'oh, don't worry about it; you're un-recouped anyway,' which means we haven't paid off the advance we've had upfront.

'Yeah, well, how much are we un-recouped?'

'Well, you're so far un-recouped that you don't want to know.'

'Why wouldn't we want to know?'

'Don't worry about it. You're un-recouped, you're in the red, so what's the difference?'

The difference is that when you're in debt, it's useful to know by how much. But back in 1982, though, such things didn't really bother us. When we'd finished touring the live album, we went to a place called Battle on the South coast of England. The place we stayed in was really bizarre, but I liked it because it was part of our heritage. The original house and all the land was given to the standard bearer of William the Conqueror for his loyalty at the Battle of Hastings. Part of the manor house where we were staying – only a small part of it unfortunately – was the original house, so it was steeped in history, as was Battle itself. The people who owned it were running it as a hotel, but it was failing badly so they came up with the idea of putting up bands with accommodation upstairs and rehearsal space in the ballroom. It was quite nice, a timber-framed kind of medieval place where we wrote »Power And The Glory«. I'm pretty sure that the woman who owned it bred hamsters because from memory now there seemed to be millions of the things all over the place.

We didn't stay there very long though, because once the album was written we were off to America to record it, leaving Battle, England, and all those fucking hamsters far behind.

Chapter Twelve

I t's impossible not to be seduced by America. Once you're there, it's impossible not to let it suck you in. And for a young British heavy metal band it was almost overwhelming. Before 1979 I'd never even sat on a plane before, and in September 1980 I was touring the States. We made great in-roads into America. Radio stations were playing us, people liked it and we were quite big. We kept pushing it, pushing it, pushing it, because it was obvious that you can't keep touring the UK over and over and over again. Of course, the first time we went there was far too early in our career but, as ever, management knew best, because management always does, right?

The thing with America is, by the end of the »Denim And Leather« tour we'd had a lot of success in England and Europe, massive success, and we really couldn't do any more at that time. We'd literally done everything. The tours couldn't get any bigger... We couldn't really go much further in the UK or Europe. An American agent had come over to see us at one of the Hammersmith shows we did and we signed an agency deal with them.

Meanwhile, Nigel Thomas had pretty much taken over the business side of Saxon and he desperately thought we should break America. In retrospect, we should have waited a little bit and consolidated Europe a bit more – as I said, I still believed there was more mileage in promoting »Wheels Of Steel« – but we were offered the Rush tour and as we were huge Rush fans we jumped at it.

It was what they call in America 'a secondary market' tour so it wasn't New York and Los Angeles but was more Southern States – Florida, New Orleans, Louisiana – and up into the Mid-West. So it wasn't a coast-to-coast tour, but that's the way Rush worked; they toured the States a lot but did it in sections. It was an amazing feeling because I think the first show was Hampton, West Virginia. It was totally sold out, 80,000 people, and it was an amazing sight to walk out onstage in what was basically a basketball stadium and see a sea of cigarette lighters. I think it must have been Rush's »Permanent Waves« tour and that was a fantastic album so they were doing good gigs and good business anyway, and we went on and did our thing and, to be fair, we did it well.

We also did some dates on the Black Sabbath/Blue Öyster Cult »Black 'N' Blue« tour, although I can't remember now if this came before or after the Rush dates. It was bizarre really – two big bands, each with their own PA and lighting rig, with seemingly endless infighting which we got caught in the middle of. It would have been a great tour to have carried on with, but, of course, it just seemed to fall apart. I did get to meet Ronnie James Dio for the first time though, who was a nice guy and who seemed to know who we were, which was great.

Organisationally though, in true Spinal Tap fashion, we had no albums to sell over there. I think what happened was that Carrere were distributed by WEA. in England – and they did a fantastic job – but in America they were on Warner Brothers, and I think the French managed to piss them right off. I think Claude Carrere put a guy in an office in Rockerfella Plaza or somewhere – a French guy – to oversee his interests and business affairs in America and I think it got right up the Americans' noses. So they printed 25,000 copies of »Wheels Of

Steel«, which contractually they were obliged to do, and didn't bother printing any more. So everything we sold after that initial 25,000 (which sold out really quickly) were imports; and imports in those days were (a) very hard to get as only specialised shops had them, and (b) fucking expensive. So from an albums' sales point of view the Rush tour wasn't that great and right then came the start of the great American debate in the Saxon camp: would we have broken America, really early on, had »Wheels Of Steel« been more freely available in the shops? We did good business, but because we hadn't sold many albums – not as many as they'd expected us to – they pulled the plug on the money so we came back home after the Rush tour and started out on the UK »Strong Arm Of The Law« tour. Had we been with an international company I think we probably would have broken America on »Wheels Of Steel«, first time out. When Iron Maiden first went to America they really pumped it hard – the Judas Priest Tour, the Scorpions tour, they did all the right tours in the early part of their career. We went back to America again and toured with Cheap Trick who were lovely guys – great band, too – but they were on a really bad decline because that sort of music was going down at that time and there weren't enough people coming through the doors. Krokus were on that tour as well, but it wasn't a metal audience, and it wasn't a big audience either, so we weren't really gaining anything. Some big mistakes were made on those first tours of America. We went out and played our souls out – so we did our bit – but the business side of it wasn't handled very well at all by our record company and management. America's a massive place and unless you play the game, unless you let the people there do what they are good at, you are not going to be successful. And Claude Carrere in particular was not willing to let go of the strings. I think most of the time he was buying American porn and shipping it back to France. Maybe that was where he made his money, shipping back American pornography; there was a sizeable collection in his office, put it that way!

Aldo Nova joined the Cheap Trick tour on some shows and those shows were totally sold out so that was pretty cool. That was a wacky band – a short, chubby bloke in like a leopard-skin catsuit: very bizarre. The album was pretty good though; I think he just did the one, because I never came across another. But that was the proof of the power of radio. And of course the MTV thing was just taking off as well: Mötley Crüe, Cinderella, Bon Jovi, all those great American bands were made by MTV, and we had to try and make videos to compete. Iron Maiden established themselves by doing all the right things at the right time, and Def Leppard established themselves by turning into an American band; »Pyromania« is a fantastic album, a pinnacle in rock music history, but there's nothing British in it, no British influence at all.

We didn't get over those early mistakes until »Power And The Glory« when we toured with a real metal band, and that was Iron Maiden. We did a few other tours. We did a tour with Molly Hatchet which again was really the wrong audience; we toured with Rainbow which was more or less the right audience but they weren't really pulling that many people; we toured with Triumph; but it wasn't really until that Maiden tour in the summer of 1983 that we really started to sell a lot of records in America. »Power And The Glory« was in the Billboard charts because finally we got to play with a band who drew exactly the same audience as us and that audience knew who we were and so it was a fantastic tour. It was Maiden's »Piece Of Mind« LP, the »World Piece Tour«, so not Bruce Dickinson's first album with them, but I think it was one of his first major tours of America. We were going on and ripping it to shreds and they were having to go on after us, so that was a lot of fun for us. Our management only signed a seven-or-so week contract for the tour, not a coast-to-coast contract, the theory being that after that time we could re-sign and carry on or go off and headline. As it happens at the end of seven weeks, after a gig in Louisville, Kentucky, we were off; Fastway, who'd been the first band on, were promoted and Coney Hatch were taken on as openers. But still, it was a pretty good tour and after that we went on our own headline tour with Accept and Heavy Pettin' which was very successful for us: a lot of sold-out shows on that tour. We were at our height then; the period around »Power And The Glory« and »Crusader« was our biggest point in America. We nearly broke it but not quite, really. It's one of those things. We had more success in Europe than anybody else at that time so we can't really complain. A lot of bands tried to break America – Status Quo, Slade, loads of them – but it's quite difficult; everything has to be in the right place and you have to have such a fantastic team behind you that really believes in you. The agent was good, but I think Carrere was totally out of its league in America and they were doing deals that were, frankly, stupid.

The audiences in America were pretty crazy though; absolute party animals, and the bigger the concert the better it was for them. It was great. The first show with Rush, we played about forty minutes, came offstage and these two girls burst into the dressing room and one of them had a rose in her mouth. I think one was of Spanish origin, the other was a blonde – a typical American blonde girl – and they burst in and said, "right, we're going to take you for a good time" so me and one of the other guys jumped into their car and off we went back to the hotel. It was totally mind-boggling: I'd been with hundreds of English girls and European girls but this pair were my indoctrination into the groupie thing in America. It was unbelievable really. Unbeknown to me they were taking quaaludes and vodka and everything else under the sun and were completely fucked up. When we went to the hotel there was a disco underway and this blonde girl said, 'c'mon, let's have a dance.'

Now it might surprise you to learn that I'm not really a dancer; I'm too gangly. But I went down to the dance floor and all of a sudden she turned into a female Rudolf Nureyev. It was unbelievable. I was stood there, you know, arms flapping, doing the shaking-maracas dance and she was like doing the splits and cartwheels. And the whole place is watching. So I'm like, 'I'm getting a bit tired now, I'm going for a sit-down' and we retired to the hotel room. I'm with the blonde and my band-mate is with the other girl. He was never that much good at sex anyway, just a come-quick-and-go-to-sleep kind of guy, and so once he'd done the business on the other bed and went to sleep, the other girl came over into our bed. I'd already had the blonde, and soon afterwards they went into the bathroom together. I'm lying on the bed, minding my own business, and he's fast-a-fucking-sleep, when both girls came back out and said, 'we're going to turn you on.' They both went down on each other, and I'm laid there, watching, and then they went down on me; it was unbelievable actually, like a schoolboy's dream come true. When you get two women sucking your cock, it's fantastic. And meanwhile, this silly bastard's fast asleep in the next bed!

AIDS hadn't been heard of back then and everything was totally balls-to-the-wall. American girls had no inhibitions whatsoever; and being English and very reserved, it just totally blew my mind. From then on, I was totally hooked on American girls and sex. Whereas most guys in the band had a beer and stayed up after a show, I usually had a girl in the room, two girls sometimes; that's basically what I used to do. In fact, I didn't spend that much time with the band on the road because mostly I was with girls. It was fantastic! I was totally – literally – fucked. Some nights I was almost collapsing on stage because I was completely exhausted, having been up all night and then just snatching a couple of hours sleep on the bus (and maybe having some groupies on the bus as well). It was like living a giant porn film. That's the only way I can describe it, like a giant, never-ending erotic dream, really. America just seduced me and corrupted me, and to be honest it would have been quite easy to have met some rich lawyer's daughter someplace, shagged my brains out and just gone off with her into obscurity… Rich obscurity, but obscurity all the same. I did have a lot of proposals to do just that, but I was living the dream I'd always wanted. I'd sacrificed so much for this, and now, as far as I was concerned, I had it all.

We first came across Metallica in March 1982. It's been said that they saw us as aloof, for the want of a better word, but it's surprising how 'knackered' gets confused with 'aloof', isn't it.

We spent most of the first half of 1982 in America, playing everywhere and anywhere. One such gig was at the Keystone in Palo Alto, where we were billed as 'the loudest band in the western hemisphere'; we also played four shows at the Whisky A Go Go, which must have been our first shows in Los Angeles. Two shows each day on two consecutive days. We were tired because we were doing interviews for the record company all day and then doing these two shows, which were important shows for us. I do remember watching Metallica: they must have been quite garagey back then, obviously influenced by songs of ours like "Motorcycle Man" and the other fast stuff. I'm sorry we didn't get chance to talk to them, especially when we found out later that Lars Ulrich in particular was such a big fan of the band, but before they sound off about us, can they honestly say that they have spoken to every band that's supported them.

There's another story that I've heard told about us from those gigs: I used to have a fan on stage; it looked like a wedge but there was a fan in it which stopped me getting too hot on stage and besides, it looked cool as well with my hair blowing back from my face. The story goes that they asked us to use it and I think our stage manager at the time told them to fuck off. But if that's the way it went, then as a band we knew nothing about it. We were far too busy on the day. Ozzy Osbourne was there too. We'd become quite good mates with him and Sharon, and having him visit us in America was great. This wasn't long after the tragic accident that had resulted in Randy's death so we were really pleased to see him and it was quite an emotional meeting. I remember when Ozzy walked in – I've got some good Ozzy stories, but then, everyone has good Ozzy stories! – we were drinking champagne; don't remember why, but we were. Anyway, Ozzy walked in, so we gave him some champagne which he drank and it just came straight back down his nose. He was already pissed anyway, he was upset, and then he asked if we'd got anything stronger and put that back as well.

So with all this going on, I can imagine that we didn't get chance to talk to Metallica, although not through any reason of malice. Believe me, I've never knowingly been a wanker to any of our support bands, ever. I would say in fact that we've gone out of our way to accommodate them most of the time. And so any sort of disrespect they thought we'd shown them certainly wasn't intended, and by now they should be big enough to realise that when you go to a town like Los Angeles for your first shows and they're sold out and the music business people are there and you've got people like Ozzy Osbourne coming and Mötley Crüe coming (who we'd never heard of but they came along anyway so that they could have their photographs taken with us) it's a complete jungle. So if I didn't say 'hello' or 'it's nice to meet you' then no slight was intended.

You can't bear a grudge in this business. It's silly. I mean, we've been screwed over by some of the best bands, but I don't bear a grudge. We played with Whitesnake at the Coatham Bowl which is basically David Coverdale's local gig in Redcar. We walked in after having had a seriously bad day – a wheel dropped off the van – and we were really late; we'd had to thumb a lift in an artic to the gig. We told them that the roadies were dealing with the van and wouldn't be long and the stage manager said something comforting like, 'you've got five minutes to set your fucking gear set up or you can fuck off.' We did it, we set up in record time, but they were just wankers really. Coverdale was great, he was really nice, but the crew were complete arseholes. But Metallica; the story I heard was that we didn't let them use this fan, we didn't talk to them… So what! Boo-hoo; big fucking deal! Generally, all throughout our career, I've tried to say hello to all our support bands because I know it means a lot to them. Metallica went on to be huge and have written some fantastic albums so does it really matter any more?

The other band back then was Ratt, and I can't say I said hello to them either. It's such a small venue, and when you do two shows in one day you're so rushed. But we weren't like REO Speedwagon; we didn't swan around on stage like God doing ballet-pirouette things, we just went for it; and to play for an hour-and-a-half full on, and then have time off for a shower and then do another show in a small, hot, sweaty club is quite difficult. At the same time you've got all these people arriving from the business and you just haven't got the time to go downstairs and say hello to everyone. I wanted a meal and a shower and to be ready for the next show (and besides, there were shitloads of girls there with hardly any clothes on too). Metallica would probably say that they played two shows as well, but they only played about thirty minutes, which is hardly the same. And one thing I will say: through all of their success, I've never, ever, said to anyone, 'well, of course, when Metallica started out they supported us.' So although I probably didn't say hello (or whatever else they expected me to say), I've never used the fact that they opened for us either; I'm not a name-dropper and that's how it is. I obviously pissed them off seriously but, there you go; it was a long time ago. Sorry, guys. What can I say?

We played with Rainbow in America as well, right about the time they recorded the »Live Between The Eyes« video. I never really knew how big Rainbow were: I guessed they were probably like us, massive in Europe with "I Surrender" and "Since You Been Gone" but not so well known in America. And I never really got on with them. We'd done some shows in our early career like Deeside Leisure Centre, and they kicked us off the Wembley gig because obviously we'd gone down too well. They just kicked us off without warning; we got there and somebody else was playing. That really is a big 'fuck you!' Obviously Ritchie Blackmore didn't give a flying fuck, and didn't even remember anything about that. So when we toured with them in America I was slightly prejudiced against him to start with because he'd already screwed us over once. I was also wary because he was so dismissive of us, but he still used to watch us every night. Why he used to do this, I don't know; just to see if we were nicking of any his licks, I expect; or, more to the point, to nick some of our moves. I used to whistle a lot, and bend over backwards on the drum riser, and he said, 'Joe wants to do that; stop doing it.' I was almost speechless. 'Hang on: you're asking me to stop doing something I've always done? Fuck you!' So of course I'd just do it even more!

I think Blackmore would be the first one to say that he was a bit nuts in that period of Rainbow. They were trying desperately to break America. I mean we used to do 3,000 to 4,000 people which was all right and, as I said, when Aldo Nova joined the tour it went from that to maybe 10,000 people. I don't think the Rainbow tour helped us too much because they weren't what was happening at that time. What was happening was what was happening in Europe, where we were in the thick of it. We were a heavy, heavy band, but in America we were made to be a little bit less heavy because, for instance, a Rush audience doesn't care how much you can headbang or scream; they're more into Music with a capital M, with intricacies and textures and moods, and we were thirty minutes of power and getting them to sing "Wheels Of Steel" – which they did, to be fair. I did get everybody to sing it. But it's not really the same music. I'm a huge Rush fan, I love their music and I love the band, but it was the wrong tour for us. We were just there because our agent was their agent and put us on. Nearly every band we toured with was the wrong band. Cheap Trick was totally the wrong band. Mötley Crüe weren't really the right band. They didn't really have heavy metal fans, diehard heavy metal fans; what they were pulling in America were school kids who were rebelling against their parents and everything else with »Shout At The Devil«. I love that album, and I'd call myself a Mötley Crüe fan, but it just wasn't the right tour at the right time for us.

Really, our chances in America were squandered. There were only a few bands you could tour with. Judas Priest was one, and Iron Maiden toured with them. There's a big grudge there and they've never played together since (from memory, I believe that Judas Priest accused Iron Maiden of ripping off their act). We toured with UFO in America; that was probably a good tour for us because although they weren't of our musical generation they were still a great rock band (and I was a huge UFO fan), but again, we're not exactly musically compatible.

So it was a tough time, band-wise. Yes, it was fantastic to be in America, where we were classed as 'nearly good-looking'! (We weren't quite good-looking enough to be full-on sex symbols, so we were always the 'English guys with a cute accent and a nice arse', but facially we were never like total babe magnets. We did try in the middle Eighties to be better-looking, but to no great effect; I don't think we ever rose out of the 'nearly good-looking' category.) But the people in charge of our career should have been guiding us and looking after us while we were doing our thing. They just weren't doing a good job, and they didn't really understand the New Wave Of British Heavy Metal thing at all. Nigel Thomas certainly didn't get it. He just thought we were like Joe Cocker – some Northern guys who needed sorting out. I don't think he ever really understood what really made us tick. He was doing what he thought was right but actually this was a new thing, an explosion of heavy metal that was happening across the world, he didn't really have his finger on the pulse. None of the management, nor anyone at Carrere Records come to that, would know who Scorpions were, or Cheap Trick, or the difference between them. It would simply be a matter of, 'are they big?'

'Yeah.'

'Well, get Saxon on the bill, then.'

They were just bad management decisions, inspired either wholly or in part by the word 'greed'. Much as I loved being on the road with Mötley Crüe and those other bands they just weren't the right tours for us in that respect. But having said all that, when Nigel Thomas died I quite missed him; although he probably didn't do us any real favours in our career he was still a character and, as I've said, I like characters.

Chapter Thirteen

he song "Power And The Glory" itself is about the Falklands War. A lot of the war songs, war lyrics, that I've written are anti-war songs. Maybe a lot of people don't realise that. "Crusader" is a bit different; that's not so much an anti-war song as a straight historical tale. "Power And The Glory", "Broken Heroes", they're really anti-war songs, saying that the generals sit on their fat arses just pushing people around a board while the common soldier dies. But that's what it's about, and it was the Falklands War that inspired it, because that was going on while we were writing and formalising the ideas.

»Power And The Glory« was the first album we made in America. We started the sessions at the end of 1982 after we'd finished touring the UK with »The Eagle Has Landed« and used a guy called Jeff Glixman to produce it, who I think worked with Kansas in the past. I really can't remember much about it because I was shagging a lot, to be honest. That's where I met Christine, my second wife. She had a Porsche 911, so I was gone. I just used to come back and do the vocals – 'just ring me when you need me guys, I'll be back' and I was off! So I can't remember much about it. I can remember the producer put the guitars in a big chipboard box to get the sound, which seems ridiculous really; by that I mean the cabinets in a box, not the guitarists (although in one case that wouldn't have been a bad idea). Also, being a Hammond organ player, he had a Hammond set up and had the annoying habit of jamming with us at the drop of a hat on this fucking Hammond. And of course being a Hammond it was always Deep Purple we'd be jamming to. I hate Hammond organs. Love Deep Purple; hate Hammond organs.

We made the album in Atlanta, Georgia, which is a fantastic town, actually, although it was the first time I'd really encountered racism. The Black versus White thing was quite strong, which I couldn't really understand. A lot of White people there still had Black servants who wouldn't look you in the eye – they'd look at the floor if they were with you.

»Power And The Glory« was the only one of those early albums which we didn't tour the UK with. We'd done the UK to death, and we needed a rest from Britain and Britain probably needed a rest from us. That said, though, we had a rather silly festive cover picture on the cover of the Christmas 1982 Kerrang!, dressed up as Santas and wise men, and did odd shows in England throughout 1983 so it wasn't as if we'd vanished off the face of the planet. It was our sixth album in three years so expectations were obviously pretty high. Apparently, although I don't remember this, in that Kerrang! feature I was quoted as saying that we were thinking of bringing out an album that was half live and half studio songs, using left-overs from »Power And The Glory« and some recent live recordings, although I don't recall anything about that now.

We did a one-off at the Royal Court Hall in Nottingham to record the »Saxon Live« video, which gave us a chance to play some of the new songs – "Power And The Glory" itself, "Red Line", "The Eagle Has Landed" and "This Town Rocks", although the title track didn't make the final video for some reason. Kerrang! hated the first single (once again, the title track of the album) but gave the album itself a great review. Strange. Sounds also liked it, giving it a four-star review and a quote of 'it's a winner all the way'.

We toured Europe, coming home for a one-off at Leeds Queen Hall, headlining a bill that also included Twisted Sister, Girlschool, Anvil, Spider and Battle Axe. The gig was memorable, if for no other reason than me being lowered from the roof on a motorbike. We did that a couple of times, because we did it again at Hammersmith Odeon during the tenth anniversary shows; we did two London shows on that tour, the Country Club and Hammersmith. A friend of mine was a TT winner called Roger Marshall and he had a deal with Yamaha. They foolishly lent me their Grand Prix bike and I came down out of the truss on that which was pretty cool. The first time we did it, in Leeds, I think it was a Harley-Davidson, but the Yamaha was worth about half-a-million quid. Both times, though, before it was lowered there was a real 'fucking hell' moment because I'm up there and it's quite wobbly – just two chains holding you up, one on the front wheel and one on the back. It's a weird sensation because as it comes down it starts to sway and I'm thinking, 'whoa, I could fall off here!'

As I mentioned earlier, »Power And The Glory« also gave us our first real tour of America, with Iron Maiden, and was the first album in the Billboard charts. So we were finally selling significant numbers of albums over there. I think we did half-a-million albums in America, which was more than our total sales in Europe of any album, and »Power And The Glory« and that Iron Maiden tour really cemented the success that we had later in America. Two nights sold out at Long Beach, California; good shows. Fucking great shows, in fact. One of our problems though was that in the UK we were considered to be more British, more 'the home-spun boys', and so when we went to America the English press did not like it; did not like it one bit. We were selling out, as far as they were concerned; they'd done the same thing to Def Leppard; you know, '»Pyromania« is too American, it's a terrible album...' »Pyromania« didn't do that well in England when it first came out; it was »Hysteria« that was their first instant big seller over here. But we liked »Pyromania« a lot, and recognised it was a really important album, even if the British press still had their knives out for the band.

We did that Iron Maiden tour, quite a long tour of major cities, but stupidly the management didn't sign the contract for the whole tour, being impatient for us to headline in our own right and make them mega-bucks, is how Paul sees it. We did six weeks with Iron Maiden, ending our stint on the tour in Louisville, Kentucky. On that last night of the tour we did two things to Maiden. Firstly, we threw coconut cream pies at them, and then we came up on stage dressed as prostitutes which was really funny. I think everybody else knew about it, apart from Bruce and it really took him by surprise (although he must have expected something as they were marching across stage dressed as Hitler and Nazis during our set). It's what you do on last nights. And it was quite funny because we obviously made really ugly women – especially Steve Dawson.

We got the gear off some groupies whom we left naked in the dressing room while we did it. We didn't wear everything obviously, we didn't go for the shoes and the pants and the tights. We just wore dresses and came on, over the top of their back line, during "22 Acacia Avenue" which is a silly song anyway. I think the sight of two moustached women coming on each side of Bruce almost took him over the edge. He's probably like me, you know, in that when he's on stage it's *his* stage, and nobody goes on there and gets in his way; and we were all over it like a rash, throwing cream pies at them and all sorts of shit. It was all in good fun, and they'd already done their thing on us anyway so ours was like a get-back at them.

I think the worst thing ever done to us was when we toured with Molly Hatchet and they dropped ping-pong balls on us for about forty minutes. God knows where they got so many ping-pong balls from. But they were dropping on us through our entire set, bouncing across the stage. I could cope with five minutes, but the whole fucking set... That was a bit much. These sort of last-night pranks, they're not really done much now because it's all taken so much more seriously, We will occasionally sweep the stage during a set, but that's about as far as it goes these days.

But I liked that Iron Maiden tour. It was a fantastic tour for us, a great tour all round and they are a great band. It was their first really massive US tour so I think they were really going for it. We should have done the whole tour but I think we were going down too well anyway. When you've got a similar band on your bill, and they're going down really well, it's a fantastic package for the crowd but there is a niggly thought in your mind that you could do it without them. We went on a tour after that with Accept supporting us as special guests and they were on »Balls To The Wall« which is another great album and they went on every night and went down fantastically. They didn't go down better than us but they went down the same and in the back of your mind, you think, 'fucking hell, we'd better get it together!' Iron Maiden certainly never went down any less than us. Most nights they were better, or at worst they were the same as us. People were singing "Denim and Leather", "Princess Of The Night" and that was the same as people singing "The Number Of The Beast".

At the same time though, the openers Fastway were niggling to get our slot so I think it was easier for Maiden to get rid of us and promote Fastway. As a decision it's easier to get rid of the band who are going down well when the contract ends rather than keep them on. It's fair enough; I have never felt any animosity towards Iron Maiden and I would have done the same. I liked going on middle of the bill on these massive tours though; it suited us because there was no pressure and we could relax, despite the fact that things were quite serious. The pressure is always on the headliner, and also, the later the show comes, the more tired the kids are for the headliner. When you are playing in front of an audience with a successful band you want it to go smoothly and you want to feel that you are having a fantastic show from the first moment without really having to work too hard to make things happen. And the thing is, me and Bruce are quite similar in the way that we work audiences. It's important to me to get everybody, right to the back, involved in what's happening; to me, that's the ultimate goal of the gig. And it's probably the same for Bruce. So when you have two bands, two guys, doing that, and I'm doing it first, in some way it steals their thunder a little bit. When you are headlining, to be brutally honest, all you want is for the band before you to go on and have a good gig; nothing more. If they're reaching right to the back, it's like, 'fuck! What can we do more than that?' It's a big leveller when an audience goes nuts for the band that's on before you, because you can't take it any higher than that. So I think from Iron Maiden's point of view it was probably better to leave us off the rest of the tour once the contract was up to stop us burning out the audiences.

But that was it. They didn't need us any more, we'd been contracted for six weeks, and when that ran out they didn't ask us to carry on. They didn't kick us off the tour, which people have said; the contract ran out, we weren't picked up and they just moved Fastway up the bill. And Fastway were selling a lot of albums. Dave King wasn't a great frontman at first but he learned quickly from me and Bruce: in fact he turned into me and Bruce after about two weeks. They had been no threat to us, as openers, and they were no threat to Iron Maiden. I liked their first album because they were just basically Led Zeppelin-ish, but then they changed a bit on the second album. They were a bit like Kingdom Come in that respect. I liked their first album because it is very reminiscent of Zeppelin, but the second was reminiscent of AC/DC, and the third was reminiscent of someone else. It's a consistency thing. I think Kingdom Come could have been a huge band, had they carried on doing the Zeppelin thing. I think Lenny Wolf is quite a talented guy.

The Iron Maiden tour though was a big break for us in terms of opening up America. We've done festivals since together, and we're big fans of theirs and they're big fans of ours. I don't think that overall though they did anything to our career for good or for bad. I think what Saxon achieved we did for ourselves. Maiden and us just co-existed, and obviously they went on to much bigger things, the biggest of them being success in America. Everybody was saying that we were selling out to America, but the same accusation was never levelled at the likes of Maiden and Judas

Priest, and in fact the one country that enabled bands like Maiden and Priest to survive was America. Being big in America makes a huge difference to what a band can do, purely because of the income you can generate, and that's one of the biggest differences between Iron Maiden and Saxon. We never had the income from the album sales in America to make our organisation truly big. We were always at the middle level, and I think that's one of the reasons why we never became massive and then sustained it. Anyone in a band will understand what I'm saying. Across Europe we were big, and in our heyday we would sell 350,000 records easily. But while we were doing that, Iron Maiden were selling three million in America; so we had to do what we did on the sales of 350,000 albums, whereas some of these bands were making millions in America and then re-investing it in themselves.

I guess the bottom line is that we were never destined to be big in America. We went straight from the Iron Maiden tour to our own headline tour and we did quite well. We did six shows in the New York area, Chicago, Los Angeles; we used to play the Santa Monica Civic, 6,000 sold out, we'd do it on a regular basis. Texas, we'd do pretty good business through there as well. So we were on the middle road to success, because suddenly the heavy metal thing in America had gone absolutely nuts and the home-grown bands were starting to come through, like Mötley Crüe. Obviously Van Halen were already huge by the time the Eighties came around anyway but were doing great business still. The older bands though were on the wane. REO Speedwagon, Alice Cooper, all those bands were going down; they were still doing well but the young kids wanted new bands, bands they could call their own. The Americans took the British style and used it, changed it, repackaged it and sold it back to us. And, you have to admit, some of those American bands were fantastic.

Back in the UK though, by the end of 1983 tour dates had been announced for a major UK tour the following February. We were coming home once more, to a storm that we'd apparently 'sold out'. It's sad how much shit the press gave us for recording a song called "Sailing To America", which is about the Pilgrim Fathers and therefore about Europe. It's a song about England, it's a song about them leaving the country to start anew. It's a song about hope. We should have called it "The Mayflower" or something like that. It's a naïve approach for the press to take. If they'd listened to the lyrics, or read them off the album sleeve, they should have got the point.

We'd written »Crusader« in Rotherham, some of it anyway, in Park Gate studios, which as Paul often points out, was Jive Bunny's studios (the people responsible for those awful megamix singles way back whenever). I think we might also have written some at Transam. Whatever, the producer Kevin Beamish came over for pre-production which was a first for us.

The »Crusader« tour was probably our biggest tour in terms of production and probably pulled the most people, both in Europe and America where we toured with Accept supporting and Pretty Maids. It was a massive tour, so we were going for it. I see »Crusader« a lot like our first album, though, in that it was very mixed. And again, we had a really wacky choice of producer. We wanted Ron Nevison to do the album, but for some reason he got drunk and fell asleep in a flight case, so the management didn't take to him and that was that. He went on to do some great work after that: but not with us, unfortunately. We wanted Mutt Lange and Def Leppard got him. We always knew what we wanted but we were never given that opportunity because management always knew better. So »Crusader« was produced by Kevin Beamish; nice guy, lovely guy. But there were a few problems during the recording mainly because I think that the jealousy thing came in quite hard with the band again. Being a singer, Kevin really took me on; it was like, 'let's go for a drink and talk about what we do' and the rest of the band weren't important to him, or so it must have seemed to them. So I would go to his house above the hills in LA and drink and talk, and I think Steve Dawson in particular got very jealous.

Beamish's production of "Crusader" itself is very weak. The song has tons of bottle, tons of bass, but he didn't get it. There's a lot more to it than you can hear on the album. And then we had a ballad on there called "Do It All For You" which was highly influenced by him: he co-wrote it with us in fact. Like our first album, »Crusader« was a bit disjointed. There were ballads and heavy metal together and some of the UK press didn't like it at all – 'sold out to America, making albums in America, how could they?' etc etc. Everyone else was making albums in America so what exactly was their point? It wasn't the heavy metal capital of the world, but it was certainly the rock capital of the world. So we figured… Well, we didn't figure anything, we just thought we'd get laid a lot! We had a great time. We stayed out by Universal Studios in some apartments. Sound City, Los Angeles, was a nice studio. We spent tons of time down at the Rainbow, got a big car and used to go out with a shitload of girls and meet the who's who of rock music, basically. Scorpions were in there, Bon Jovi were in there, everyone who was anyone was in there, and we were chatting and talking and it was a great melting pot on Sunset Strip. It was just the place to be at the time and we loved it really. Great pizza too!

We recorded »Crusader« very quickly. We recorded albums then like we do now, in six to seven weeks or so. I don't think the people there could handle our way of writing songs though, nor the way that we played. We played very aggressively and very in-your-face and we really weren't subtle. The album featured two 'firsts' for us; one was a cover version. Nigel dug out a Sweet album and we started messing about with "Set Me Free". Like everybody of our generation we were always quite into Sweet B-sides and album tracks as they always seemed to be quite rocky and much heavier than their commercial singles. I think we did a pretty good version of it, although it didn't cause any great stir really. I think it's good doing cover versions, if you don't attach too much to them and don't make that big a deal out of it. It's like "Ride Like The Wind" – that was a fantastic cover and it got tons of airplay all over the world so people keyed in on it, but actually it was never meant to be the main track on the album which is what it went on to become. But it's a great version. People got carried away about it; 'it's Christopher Cross – he's not heavy metal.' But that was the whole point; that's why we did it. There'd be no point covering "Smoke On The Water", would there?

The other 'first' was the aforementioned radio-friendly ballad. I really don't think we can do ballads justice even now – and we are a much better band now Doug Scarrat's with us. If we play laid back, it tends to be more bluesy: we're really not good at creating emotions that, say, Journey create. I don't really have the voice that makes women weep; I probably have a voice that makes women run out the fucking door! I think when I sing soft, I can be quite gentle, but most of the time I'm screaming my bollocks off really. I don't think that all those trials we went through of writing love songs worked very often, and I don't think people wanted us to do them anyway. The nearest thing we got to a nice song was "Northern Lady" which was a huge song in America. But we were more well-known for things like "This Town Rocks" – that was our biggest hit in America off the »Power And The Glory« album; it got massive airplay and radio stations used to use it as part of their jingles. It was a really big song for us, which is strange because we wrote it in about twenty minutes. It was an anthem in America and when we played places like Long Beach and I asked 'does Long Beach know how to rock?' the place went nuts. All hell broke out. And that's what we wrote these songs for – to be played live. Sometimes songs like that don't really work on vinyl; they're not written to be heard, they're written to be experienced live.

But I like »Crusader«. I listen to it quite regularly, and it's cool; once you get over the production cutting your balls off, it's got some fantastic moments. "Rock City" is a great song. It's brilliant actually: I'm not 100% sure it's Saxon though, but it is a great song. Kerrang! to be fair gave the album a good review, although a lot of the writers hated it, and no-one at Sounds seemed to like it at all. Still, the tour was great, a big production too with castle battlements and stuff like that.

The problem was though, we were experimenting because we were being led by people who didn't know where they were going. So we were going down the same road as them, which was actually going nowhere in a fucking fog. Nobody ever said to us at that time: 'what's the composition of the album? Is that where you want to be at this particular point in your career? Do you think that all these songs are representative of what the band are?' That's what the management should have been saying; that's what we do now, and have been doing for quite a long time. But back then, nobody did it; there was a complete lack of guidance. Producers and management, their job is to guide their bands and advise them in their path. Some bands have fantastic guys and although it's not always a happy relationship and it can get a bit rocky from time to time, the path they take is the right path. I think it keeps coming back to the fact that the producers that were chosen for us weren't right. Many times we'd talk amongst ourselves and think, 'let's just fuck off; I don't like what's happening here. Let's just get on a plane and go. What are they going to do; smack our hands?' But we never did, which is a shame. I was always in favour of the 'what can they do?' approach. Because there was always an us-or-them mentality, there always had to be a boss. And the boss always had to be hated. It was the Working Class thing all the time. They were the boss, so it was their fault. They gave us the money. It didn't even feel like our money (even though it was); it was their money they were giving us. And that mentality was always the same with early Saxon. It was always like, 'well where does the money come from?'

'Well, he gives it to us.'

'Oh well, he must be the boss then.'

That was our mindset, and so we basically did as we were told. Personally, there were lots of things I didn't want to do but as a band we just went and did what they wanted us to do; we were just brow-beaten into it really. Like I said, though, I do like »Crusader«; there's nothing wrong with the album. I just think that – and I mean, everybody in retrospect is correct, aren't they – the advice and the guidance and the choice of people to work with was wrong. But ironically it was probably our biggest album.

Because the UK press were so vitriolic though, it did get to us a bit after a while, and we did start to think that maybe we were writing shit albums. The views that were coming back to us did affect us; we would never have admitted it because we used to say we didn't give a shit, and in fact we didn't in one way because we did what we wanted anyway. But I don't think they understood what we were trying to do. We were never ones for washing dirty laundry in public, and I think that the songwriting was still at a high standard. I think "Crusader" is a great rock song, and I think the standard we'd set ourselves was still there. I just think we were fighting against a manager who really wanted us to be something different. If we'd stayed the same and written what Doug calls 'naïve rock songs' we'd have been panned anyway, so it was a lose/lose situation; »Crusader« was our biggest album and the tour we did was massive but the press were waiting and actually did us a lot of damage. And they damaged themselves as well to an extent, because by screwing us over they were screwing over the very thing that they liked and so shot themselves in the foot. Hyping up Mötley Crüe and Cinderella and Aerosmith is all well and good but those bands couldn't give a flying fuck about the UK audiences – just waltzed in, took all the cash and went again. Their loyalty was to America.

Everybody took a rough ride through the late Eighties. We didn't take a dive as far as live shows went, but the albums didn't sell as many because the reviews weren't as good, and a lot of people who were 'faddy' didn't buy albums that copped bad reviews. But the hardcore stayed loyal, and we never, ever had a UK tour that the fans didn't support. We were always flying the flag for Britain – 'yeah, we're in America but we're a British band' – but the UK press seemed to think we were turning American. But in our mind we were Union Jacks on stage; in interviews it was 'Britain this, England that,' we felt we were still at the forefront of a British invasion. It was the press that was misunderstanding us, not the other way round.

There's only a handful of bands left from all of those that emerged at that time, and I am a big believer that the reason is because we never really, really sold out, and we didn't compromise. We were just trying different things as songwriters –

it's as innocent as that really – and the press perceived us to be more American... I mean, "Suzie Hold On" is quite catchy; it's a sickly fucking pop song if you look at its bare essentials, and nobody said that was selling out to America. So basically I just think one guy said it and everybody took the lead from it, and from there it became a big thing. Really it galvanised us into a 'fuck you' attitude. Paul's right, when he once said that England should learn to be proud of its heritage because from The Beatles through Led Zeppelin to Goldfrapp we've been selling music to America for years, and long may it continue: bands should play the music that they believe in and do it with conviction.

There's only really three bands left from that period of the late Seventies/early Eighties – Def Leppard, Iron Maiden and Saxon. They're the only bands left from those days. The rest packed it in and went to be butchers or carpenters or whatever and then came back when it became popular again. It's bands like us that stuck to it and kept hammering away all through the years, hammering away at what we believed in to make it come around again. I just think that those three bands have stuck to their principles, stayed together – some members come, some members have gone, but the band still exists. There's nothing left of that movement but we three bands, the three bands that everybody remembers. (You can't include Motörhead, Judas Priest and those bands in there because they were huge before then.)

And why those three bands? It's got to be the songs and the songwriting and the fact that we moved people. We're still big and people still buy our records and those albums have not been deleted. They are classic albums. I just think that it's very strange that the three bands that I knew the best are the three bands that are still there. We didn't really know, you know, Tygers Of Pan Tang, Praying Mantis, Witchfynde, etc; they were on the fringe. Some of those bands profess to have been massive in the Eighties but in reality they weren't, they were middle order bands. I'm not saying they weren't great bands, but they just didn't have that extra oomph to get them up there really. They obviously didn't have the financial stability to stay together either, and so people had to get jobs. That's really what they had to do.

So it does rankle a bit when bands get back together, like Whitesnake or Twisted Sister, and come and do a few major festivals when they've done nothing for ten years. And suddenly the music is popular again and they come out of the woodwork and it's people like us who've been working consistently over twenty-five years that's helped bring it back in the first place. It does annoy me a bit that they don't ever say in their interviews, 'ah well, if it wasn't for bands like Iron Maiden and Saxon who kept it all going, we wouldn't be here.' They could easily say that because actually it's true. Ronnie James Dio didn't give up and get a job, did he, stamping tickets in a travel agent or something; he's been there at the cutting edge all the time. Lemmy hasn't gone off driving a bus, has he? He's been there sacrificing his life for music, basically, and for his fans, and that's what it's all about really. It's not about looking pretty or what guitar you play, it's about sacrificing everything for your art – that's what it's all about. When we walk onstage as a band in front of 50,000 people, those people go, 'yes! They've been here doing this for twenty-five years,' and they say the same thing about Iron Maiden. 'This is a band from the Eighties playing our music and they're still together; they're not here just to sing a few old nostalgic songs,' and to me that's what counts. I think you should have a lot of respect for people who have stayed in the business for so long. To be able to sit here at the end of twenty-five years and look back is no mean feat.

As I've said before, people pick up on the fact that we never broke America but at the end of the day, it's not that big a deal, is it? Lots of bands didn't break America. The fact is, we're still here. And that's what counts.

Chapter Fourteen

he Mötley Crüe tour was the highpoint of sexual adventures, but America really was where most of the groupies were. And like I said, I nearly died from too much sex and too many shows. I really got ill actually and had to pack it in for a couple of days because I was really exhausted. It is like a drug actually – once you start, you can't stop. 'Semen deficiency,' Paul called it. I remember one tour we did, we had a tour manager called Steve Wood, he was a womanising bastard as well, and we had a competition on one tour of America as to who could shag the most girls in thirty days. We started on day one, and we'd be doing the gig and I'd be singing away, and he'd suddenly appear in the middle of the audience with a blonde girl mouthing 'done her!' We caught him cheating because he shagged a receptionist twice which didn't count. But he did 28 girls and I did 36 in thirty days, so the band won, right. You can't let the crew win. But that's how it was in America. Some people might think that's a really shitty way to treat women, but they just wanted to party. There wasn't much seduction going on; there was no AIDS and there wasn't much to stop you really. We got on the Mötley Crüe tour bus and Paul said to the driver, 'it's a bit Spartan on here, isn't it? Where are the carpets?' and the driver replied, 'it's so the beer and semen can run down the stairwell when I brake.'

It was a good time, the Eighties, for the groupies in America, and as we used to tour quite a lot we had regular groupies who were obviously with other bands as well, but when you were in town they were your band's groupies, which was quite nice really. It was a quite satisfactory arrangement all-in-all. It's all so shallow really though, because I've spent a lot of my life with different girls but in actual fact it doesn't mean anything. You might as well have a wank because it's just a fun thing. I didn't drink so basically I just ended up with girls all the time. It's like a drug though. You know how you're up for a cigarette when you haven't got one, it was the same with sex. If I didn't have a girl after the gig it was 'GOTTA HAVE A GIRL! GET A FUCKING GIRL FOR ME! I NEED ONE! WHAT AM I GOING TO FUCKING DO!' Crazy, really. I remember quite a few of them, special ones, but most of them I can't remember at all. But you wouldn't, would you. One night stands; one hour stands... But like I said, every bloke should get to do that, really. It's sad that every guy hasn't been able to do that because it's such a fantastic thing really, to have two gorgeous girls sucking your dick and then going down on each other, and you can take your pick which one you shag, or which one you shag first... For a bloke it's the ultimate turn on, and I did that so many times. And it wasn't just me; the whole band was at it. We were just young lads having a good time, sowing wild oats for England really! And the girls loved it. The routine was virtually always the same: 'you guys from England?'

'Uh, yeah.'

'Did you drive here? I just love your accent.'

'OK... Want to see the inside of the bus?'

So the whole mental attitude of English guys suddenly in America faced by hundreds of women that just loved your accent, loved everything about you, long hair, the rock band, everything, it's just like you've died and gone to heaven. That's how it was, and I've heard other people say the same thing. I don't really know if the guys in Iron Maiden were like that, but we were totally corrupted by America.

In terms of sex, there were certain countries that did, and certain countries that didn't. Germany was good for girls, quite a lot of girls there, Scandinavia was good, 90% of our audience there was girls. Spain – no; good Catholic girls. Italy was OK; bad Catholic girls! I did have a liaison with an Italian girl that was fantastic. I remember coming off stage after we'd finished and a girl was bouncing up and down on the seats, trying to get my attention, and she was really gorgeous, and she was taller than me which is a bit rare, and she basically dragged me back to the room, fucked my brains out and just left. I tried to find out who she was because she was really hot, but never did… France wasn't great. I did have a liaison with a circus girl in France, she was quite nice. Bit of a contortionist. I remember one night we were screwing in the shower and something must have dropped into the plug. We could hear this shouting and screaming downstairs and had no idea what it was so we carried on and I heard her go something like, 'sacré bleu!' or something, and then I realised that the whole room was knee-deep in water. It just flooded everywhere and there were people running about downstairs and we just got some big pieces of wood and were starting to scrape the water, both bollock naked, back into the shower. And we could hear people thundering up the stairs and banging on the door. Cost us an arm and a leg, that did. But it was pretty funny actually. No idea what her name was… I'm sure we had lots of French girls but it was the America girls that were always partying. I have great respect for all the girls we met. They just wanted a good time and so did we so it was a mutual thing. Most of them were on the Pill (obviously you check before getting started) so there were no pregnancy problems.

The Mötley Crüe tour was the height of our debauchery. I think because they drew a lot of women but even they couldn't deal with them all so there was a massive overspill. We didn't really know them at first but they were huge fans of ours; I think Nikki Sixx was the guy who asked for us to do the tour. But they were up-and-coming, »Shout At The Devil« was going through the roof, and we joined them for the US leg of the »Crusader« tour in April/May 1984.

It was a very strange tour. Totally American, more so than any tour we've ever done. 95% girls, and the other 5% were blokes dressed like girls anyway, so it was a bit like being with a pop band really in terms of adulation and being the biggest thing on the planet at that time. The tour was long and went right through the Bible Belt so we had all the people outside with the banners, protesting and calling it the Devil's music. And of course Mötley Crüe played right up to it. All the stories you hear about them, they're all totally true. Complete debauchery bastards; wild parties. And of course we dived in there head-first as well!

They were nice guys, a good band too. The guitarist Mick Mars was a bit of a grump but it was a successful tour for us. Like I said, there were a lot of protests though. They didn't really bother us because they were aiming at Mötley Crüe, although we did get some shit sometimes. We were different, though. We didn't wear make-up and look like girls, we weren't a glam band; we were more leather jackets and ridiculously tight trousers and hand-made boots from London – that was our type of look. But the first gig we did, we'd done our set, we'd gone down well, and outside there were hundreds of Evangelists. I can't remember where it was, it might have been Chicago. Anyway, meanwhile, Mötley Crüe are onstage, doing all this 'we're going to eat some Chicago pussy tonight!' and the place went wild, and all these protesters must have been thinking, 'oh, for fuck's sake!'

The band were totally outrageous and although we toured with them for quite a long time, it was unbelievable really and I don't think we ever got used to it. Our tour bus was full of women from morning till night. Both tour buses used to travel together and it wasn't unusual to stop off at a restaurant and meet a nice waitress who'd say, 'you guys in a band?'

And we'd reply, of course, 'yeah, do you want to see the tour bus?'

And we'd end up shaging her in the back lounge within, like, six minutes. Total Sodom and Gomorrah. Fantastic! A testament to the power of MTV, and the bad boy reputation really. And the thing with Mötley Crüe was that the more conservative the town, the wilder the people went. There's nothing better than a shy girl who suddenly lets it go. It's always the shy ones who are the naughtiest girls. The loud-mouthed ones aren't always that good. Sad but true. And we were absolute bastards; we used to seduce tons of guys' girlfriends. The rule was that the girls could come on the tour bus but boyfriends couldn't. So the girls would be waving to their boyfriends out the back window while someone was giving her one from behind. It was complete and total debauchery. Why we didn't get arrested, I'll never know. The police came on the bus many times, and said, 'look, we don't care what you do; just go somewhere quiet and stop making so much noise.' The Mötley Crüe tour was an absolute wall of sex. It was unbelievable. I can't really talk for everyone else because they were married, but I was totally exhausted the entire time. There were days when I couldn't walk, I was so tired.

For the first time, we had a party room, an idea we took from Mötley Crüe. We just had an extra room and we'd put all the good-looking women in there (no ugly ones, no guys; they were our only criteria) so I'd be with one in the room, and say, 'do you want to go back to the party?' And I'd phone JJ our guy and say, 'in about ten minutes, send another one down.' It was constant; no let-up any of the time. Wholly unbelievable. You never get over that sort of thing, really. It was a great time and I wouldn't have missed it for the world. Every bloke should get to do that. If there's ever a time in which there's a place you can go to have an implant put in your brain, like in that film »Total Recall« that would be the one to have – to be on an early 1980s Mötley Crüe tour. We'd go out to a club and the place used to explode when we'd walk in. Obviously it was for them: a few people would ask for our autographs but mostly it was girls going for Mötley Crüe. I remember us playing this gig and I looked up at the side of the stage and Tommy Lee's there, having a blow job while he's watching us. Talk about off-putting!

Chapter Fifteen

A lot of our career can be characterised by 'you can have anything but no fucking cash'! Nigel Thomas was pretty much holding the purse-strings, but the thing with Nigel is that he did have a massive influence on our career, and on me in particular. He was an Oxford graduate, totally different to where we came from, and he turned me on to the social scene in London. We used to go to happening clubs of the time where I met all sorts of people like Ridley Scott, Richard Branson... Because we were quite big at that time, it was cool for people to be seen out with a famous rock star – well, still is, actually – and I had some fantastic times. Nigel basically coached me to be a bit more, well, sophisticated, for the want of a better word. That side of him was fantastic because he was forever having meetings or business lunches or dinners with a lot of influential people of the time: he knew a lot of people and he helped me overcome my natural shyness and feel comfortable in that sort of company.

I think that because I had a friendship with Nigel Thomas, it impacted on the band in terms of petty jealousies. He had a manor house in the Cotswolds, in Stow-on-the-Wold or thereabouts, and I used to go there quite a lot with various girlfriends. I think a lot of jealousy started within the band at that time because I was becoming a bit more independent from them. It was not so much 'all the gang together' now, although don't forget that they were married and I wasn't at that point, so I was footloose and fancy free and could do whatever I wanted. So I think a lot of jealousy started at that point, basically with Graham Oliver and Steve Dawson.

At the same time, most people in the media were drawn towards me more than the other guys. I was better at communicating, better at putting my point across, because that's my job. So I think a lot of jealousies started to appear, and a few cracks too, because I had become the focal point of the band. At the same time, to be honest, I was getting to feel that it was me who had to give up time to do interviews while they loafed around, and it's quite tiring actually; all the interviews ended up being about life, the universe and everything as I saw it, which was not the way I'd thought it was going to be when we started the band. At the start we were all in it together, and I always thought that if anyone in the band got the front cover of a magazine, that was great. But there's a trick to interviews, to getting your point across. At best you have to tell people what they really want to hear; but if somebody asks you a question and you don't like it, you answer it with the answer you want to give, regardless of what the question was in the first place. That's the secret, but it's not exactly rocket science. I got caught early on a number of times, but soon found out how it's done. For the rest of the band, it was all a bit of a hoot doing interviews and all that stuff, but for me it seemed to be part of my job, and I had to do it because a lot of the time nobody else would.

So maybe some small jealousies started to appear: nothing too blatant, but I think that's when the cracks first began to appear in that band. They didn't want to get involved in press conferences and interviews and stuff like that. They just did not want to get involved. They were quite willing to let me – make me, in fact – do all the interviews and all the business meetings, and then they started to complain when I got all the attention, or if the business meeting didn't work out. That's how they were and that's how it was. I felt I was stuck in the middle of a lose/lose situation, compounded by changes around the band.

1985's »Innocence Is No Excuse« was our first album with EMI and at that time we obviously thought we'd moved on to better things from Carrere. It was a huge deal because EMI bought the entire back catalogue, but it just dragged on and on, as these things do. A snippet in Kerrang! in July 1985 both publicised the forthcoming album and tour while pointing out that a court battle continued between us and Carrere, with Carrere still claiming that we were signed to them.

Nigel Thomas didn't like Carrere. They were far too small for him, and French. I didn't have a problem with who the parent company was because Carrere was quite successful actually. They had some massive disco hits, a couple of Number 1s, but he wasn't happy with them. I thought they did well with »Power And The Glory« and »Crusader« because neither really received critical acclaim – in fact they both got slagged a bit – but Carrere hammered the promotion of those albums and they were very successful; a classic example of what EMI didn't do later on. Carrere really, really went for it, because they'd obviously spend a lot of money on those albums and they couldn't really afford us to slip. We were their main act at that time, so they did throw money at those albums to promote them and as a result »Power And The Glory« charted in America and »Crusader« was a big-selling album although production-wise it's quite soft.

But anyway, he wanted – HE wanted – to leave Carrere. The Carrere deal was running out, probably one more album with a really low advance, and I think he wanted to do a mega-deal of half-a-million pounds or something like that; that's what he was after. As he was looking for a way out of Carrere, they were going to release a live album, and in the contract they were supposed to pay us £30,000 if they did. They denied all knowledge of such a release but somebody in the organisation sent Nigel Thomas a memo from the top that said, 'just release the album' so they were totally screwed: we had a letter from the boss, Claude Carrere, giving them the go-ahead to do it. So they lost. I think they did a deal on the steps of the court and I think we had to pay – because they'd given us the £30,000 – I think we had to pay that back and give them something else, six months' pay or something, but we were out. We were going to go straight into a deal with Zomba Records but for some reason it didn't happen; I don't know what happened but we didn't go through with it so we were out in nowheres-ville with no deal. Nigel Thomas supported us actually through doing publishing deals – supporting us with his money which was obviously actually ours – but we had about eight months off during which I was writing »Innocence Is No Excuse« with Steve Dawson at my vicarage.

Within a year of us leaving, Carrere put out the »Strong Arm Metal« compilation which was heavily slated. But of course the record company at that point is never bothered about being slated; it's the bands who are bothered about being criticised. The record company – the ex-record company – never gives a shit. The criticism follows the band, you see, and apart from pressing it and printing a few sleeves, that album cost Carrere nothing. But you can't stop it; the band can't stop it. You did a deal, they've got the rights for however many years the contract says and they can do what the hell they like. So the people at EMI can do whatever they want and they don't have to talk to me. In fact, they didn't talk to me. Only recently, with the re-release of »The Eagle Has Landed«, which I wrote a short intro for, have they actually recognised my existence; that's the first time ever that EMI has talked to us.

So we were off Carrere. In the long run, I don't know whether changing labels was such a good move, because we were much more successful on Carrere than on EMI, much more successful, and they were an independent label. I just think they had serious problems in America with attitudes and personalities and the French mentality, wanting to do everything a certain way. The

Americans hated it, which probably is another reason why we never broke through in America. As I said, I remember being taken to a record store to see »Wheels Of Steel« in the racks, and there were no albums in the sleeves; the Carrere deal, we found out later, was that Warner Brothers had to make a minimum of 25,000 records and sell them. That was the deal; and that's what they did. They printed 25,000, sold them in a couple of weeks because we were quite hot at the time, and that's it. Didn't bother to make any more. It was all politics. So after that Carrere went with somebody else, I can't remember who; probably CBS. Carrere was always trying to get in there with the big players but it never really happened. They had an office in the same building as Warner Brothers and the French guy there, Jean-Claude – good-looking, smart, wore his jacket on his shoulders, cravat, obviously shagging his brains out, sitting in his office twiddling a pencil all day (not a bad way to earn a living) – would take me out to dinner with Warner Bros executives and all they wanted to do was sign the band direct because that's what their game was. And Nigel Thomas was up for it, but he just couldn't get us out of the contract at that time. We were Carrere's biggest act and they wanted us to break America not only because that's where the big money was, but also because it would have opened so many more doors for them.

So, for some time we didn't do much, just started writing the next album. Steve Dawson and I wrote the most of »Innocence Is No Excuse« at my place. We were off the road for quite some time, while we were negotiating with different labels. We were taken with this deal with Zomba Records because part of the deal was that Mutt Lange would do the album; but then EMI came into the picture and basically their deal was to buy the entire catalogue for a large amount of money, sign the band to a three-album deal and pay out quite a big advance. And that sealed it really. I think the album budget was a couple of hundred thousand pounds so we were able to do pretty much what we wanted – and basically we went nuts and spent it all. We didn't want to record in the States again – well, we certainly didn't want another American producer –

and couldn't afford to record in the UK because of the tax laws at the time, so we recorded it at Union Studios in Munich and lived in the Munich Hilton for three months. The food bill alone was DM30,000, and I think the hotel bill was DM60,000. Over twenty grand. Just generally over-indulging ourselves really; you know, three rental cars to get to and fro, that sort of thing. It was good fun though. In the process, we discovered you could go out at 9 o'clock in Munich and stay out till 9 o'clock in the morning.

We seemed to have unlimited funds – still no cash! – but unlimited funds to make the album. And we were paid a salary too; I think at that point we were on about a grand a month, or between a grand and £1,500 a month, which was a pretty good wage at that time. So we didn't feel we were being squeezed any more, like we were in the early days. I remember going to the EMI convention. EMI had signed Marillion and they were playing at this thing and they must have been playing Donington around that time. Must have been around 1985. We met Maiden there, and they seemed genuinely pleased that we were on EMI, so we were quite happy. Suddenly, quite out of the blue, we got changed to Parlophone which was a bit weird. It was the same label, EMI, but a subsidiary working out of a different part of the building. It had a reputation for being a bit 'arty'. They had more of the new romantic stuff. All of a sudden it didn't seem so great any more. The people were nice to us but they really weren't totally committed. The tour was big but we'd spent a lot of money already; I realised that we'd spent far too much recording the album, which still didn't even have a title.

In May 1985 Kerrang! ran a feature in which I said that we'd hadn't agreed on a title as yet, although "Give It Everything You've Got" or "Everybody Up" were the songs we might name it after. In the event, by the time it was released, it was called »Innocence Is No Excuse«.

I think the title came from the Carrere law case. I think what it really means is that the band had been pulled along and manipulated and were quite innocent in their motives but obviously that's no excuse. So that's where it comes from. It would have been all right to have called it after one of the tracks on the album, which we were used to by this time, although now we were on Parlophone, who were a little bit more arty, and maybe this gave us a bit more licence. Besides, probably more to the point, nobody could decide which was going to be the title track. We could have gone »Rocking Again« or »Back On The Streets« which was the lead single. I think I liked »Back On The Streets« as a title, but it would imply that we'd been away, so the record company might have thought that was a bit negative.

"Back On The Streets" did all right for us, it wasn't by any means unsuccessful as a single, and it was followed by a massive tour actually. But I think the album starting with "Rocking Again" was wrong; but »Innocence Is No Excuse« is a more sophisticated title and I think they were aiming for a more sophisticated album. I think Steve Dawson in particular thought we'd finally got to the pinnacle; you know, at last we were with a real company. I had my doubts about it though because I didn't like being put on Parlophone, I didn't think much of the producer Simon Hanhart, who was a nice enough guy and a protégé of Mutt Lange, but the project was too big for someone at such an early stage of his career. I didn't really like the »Innocence Is No Excuse« photographs: although I liked the model, I didn't think the photographs or the concept fitted with the album. And I thought the track listing of the album was wrong, as I said. I thought that it should have started with "Back On The Streets" and finished with "Rocking Again"; as it was, it started with a ballad which was a bit strange. It was a bit different for the time, I guess, but for the first album on EMI we needed to make an impact, we needed to hit 'em running and hit 'em hard, and although it's not a soft album, it's just geared more that way because of the way it's laid out. First impressions are everything, and opening with 'oooh-ooh-oooh' – I'm sure most people would have been thinking, 'what the fuck's this?', you know? 'They're meant to be fucking warriors; what's happened to them? Gone wimpy all of a sudden?'

And with all this, Nigel Thomas was trying to change the logo from the brutal, warrior type of thing to a more subtle depiction of the name. A bit pointless really: a poor example I suppose, but shit is shit: you can call it 'manure' if you like, but it's still shit. You know, you can't hide what the name means really, so what was the point of trying to change the logo. It was all a bit odd in my opinion.

»Innocence Is No Excuse«... Some people like it, but for me it didn't work: not at all. It wasn't the EMI debut it should have been. By this time, I was totally paranoid about us losing fans, and in retrospect I was right. It was a shame because at that time EMI had got Maiden, Saxon, Marillion, all the great bands that were happening and it's quite sad that we went down the wrong road. Somebody should have said to us, 'now, look; you need to get back to the »Strong Arm Of The Law« days. Go in the studio and write an album like that.' But unfortunately, by the time we'd signed the EMI deal the album was written. We'd already written it while we were waiting for things to happen, although we weren't really writing an album, we were just writing songs because otherwise we'd have been bored stupid waiting for a deal to be sorted out. As it was we had the best part of a year off which didn't do our career any good because we started to lose ground in the press.

We got back on the road though with a massive sold-out tour and a two-hour set which incorporated a lot of the new material. Things kicked off in Spain, our first live shows in over a year, before hitting the UK in September. The BBC recorded one of the shows at the old Hammersmith Odeon in London and so I got the audience to shout 'Rock!... With Tommy Vance!' which he used as a jingle for many years. The other bit of tour trivia was that the live footage for the video for "Broken Heroes" was shot at the Brighton Dome on the last night in the UK. We got invited to do Hungary, Poland, Yugoslavia, which was a fantastic experience. Aside from Maiden, we were the first band to go in behind the Iron Curtain, I think, and it was all so different. Big venues, 15,000 a night, fantastic fans too. We had a few problems with the police though as they used to draw a line across the front which the fans couldn't cross and if they did they got belted with a truncheon, which was totally against our mentality of having a good time. The 'System' there was horrendous. But the kids loved the gigs, and 15,000 people singing "Denim And Leather" is pretty fucking cool.

I think the rest of the band were quite happy with what was going on at this stage and with where they were but as I said, I wasn't really happy with »Innocence Is No Excuse«. The review in Sounds said the album featured "some welcome fresh-faced ideas... We can safely assume that this time around Saxon are out for blood," and Kerrang! called it "a fine album... their best for four years." But deep down, I wasn't happy at all. I didn't think it was the right album to do at the time. I though we should have been back more to a heads-down »Wheels Of Steel« or »Strong Arm Of The Law« type of thing for EMI. But I think maybe Parlophone wanted something like »Innocence Is No Excuse« because it was so different to Maiden. I mean, »Innocence Is No Excuse« is nothing like anything Iron Maiden ever did, full stop, and I think that's exactly what the label wanted because it was a very different product. A bit manipulative perhaps, but to be fair it went on to be a massive album and it was a great tour too, with Pretty Maids as support.

Pretty Maids were a good band. They had one fantastic song, "Red Hot And Heavy", a great song, but they never really followed it up. But a good band, and total superstars too. We did have a problem when we played in their home town in Denmark, because they'd already sold it out themselves beforehand and they thought that they should have had a drum riser and been treated with a bit more respect for their position. Their manager was a guy called Eric Thomas who was a famous guy who did all the tours of Scandinavia at the time, and he told them they were being fucking stupid. 'Just play it. You've played all the other shows, just play this one the same.' But they got pissed off with us – and probably still are. In this case, it wasn't our fault though, it was their manager. They could have just said they weren't playing it which would have been fair instead of getting pissed off because we didn't let them use our drum riser and our backline and give them more room. That aside though, it was a good tour, a complete sell-out tour.

I remember the first time we went to Scandinavia, which must have been on the »Wheels Of Steel« or »Strong Arm Of The Law« tour, we had our Malcolm Hill PA. Don't forget, this was quite a big PA at the time for the theatres in England for up to about 4,000 people, but when we got to Scandinavia though the first gig was in Stockholm and we'd sold out a stadium – wow! 15,000 people – and the PA looked so small in there. We were totally gobsmacked. We had no idea that we were that big. I also remember on that tour some girl picked me up. I took her up to the room, which in Sweden was almost impossible at that time. You couldn't get girls into your room there; it was considered totally non-kosher to take a girl up to your room and they had these huge security guards in hotels whenever rock bands were booked in (we were in the Sheraton, incidentally, which was known as 'Stalag 13' by the bands). Anyway, I managed to get this girl up by bribing somebody and had quite a nice time, all-in-all.

What I didn't know was that she was a journalist, and the day after there was a blow-by-blow account of the night in the daily paper. It was horrendous. Luckily it was all right, but it could have been disastrous for my sex life. Can you imagine opening the newspaper and reading something like: 'he fell asleep and I ended up watching TV'! But as it happened it was a good session: 'He slipped his towel off and dah-dah-dah...' so luckily it was OK. She said later that she was really sorry to do that to me, and at the time I thought, 'fucking bitch' but actually on reflection it was pretty cool. It could have been a lot worse, after all; sexually, it could have been the death of me!

Meanwhile, back in the UK, Parlophone followed the release of "Back On The Streets" (reviewed in Kerrang! by Ronnie James Dio, by the way: 'a good song and well produced. Biff's singing fine, there's a nice guitar solo and I hope it happens for them...') with a 12 inch 'club mix' reviewed three issues later by Ratt's Robbin Crosby and Jon Bon Jovi. Obviously the writers on the magazine couldn't be bothered. They had a phase of using guest reviewers, which in this case co-incided with the mid-Eighties phase of club remixes. It's a bit like the double-sided CDs that they've been doing. It's faddy. Everybody had club mixes, and don't forget we were on Parlophone and they were like into that sort of arty thing. It was a bizarre thing to do, but they were rather bizarre times. They wanted to capitalise on it, and it might have worked. It didn't though, and I think the review was right. Robbin Crosby called it a 'rock song that's been ruined' and Jon Bon Jovi said that he liked 'what he could hear of the actual song inside the complicated mix.' After that, the label released "Rock 'N' Roll Gypsy". For once, we had recorded more songs that we needed – I think I'm quoted somewhere as saying we had written twenty-five songs or so because we had had so much time on our hands – so the singles had previously unreleased songs on the B-sides, rather than live versions or album tracks. "Back On The Streets" featured "Live Fast Die Young", and "Rock 'N' Roll Gypsy" was backed with "Krakatoa" and the "Heavy Metal Thunder" medley which we'd played live on the tour. (They'd run out of unreleased stuff by the time they released "Broken Heroes" so they just pulled "Give It Everything You've Got" off the album.) Although "Krakatoa" was recorded after the album, I think, it's a shame that those songs couldn't have been included on »Innocence Is No Excuse« as, because they were heavier, they would have given the album a bit more of a heavy flavour. As it is, they're destined to be no more than quite collectable flip-sides.

Things weren't exactly all wine and roses in the band though, and, after Pete Gill, the next person in the Saxon departure lounge was Steve Dawson.

When Saxon first started, especially »Wheels Of Steel«, I was very much hands-on on the musical side, a lot of the riffs and things would be co-written by me anyway, playing guitar or bass – I used to play guitar a lot on the writing sessions. Now I get the guitarists to do the music because that's what they should be doing – lazy bastards! – and that's how it works for us. But back then it was pretty much hands-on for everybody. Although I wrote all the lyrics, I would have a lyric-writing partner for a soundboard, and because I'm not very good at writing lyrics down. I'm very good at lying on a sofa and spouting lyrics, so it's very good if someone can write them down as I'm saying them. I do that a lot, and my partner in the early days was either Steve Dawson or the guitar tech, or later Pete Hinton. I wrote "Hungry Years" with Pete Hinton writing down what I said, and he obviously added a couple of words here or there, but that's still how I work. At the moment my writing partner would be Doug. He's quite good with words; you have to have someone who's clever with English. I mean, not everything has to rhyme, but it is good to have a second person to bounce everything off. But I used to write the bulk of the lyrics with Steve Dawson in the early days. His contribution wasn't that great: mainly I'd shout the stuff out and he'd write it down and make comments. His biggest lyrical contribution was that every time he used to have something that rhymed with, say, 'height' his answer was always 'STAND UP AND FIGHT!' That was his classic line – 'stand up and fight!' I'd say, 'look, Steve, you can't say stand up and fight in every fucking song!'

But after »Innocence Is No Excuse« he started to go a bit nuts. He began wearing polka dot jackets and a red trilby with a green feather in it and playing a trumpet a lot. And to be honest he was just getting on people's nerves a bit on that tour and it was a long, long tour, believe me. It was as if his personality was changing. Also, he kept phoning EMI and complaining about why the single wasn't in the charts, which I've got no problem with (I thought it was quite funny actually) but the management hated. They saw him as going behind their backs which created a lot of tension between him and them.

Steve Dawson was and still is a real character. On and off stage he was well liked, he did what he did and he did it very well. But he started acting strangely, smashing equipment on stage and getting really pissed off all the time. Generally Steve acts really tough but is in fact quite soft – he's one of those sort of guys. But he was smashing up my mikestands and eventually I had a major argument with him and it ended up with a 'fuck it, it's either him or me' scenario, I decided I was not going to carry on touring like that any more, with him smashing things up and arguing every night. So they chose me and the management sacked him.

I think in retrospect if he'd cooled off for a few days it would have been all right; it would have worked itself out. But it was just one of those tired, exhausted times, quite emotional, when things go to the edge and sometimes you go over. It happens, and you have a blazing row and sometimes bands split up and sometimes they get over it. But management jumped on him like a ton of bricks because they didn't like him anyway and they sacked him. I never really saw him again, and have never spoken to him since.

We should have had a meeting and talked it over with him, and told him he was pushing it and getting in everyone's space, and I think it could have been sorted out. But it didn't happen that way. I don't know why he didn't insist that he kept his job, as I wasn't there when they sacked him. If I'd have been him I would have demanded to see the band but he didn't, he just fucked off. Maybe he was scared… I don't know. I don't know if they paid him anything. Probably not.

We had a meeting shortly after the management canned him, took a vote to sack him and all agreed it was for the best. Again, management forced the issue really quickly after we finished the tour when we were really still quite wired. A highly manipulative move. When he left, it was sad really, although having said that I don't think we'd be what we are today if he was still with us, because both Nibbs Carter and Doug have opened up a much more musical path for us as a band, and that is much more enjoyable.

Chapter Sixteen

A s I said, the »Innocence Is No Excuse« tour was big but we'd spent too much money on that album, so the next one »Rock The Nations« we wrote very quickly at Rockfield in Wales and recorded very quickly at Wisseloord in Holland. It's a strange album. I think it's where we were trying to go back to a more rockier time, but again the choice of producer wasn't right. Nigel Thomas went for somebody he'd known in the past, and that was Gary Lions. He had a track record but not a track record that was consistent; it was, well, patchy. He was a great producer technically but I think we needed somebody who had a direction and could be the sixth member of the band, guiding us, which is what a producer should do. But that didn't happen and so the album is a bit of everything really, a clash of different influences. There's some quite nice sort of poppy rock songs on there and there's some heavy songs, so it was a mixture really. I like the album but again it's a little directionless; or if there is a direction on it, it's a bit fucking vague! It charted well, higher than »Innocence Is No Excuse«, but the

»Innocence…« tour was very successful so our profile probably went back up a bit and the album sold well on the strength of that.

I think there's some great songs on there like "Rock The Nations" itself (which is basically just a song about being on the road and which came about because we just seemed to be constantly touring and touring and touring) and "Battle Cry" so we were still writing stadium rock things, the anthemic songs that we did well, but we were trying to get back more to a rock 'n' roll-based thing rather than a studio-based thing. It worked in one respect because the album did well and we undertook another massive sold-out tour on the strength of it. Loudness supported us, the Japanese band, which gave us a 'why you no crapping' catchphrase which we did to death. Great band though: nice guys and a great drummer too. He totally freaked Nigel out; he was shit scared of their drummer. By this time, though, we had basically given up trying to break America. I don't think EMI were that interested anyway. Although the EMI albums sold more over there than the Carrere records, we no longer did the big tours of America. All that had gone.

»Rock The Nations« was by no means our best album, but working with Gary Lions was one of the best times I've ever spent making a record. He was an absolute nutter in the studio. He insisted on having his wife and child sitting in on the album while we were trying to mix it; he'd line up vodkas on the desk and bang 'em back… He was always playing practical jokes, and we loved it really. One evening he opened Graham Oliver's hotel windows – we were staying on a lake in Hilversum, Holland, with mosquitoes the size of dragonflies – and turned the room lights on so that night Graham was bitten to pieces, almost eaten alive. It's also the period when we met Elton John. Because Lions had produced the Elton John and Kiki Dee album, he knew him, insisting on calling him 'Reg' all the time. It was in that time that Elton John was flying backwards and forwards to royal marriages all over the place so he had a helicopter parked in the back garden. As you do. He and his band knew us though, we were heavy rockers so they had quite a bit of respect for us.

SAXON
HEAVY METAL THUNDER

SAXON
...ILLING GROUND

SAXON
FOREVER FREE

SAXON
LIONHEART

28 TIMES I'VE SEEN YOU BASTARDS AND YOU'RE STILL THE FUCKIN BEST 2.0s CAPRIS ARE THE BOLLOCKS SEE YOU IN NORWICH FOR 29

We ended up having eating contests with them. Unbeknown to them, Roxette wanted to use the main studio where we were recording for the weekend to mix some track and we said no; we were trying to record an album, after all. So their head honcho said that he was willing to pay for all our food for the rest of the session if we agreed. 'OK, fair enough then.' So we pushed off on a boat for a couple of days while they worked on some hit they went on to have, and when we came back, for the next two or three weeks we had all this food brought in from very exotic restaurants. The Elton John crew noticed this and started to compete, and after a while it was like a battle as to who could order the most extravagant food. But of course we weren't paying for it. So we'd have amazing food really, and they'd be like, 'that looks good,' so the next night they'd order that and we'd go for something even more outrageous –pig with an apple in its mouth or something – and it just went on and on without them ever twigging that ours was all for free. Meanwhile, we had a song called "Party Till You Puke", just a bullshit song really, and Gary Lions said, 'I'll ask Reg to play on it.' And he did. His crew brought in the piano, he walked in, played the piece, and left. While he was waiting, "Northern Lady" was running and he was playing along to it, just twiddling around really, and obviously Gary Lions, being a total professional, recorded it. We sampled it – samplers were just coming out then – and put it on the track; I don't even know if he knows to this day that he's on that track. But there, he played on "Party Till You Puke" which was a bit radical for Elton John. I don't think he liked Gary Lions calling him Reg though...

About the time the album was released, in August 1986 we headlined the Reading festival. In those days it wasn't the festival it was before and it wasn't the festival that it is now – it was in a period of transition. But it was good. I liked it and I think we did very well. The BBC recorded it and aired a chunk of us on »The Friday Rock Show«. And if nothing else, it blew away the memories of our previous major UK festival appearance, our second performance at Castle Donington, in 1982.

I think that the band had started to lose some popularity in England by the time of the third Monsters Of Rock festival, and it wasn't a good gig for us at all. On reflection, we shouldn't have done it, but again, that's the wonder of hindsight. We played in Dallas on the Thursday, flew to Gatwick and chartered a plane to Donington, slept for a few hours once we'd landed, and played the gig the next day.

The spot that we'd been asked to play was second on to Status Quo, but Ian Gillan kicked up a fuss and said he should be there as he'd been in the business longer and probably his management wanted him to go second for career purposes so we agreed. We got paid much more than he did so it was obviously a principle thing for his management – it's possible that Gillan himself didn't know any of this. But we were pretty big ourselves at that time. So we went on as third on the bill, after Anvil, Uriah Heep and, bizarrely, Hawkwind.

Status Quo's crew were fucking awful and went out of their way to ruin our gig. They were checking the lights and doing line-checks while we were on stage, and a guy jumped out of the truss and landed right in our guitar stack, putting all the guitars out of tune. At another point some guy walked on stage... If anyone's got a tape of us at Donington 1982 it's quite apparent we were being fucked over. Then a member of their crew came up to me and said, 'time's up mate, you've got to get off.' So I said to the crowd, 'they're asking us to leave; they're trying to get us off.' I think we did a couple more songs after that and then walked off. I was absolutely gutted really and I think I was probably crying in the dressing room once we came off stage. The promoter came in, the head guy, and I just told him to fuck off. The next night we were playing New York, headlining the Capitol Theatre, so we just went straight back to America.

It was a really bad gig for us. It wasn't what it should have been; we were hoping it would be a great home-coming gig really. And to have the headline act – or their crew actually; I don't suppose Status Quo knew what had gone on – screwing us over and mind-fucking me completely, telling us that somebody said we had to get off, and that our time was up… The guitars were out of tune, the whole thing was horrendous. I knew that we were blowing it and, I mean, we knew that people's expectations were so high. Our stage clothes had gone missing as well so I had to go on in this black and white striped monstrosity. It was a total cluster fuck for us. One of the keys to Saxon is to have a great time, and be confident with that. We're a good time band in essence and when we're not happy I think it shows.

Again, bad management; we shouldn't have tried to do so much, sandwiching it in the middle of some American gigs. We were so exhausted, so jetlagged, and with everything else going on it was too much for me. I couldn't handle it. We shouldn't have done it really. We should have waited, but with the management there was always this 'let's do everything now and get great money' mentality. On reflection, it was a bit too quick for us to have been there again, and ideally we'd have liked to have done it say in 1984 or 1985 as headliners. I think we'd liked to have slowly built up our strength, not throw it all down on the table within a year – 'there you are then, there's the three albums »Wheels Of Steel«, »Strong Arm Of The Law«, »Denim And Leather«, what about that then; let's have a hundred grand.' We were much more about relaxing, taking a break, but we weren't allowed to do that. We were brow-beaten into doing a job and I think it's amazing that we're still around, given the way we were treated back then; I could have easily at that time said 'fuck it' and walked, and I probably could have done at that time actually. But I didn't, and because as a band we were so connected with our fans, bad gigs and things like that really disturbed us, or me anyway. I remember playing Sheffield once; we always had a great rapport with our Sheffield fans because it was basically our home-town gig, and the venue brought in the security from Manchester Apollo who were really hard and they were beating kids up in the audience while I was on stage, jumping down to try and stop it. I was crying in the dressing room after the show. I just could not believe that these people were doing this to our audience.

As I said, as a band we are always quite connected to our audience and I think that when we lose that connection it doesn't go that well for us. Everyone normally thinks of Saxon as a great live band, but there have been times when things haven't been great and I think the second Donington was one of those. Maybe the people who were there might disagree, might think I was imagining it, and that would be great if it didn't affect the audience the way I think it did. But I get this feeling that it was a pivotal point where the boys that could do no wrong really screwed up and lost it. The reviews were quite positive, but that's not what it's about. It's about the feeling between the audience and the band; sometimes the reviewers get it, sometimes they don't. But for me being told to get off stage at that point in our career was like 'who the fuck are you? Some wanker who sets lights or something.' They had no respect for us whatsoever – 'get the fuck off and let's get our band on' – and unfortunately none of our people was around the stage area. By the time we'd walked off they'd come over to see what the problem was, but we'd had to deal with all this shit ourselves. Had we stayed on it would only have got worse because the guitars were miles out of tune. It was horrendous. And Paul was pissed off, smashing guitars, knocking necks off and throwing them across the stage, so it wasn't good. No happy, clappy fucking party atmosphere there. Sometimes on nights like that it is possible for the band to bring it all back together. At other times, you can play a gig in front of four people and a dog and it's a fantastic night because the empathy between each musician is there – you know, you can just play for yourselves. But at Donington that second time, the band was very disjointed and it wasn't great. We were too tired, we were trying to do too much, and the management expected too much of us. And still today people think that we can do anything – two shows in one day, anything. They just think we're indestructible and it's not good news for anyone to think that about an artist.

By Reading '86 though the band had changed from a heavier animal into more of a – how to describe it? – softer version of what we had been. But Reading was good for us. I do have a love-hate relationship with festivals though – I like them but I hate them at the same time. On the one hand there is a fantastic sense of size and scale and the massive numbers of people connecting, but if it's raining or cold and you're the last one on and people start to leave it can be horrendous. Or everyone starts throwing mudballs around and you're watching them thinking, 'oh God, those fucking things are coming this way any minute now!' They can be fantastically happy events or they can turn really ugly, and you really can't tell how they are going to go. I do like playing festivals, but I've never really met any singer who likes singing outside. It's either too windy, too cold, too hot… There are just too many variables to singing outside. It's a strange experience. And for a frontman it can be a frightening experience, although it doesn't particularly bother me because I thrive on that challenge, but it can be really frightening actually. If you are not going down very well, if people are wandering off and not focussed on you… I've seen some bands totally blow it at festivals because people aren't listening basically. Where you go on during the day is everything. If it's a big festival where people have been there since 11 o'clock in the morning and you're on at twelve o'clock at night, it's hopeless. It's much better to go on at nine or ten o'clock at which point everyone's had enough of the daylight bands but still aren't too tired. Besides, I don't think anybody actually headlines a festival. Obviously the spin on it is that there is a headliner, but generally it's one whole event where people like to go, sleep in a tent, sit on straw and do what their parents don't want them to do. It's just a massive meeting of people with music; Glastonbury, Wacken, no-one gives a flying fuck who's headlining, as long as there's a good selection of bands and they're all at a fairly good level. Really it's all about the event.

We had a new bass player by this time, of course. As I said, Steve Dawson left after »Innocence Is No Excuse«. He was very disappointed with EMI's performance, although I don't know why he was so dissatisfied – it was an absolutely massive tour, and very successful. I know the lack of real chart success as far as singles were concerned got to him, but it didn't really bother me and I think we should have been fairly happy with the result really. It was a long tour though, the schedule was quite gruelling and on the last bit I think that friction was there and it was a bit like a boil that had to be lanced. The feeling within the band and the management was to get back in and write another album which I think in retrospect was a mistake.

We didn't have a bass player and I didn't want to rush into finding one. I think really we didn't think that Steve Dawson would go. It was a bit of a surprise to us and I suppose in the back of my mind was the fact that he'd probably be asking for his job back in a few months but it obviously didn't happen because of the management's view of him. So we wrote the album as a four-piece with me playing bass, and then it was a natural thing for me to play bass on the album. And it was good fun actually. Meanwhile, everybody on the planet knew that Steve had left the band so we got tons and tons and tons of demo tapes. Paul Johnson was a good bass player and the management and record company wanted an 'unknown' to join the band because they could make quite a big deal out of it in the press, which is a bit cheesy really, but it worked out pretty well in the short term. He wasn't really a songwriter but he was a good looking lad, a good bass player and a nice guy too. I think the problem was that we embarked on quite a long tour as soon as the album came out and he was blown away by it. He couldn't really handle it. It was too big for him; you know, everything in excess. He just went totally barmy, which is fair enough. He was falling in love every day. He wasn't really heavily drinking but he was just too far 'out there'. It's to be expected really: for somebody who'd only really ever played in bar bands to be suddenly thrust in front of big audiences…It was just too much. I just think his head wasn't in the right place, and it wasn't a great time anyway for the band, to be fair to him.

By this time, we weren't at our most confident, and neither was the management or the record company. EMI were unhappy with the performance of »Innocence Is No Excuse«; they'd expected it to be bigger and so for »Rock The Nations« they didn't really spend the same amount of money on promotion. And the production on

»Rock The Nations« was a bit disappointing. It's good, but after »Innocence…« it sounds a bit demo-ish; It wasn't »Innocence Is No Excuse« that failed for EMI – it was actually »Rock The Nations«. You can't have an album like »Innocence Is No Excuse« which is a massive production, big sound, and then come out with an album that's quite raw, with this almost demo-like production. I think we put people off because the consistency's not there – and throughout our career we have had a consistency problem without a doubt. We've proved it time and time again. We have a great album, then we push the self-destruct button and the next album isn't as good compared to it. I have to blame myself for a lot of it because you can't say that you're the leader of the band and then share the responsibility for the fuck-ups. You can't do that. I blame myself for that and I think maybe because I'm quite passionate when I'm doing something I could have been going blindly but enthusiastically down the wrong road. But some of that comes back to management; I think if your manager's just sat in the office letting the band do what they want and not offering them any advice whatsoever then I think that's no good either. You need outside ears. You need somebody who's in tune with the band and I always thought that Rod Smallwood and Iron Maiden were always in tune. Whether they were or not on the inside I don't know, but it always seemed as though the management was making the right decisions for the band's career. I think they are probably quite a 'hierarchy' band as well; I think Steve Harris probably runs the band, and that within that, certain partnerships 'happen' and they work. The Blechner-Poxon thing worked for us in the early days of Carrere, but then we went a bit higher and nothing moved with it. On reflection, it would have been better if a management company had been started with Blechner-Poxon and Nigel Thomas together which could have been more global and had a large roster of bands – with us just being one of those bands. I think that would have worked better for us and it would have been quite successful all round because with them just managing one band they were 'over-focussed' on us. We were the only cash cow they had, and when you have just one cash cow you inevitably milk the poor bastard to death

– and that's what happened to us. We were tired, over-worked, and sending out confused messages to the fans over our direction. Yet the most bizarre thing is that »Rock The Nations« actually got some great press reviews. One magazine, Crash in Germany, referred to »Innocence Is No Excuse« as 'just a single glitch' and noted that »Rock The Nations« was a return to 'hard, metallic and yet melodic rock', giving it a full-marks review.

Paul Johnson played on »Destiny«, but by that time Nigel had left for the first time – I think he left after the »Rock The Nations« tour. So now we had no drummer. Paul Johnson knew someone, and that was Nigel Durham. He was a good drummer – more in the style of Tommy Lee which is no bad thing. We started having money problems with him and Paul though. They thought that whether they did anything or not, they should be paid; and at the time we weren't making a great deal of money anyway. They weren't particularly off with me, but they were always at odds with the management because we were earning much more money from publishing from the back catalogue, and this didn't seem fair to them. I think they did something really silly: when we were doing some studio work I think they nicked all the gear and held it to ransom or something like that for £1,000. I think Nigel Thomas paid them, but it was stupidity really. Certainly not a way to endear yourselves.

Also, when some people join bands, they quickly become settled in and find a niche for themselves without giving anything back to the band. They take it all but don't really get involved in song writing, they don't get involved in the planning and discussions about tours and the other hundred-and-one things that are involved in running a band. They leave that all to other people, and then piss and moan when it doesn't go the way they want. I think Paul in particular thought he'd landed himself a cushy number, and had 'made it', basically. But in reality, it wasn't a great period for the band and it would have been better to have been more consistent member-wise during that period. As I said, we were sending confusing messages to people. It was a particularly hard time for us and it was a bit unfair on them to have to be the plaster over the cracks.

At the end of the day, both Paul Johnson and Nigel Durham did all right; it just didn't work out for them. But Johnson didn't have enough charisma to pull anything to us. He didn't bring anything to the band; he was just the bassist as far as credibility goes. The management really went to town in the press that he was a tyre fitter or something one day and playing for Saxon the next, which is all right for a daily paper-type angle but probably not what serious rock fans wanted to read. They'd have probably been happier to see something like the Guns N' Roses bass player had joined the band, someone with a bit of credibility. Johnson and Durham saw us through to the end of the »Destiny« tour, although that was to be the drummer's first and last tour with us.

Back at corporate HQ, I think EMI made a decision after »Rock The Nations« that we were probably for the chop. The album sales must have been good but not as good as they were with Carrere; I mean, »Crusader« was a massive seller. But anyway, EMI must have told our management, 'one last try or that's that, so you need to make a killer album.' Again, the producer that they chose for the album – Stephan Galfas – was a very nice bloke but didn't really get it. And our management never really understood that you need much longer to actually write the songs than you do to record the album. They really weren't song-orientated so anything we wrote was all right as far as they were concerned. There wasn't anyone within the outfit saying, 'no, that's crap; it's a great song for somebody else but it's not a good song for you so write something else and let's get a direction'. Again, it comes down to direction, and »Destiny« is sadly lacking in it. Management more or less left us to our own devices and as musicians we just wrote songs basically, anything, and went on to record them. The high point of »Destiny« for me was "Ride Like The Wind". I went to everybody and suggested a cover of "Ride Like The Wind" and everyone thought I was out of my mind.

'But that's Christopher Cross'.

'I know it is; I've got the album. It's a brilliant album!'

So Paul and I worked out an arrangement and were quite proud of turning it into a "Wheels Of Steel" type song. Even now, I still think our version is a great rock song. Even Christopher Cross liked it, and he should know.

Also on »Destiny« is a song about the Titanic called "SOS" which is a great song too. But the rest of the album is pretty wacky and a lot of the songs on it are mis-understood. Galfas was a typical American producer and his hero was the guy who did the Meat Loaf stuff – Jim Steinman – so he did our album in that vein, which is pretty much how Steinman did the Def Leppard album that got thrown away. (I actually heard that album, by the way, but that's another story.) Galfas brought in session singers for backing vocals, keyboard players, and all the drums are sampled, triggered, so he had somebody working at night doing all the triggers and it must have become like a production line at that end of the process. Meanwhile, nobody bothered about us, the band.

At the end of the day, it's a good album, but it is more of a Meat Loaf album than a Saxon album. It's really over-produced. I like the songs, but to me it's a bit sickly, a bit syrupy. It is heavy in parts and although it's a good sound, it's not a fantastic sound. It didn't do well, and that basically was the last big tour we did. Some of the gigs we did were much the same as ever, but some were a lot smaller. I remember having a conversation with the band and Nigel Thomas in Paris, where we'd been used to playing the Zenith which is 4,000 to 5,000 people; now we were playing a small club because he'd stuck together a tour of any old shit, and I told them I was not going to continue like this and see the band and its legacy destroying itself and slipping into oblivion.

'I'm stopping it now. I'm not doing anything else with this band until we decide to get our shit together or that's it,' I said.

And we stopped the fucking tour, came home and that was that.

Part Three:
Never Surrender

Chapter Seventeen

*A*fter the »Destiny« tour we didn't do anything for a while as a band. There was a live album released in America called »Rock 'N' Roll Gypsies«, a commitment to a record company there. We'd recorded a few shows on the »Destiny« tour in America as well as some shows in Eastern Europe, although the final CD only came from shows in Hungary. It was only actually released in America at that time as a contractual obligation, and that was the last thing we did.

I was quite disillusioned at that point, and I really needed a break. I retreated to this huge Georgian vicarage that I'd bought in Lincolnshire; the property was so cheap there that I could have a big leave-me-alone wall around it and I spent my time restoring it, throwing myself into that instead of the band. I needed some time out and at the same time I found that restoring this vicarage was an extremely good outlet for my creativity. At about the same time they began work on the Sheffield Supertram, and they were ripping the middle out of the city to make way for the project. Some friends of mine were involved in architectural salvage and reclamation, getting all the original stuff out of the houses they were tearing down – fireplaces, doors and some church architecture too; all very gothic. I was sourcing materials to do up this vicarage, which was huge, and they asked if they could store what they'd reclaimed at my place and if I could sell it for them. So I agreed, and it was really successful. I could obviously pick and choose what I wanted, and I sold the rest on. I did that for a while, and as I was still doing my place up I could keep all the good stuff and sell on the rest.

Not only did this stimulate my creativity, but it was good fun too. I sold my house for a huge profit and thought that it was pretty easy money so I bought another place, a William and Mary house and did the same thing; I started making quite good money on the deals: maybe £100,000 profit on the sale of one house, which was much more than I'd made in Saxon. I was laughing really. I could afford to live, I was still being creative, and I was able to have a rest from the endless album-tour-album-tour treadmill. I don't think the rest of the band – well, by now of course the band only really consisted of Paul and Graham – were too happy (although they never actually said anything to me about it). But what was the alternative? To go right back down and start playing the bars and pubs again? No, thank you. I think Graham and Paul were keen to put together a side project but nothing ever came of it. We were receiving royalties so no-one was starving, and the rest was the best thing that could have happened to me at that time. I needed to do something else to give my mind some space. I think I took about a year, a year-and-a-half, off, just to do something different from what I'd been doing for quite a few years without any breaks whatsoever. However, although it was good for me, in reality I was just treading water because nothing was happening musically, and music had been part of my life for so long now that I knew I couldn't live without it.

Out of the blue a guy we knew from Germany called Rainer Hänsel (who would go on to be quite influential in the Saxon story in the early Nineties) got in touch with me and said he had a tour for us – the Manowar tour of Germany. At that time of course we didn't have an album out, but Roadrunner Records bought the European rights to »Rock 'N' Roll Gypsies« and issued it to co-incide with these dates.

That tour of Germany was a massive turning point for us. We just went on and did a greatest hits show, fifty-odd minutes, in front of 7,000 to 8,000 people a night, and as we hadn't really played in Germany to a lot of people for quite a while, it was a massive 'hello' once more. The fans just went nuts – completely fucking nuts – and it was a fantastic tour. I wasn't really very aware of Manowar; I know that Dave Poxon had something to do with them at some point, maybe brought them to England, but I never really heard much about them. But we did the tour with them and it was absolutely amazing. We went down really well and Manowar had to follow us which must have been difficult for them to say the least.

On the back of that we did the »Tenth Anniversary Tour«, one of those tours that started off quite small but became massive as it went along – we did sixty shows in the UK. It was unbelievable. But when we spilt with Blechner-Poxon, our managers in the early days, and went with the guy they'd installed as our business manager, Nigel Thomas, there was some bill outstanding; I've no idea what it was for, but it was about £30,000 or something which Nigel Thomas had agreed to pay over a period of time. Obviously, he didn't. So when we started the »Tenth Anniversary Tour« Blechner and Poxon decided to sue us for the full amount plus interest which by that time was about £70,000. I think the first we knew of it was when the bailiffs came to one of the shows and threatened to impound all the gear, including all the trucks which obviously weren't even ours. To keep things moving, we reached a compromise where we gave them a cheque there and then for £5,000, and all through the tour they would turn up and we'd pay off a little more here and there. We got quite friendly with them actually; friendly with the bailiffs – that's a pretty wacky concept, really.

'You alright, Biff?'

'Yeah, I'm fine. You OK?'

'Yeah. You got any money today?'

'Don't know. I'll go and see the t-shirt guys.'

And so I'd give them another five grand or so. And that's how it went through the sixty dates. We should have made a lot of money but in actual fact it all went on paying off this debt. I think we left about ten quid outstanding, at the end of the tour, and I have this feeling that one day, in many years' time, they'll probably come back and say that with interest that tenner's become seventy grand again!

To be honest, it seemed fucking unfair at the time, but we had to pay it and that was that. As you can imagine, the suppliers, the PA company and the trucking company weren't very happy, and we had to do some really fast talking with them. The tour though was really good for us: sold out everywhere, which was quite a surprise for us. In London we sold out both the Town & Country Club and Hammersmith Odeon. We sold out the big Reading Leisure Centre… Loads of big venues we sold out, and in effect we were working for the bailiffs. Somewhere along the line, the merchandising company didn't turn up so we sued them and got out of that deal because they weren't paying us either.

So now we were pretty sorted in terms of the legalities, although to be fair we were a band without a record deal and without a merchandising deal. Rainer again turned up trumps, coming to see me and announcing that Virgin Records in Germany wanted to sign us, and we stayed with them for the next three albums. We were a bit pissed off with Nigel Thomas over publishing, so we signed a publishing deal with Virgin Records as well, and because we thought Nigel Thomas probably still had the publishing rights, we gave all the credits on the first album to Nibbs. So although the »Solid Ball Of Rock« album looks like it was written almost entirely by Nibbs, in actual fact it wasn't – despite the fact he scores so many writing credits; it was just a way of getting round things because Nibbs was in no way shape or form signed to or connected with Nigel Thomas. It made no real difference in the end as he still got half of it anyway; Virgin Publishing 'phoned me up and said that they'd had a letter from him, claiming that he had the rights to this album. We'd already collected £30,000 – it was a big album, »Solid

Ball Of Rock« – and they said that they we going to send it on to us anyway because they didn't want him to have it. So he got half of the royalty payments and we got half, which was quite OK; probably one of the best deals we'd had in a long time.

We'd started writing this 'comeback' album – anyone in a band will know that after a while they're all fucking comeback albums! – »Solid Ball Of Rock« at Chapel Studios in Lincolnshire. It wasn't too much back then but it's where The Darkness did their first album, and Wet Wet Wet used it too. At that time it was owned by a guy called Bram Tchaikovsky who used to be the guitarist in The Motors; they'd been quite popular during the punk period. Alongside our own compositions we picked up on a song of Tchaikovsky's called "Solid Ball Of Rock" which I thought would be good for us to do.

Nigel Glockler was back in and it was Nibbs's first appearance with the band. Nibbs came from Chapel Studios, he was hanging about there all the time and if anybody wanted a bass player he basically did their session. So he was a skilled session player, as well as a skilled drinking master. We asked him to join which he obviously jumped at and he's not really looked back. I think Nibbs is the best bass player we've ever had, and he is a great songwriter as well, although a lot of his stuff we can't use unfortunately because his song-writing style is very Kings X-y. In fact, it's a cross between Kings X and Slayer, if you can imagine that. But it's good stuff, and because we've got so much material we might do some sort of side project together one day; it's certainly something we've talked about.

Nibbs is a lovely wild man, that's what he is really. He is a fantastic musician and he's a complete nutter as well. He just loves to play music, he loves to listen to music… He can drive you mad actually. He would listen to music twenty-four hours a day if he could. He never stops. That's the sort of guy he is. Once he likes something he plays it to death: if he's into the new Slayer album or something it's on the bus twenty-four hours a day. He's that sort of guy; he's really obsessive about music. But he's a great musician and I thought he brought… I mean, you can't really say what Steve Dawson brought because he was in the first original band so he was there all the time, but I think Nibbs has brought a lot to the band, certainly a lot of energy. Also, he hasn't had the same musical background that we've had and doesn't really know the bands we knew because he wasn't old enough. So he really hasn't had a Zeppelin, Sabbath, Cream, Mountain, upbringing. His sort of band, the stuff he grew up with, was Rush; he learned to pay bass from the Rush albums. So he comes from that era and brings a different influence to us as a band.

So it was 1990, and all of a sudden we were back. »Solid Ball Of Rock« was a massive album, and we began to sell a lot of records again; it was the perfect album at the perfect time. We recorded it with a producer called Kalle Trappe at Karo Studio in Hamburg. He was a musician in his own right and had been in quite a successful German band, and before we went in to record he'd produced a Blind Guardian album which we liked the sound of. It was a nice studio, and in classic old Saxon style was in the middle of nowhere with no distractions; when we went to LA to record, and New York, we all went nuts really and I think as a result sometimes the music suffered. The food was great, and the girls were nice, but the albums could have been more focussed.

Karo suited us at that time and Kalle was a great guy; very old-school, and me and him gelled straight away. It was Rainer's first album with us and he set himself up as the band's mentor, and in fact for »Solid Ball Of Rock« he did very well. I think he fell out with Kalle Trapp so for the second album for Virgin, »Forever Free« he wanted us to work with some unknown guy in Austria, and he was an absolute fucking nut. Herwig Ursin was his name. His claim to fame was that he was re-starting the Austrian film industry, because we all know what sort of films they made in the past. He was also recording the Austrian Philharmonic Orchestra, and because the old Austrian film studios were vacant and derelict, he was trying to make a deal so that he got tons of money off the Austrian government to restore these studios to their former glory; and in doing that it would give the Austrian Philharmonic a base as well, so it was a pretty good scam – I mean, deal! In the middle of all this scheming though we were trying to make an album. The studio was in an old tarmac factory – still had the chimney and everything – and all I can remember of that album really was being dropped off early in the morning by Herwig Ursin saying, 'I'll be back soon,' and just hanging about in this studio in the middle of nowhere until he'd turn up at ten o'clock at night for us to do a vocal or something and then he'd go off to a gay club. 'No, that's OK, Herwig; I don't really want to go there. Just drop me off back at the hotel, please.'

It got so bad that I was complaining to Rainer all the time but Ursin was so cheap because I think he needed instant cash for a deposit on another building. I think he did the whole thing for DM 60,000 but he really wasn't into the music at all. He was a nice enough guy but he didn't give it the time it needed and he wasn't really a rocker at all. So I think the album suffered a little bit because of that, although I love the title track: "Forever Free" is a great song. And because that album came after a big selling album it sold a lot on the strength of its predecessor. That's always the case. You are only as big as your last album, so if you have a big album like »Solid Ball Of Rock« then everybody rushes out and buys the next one »Forever Free« and discovers it isn't as good. So the third one, which is great, well, the people who bought »Forever Free« don't go out and buy it. So whatever you think of »Forever Free«, it was a mistake to do the album with Ursin in Vienna. I would never recommend to anyone that they record in Vienna; it's so boring. The funniest thing that happened while we were there was at a party. There's a really famous guy called Wolfgang Ambros and Ursin did his album and Rainer did the tour. He's a big star over there, very famous indeed. We ended up at this party in this café with this Austrian band doing a showcase gig, and suddenly Ambros bursts in. Now don't forget, this guy is really big, and he knows it, too. 'Fucking hell,' he announces as he strides in, 'I've just driven a thousand kilometres,' and Nibbs, being Nibbs, asks politely, 'are you a truck driver then?' Wolfgang Ambros just stared at him and then stormed straight back out of the room. It was so funny! That's just so

Nibbs. I mean, I'd met Ambros, and his band were at another studio at the complex, but Nibbs had just come over to do the bass guitar and was, of course, inebriated. We all collapsed under the table laughing. Needless to say, we didn't see Wolfgang Ambros again.

Aside from the title track though, I thought »Forever Free« was going so badly that I insisted on bringing Pete Hinton in to see if he could do anything with it. We hadn't seen Pete for a long time and it was nice to have him back, but he couldn't work with the guy either. There's got to be a connection or chemistry between the band and the producer for it to work properly. With »Solid Ball Of Rock«, we actually wrote some of the album at John Parr's studio in Yorkshire and we were thinking about letting him produce it. He came to listen to a few tracks – he's a nice guy, John Parr – but it just wasn't his thing at all. We played him "Solid Ball Of Rock" and "I Just Can't Get Enough" and he was like, 'nah, I don't see it.' But that's good, because this business is so full of bullshit and most people would go, 'yeah, I think it's great; I'll do it for a hundred grand.' At least he was honest.

As I said, »Forever Free« was quite a big selling album. The title track is a massive favourite because it's a good sentiment song, and that was one of the first times I'd written a biking song like that for quite a while, and to get back to that 'wind in your hair' type thing was really great to do. It's a great rock track, and one I really do like. To be truthful though, I really can't remember what else is on that album aside from "Iron Wheels". I wrote a song on »Destiny« called "Calm Before The Storm" which used those lyrics but I thought I undersold them; I threw them away on what was not the best vehicle for them. Me and Nigel Glockler wrote "Iron Wheels"; he wrote the acoustic part and I decided to re-write those verses because they're about my father. Well, not so much about my father as about my father's generation. It's a song about Yorkshire and the decline of the county's traditional industries – the fishing fleets and the coal mines… The end of what was there when I was young. I think I threw the concept and the sentiment away on the first song so I used it again and reworked it a little for "Iron Wheels." And I like that song; I think its probably got some of the best lyrics I've ever written. "Iron Wheels" was put out as a single, and although we don't play it any more it used to go down really well. If you listen to »The Eagle Has Landed Part II« there's a fantastic version on there, and the audience is really going for it.

Some of what I like about that song is the kind of folk angle. When I was younger I was really into folk music from Yorkshire, that kind of Mike Harding sound, and used to go to lots of ceilidhs in those days because it was the thing – Friday night was ceilidh night. It was supposed to be Celtic music but it generally wasn't. But I was quite into folk music – electric folk – and still am, actually. When I was in the Iron Mad Wilkinson Band we did gigs at universities with bands like String Driven Thing, East Of Eden, Lindisfarne… And if you think about it, the Blind Guardian stuff is quite folky in its way. But I quite like English folk, I think it is quite unique. The Irish and Scottish folk music is better known but there is a lot of good English folk with Celtic roots. I think that's why I like so many bands that incorporate folk influences, although we don't ourselves because the other guys aren't into it and don't give a shit about it. Heathens! But the lyrics are really earthy (like real country and western lyrics are), and I quite like that too – the real stuff, where the lyrics tell a real story, not the commercial radio-friendly shit. And "Iron Wheels" does the same. But I like that sort of influence and I don't think it comes out in our music enough. I think that's why I like Blind Guardian because they often go into a traditional English-Irish kind of feel and I quite like that. I think we could use it more, but, as I said, none of our guys are into it. That said, it happens when we do acoustic things like "Jack Tars" on »Lionheart«.

Don't get me wrong, I don't think »Forever Free« is a bad album, I just think that the production is unfocussed. But that's my memories of »Forever Free«; long days waiting for people to arrive, and poor Pete Hinton trying to pull something out of a hat and failing miserably while the producer had been given a lump of cash and was just going through the motions. We did tour with the album, but to tell the truth, I can't remember much about it. In retrospect, we should have gone back to Kalle Trapp because we went back to him for the next album »Dogs Of War« and it's much better altogether: the flow of it is better, the focus is better, the guy doing it is more in tune with what we want. And I think really »Dogs Of War« gives an indication of where we were going. The title track is quite an aggressive track; in fact, it's quite an aggressive album. I think »Dogs Of War« was our first step back into the earlier, intense music that we were famous for. We ended up back at Karo because there was no way, no fucking way, I was going back to that nutcase in Austria, and the result was a really good album. I like »Dogs Of War« and also it's more pertinent to what was happening around us in the world. »Solid Ball Of Rock« is more a good times rock 'n' roll album, whereas »Dogs Of War« is much more relevant. The title track was about the disintegration of Yugoslavia, and I was writing lyrics again about things I was seeing around me rather than writing lyrics based on a good sentiment. I mean, I didn't write "Solid Ball Of Rock" anyway, but that album is much more rock 'n' roll than »Dogs Of War«. If you listen to »Dogs Of War« although there are some what you might call rock 'n' roll songs on there, the whole thing's much more on the edge; »Dogs Of War« is much more in-your-face. It doesn't rely so much on pretty little riffs – we just kept a riff grinding for a long time and didn't give a shit, much more how we used to be. I think we moved back to that, consciously or unconsciously; well, someone wasn't so much moved back to that as dragged back to that, as the thing with Graham Oliver began to come to a head. »Forever Free« has its moments, but it's a bit more 'out there' really; if you listen to it as an album, as a collection of songs, there's only maybe one or two songs on reflection that I wouldn't have done. I guess it's like the 'forgotten album', because it doesn't really have a defining moment. The title track is a great song, but it doesn't have a connection through it, there's no link through the album. It's not focussed; it's a mish-mash; an odd collection of songs with no real thread.

I can't remember how much UK touring we were doing at this time. »Solid Ball Of Rock« was quite a big album in England and sold a lot of copies – I think we did 23,000 in the UK which at that time was pretty damn good. As I said, we sold out a lot of shows and in

Europe, especially in Germany, it came straight after the hugely successful Manowar tour so we were quite happening. I was very pleased with the lyrics I wrote to "Requiem (We Will Remember)"; as I mentioned before, Graham wanted me to write it specifically about Jimi Hendrix but I wanted something more ambiguous, something about all the people who'd died but whose music lives on – especially as the digital age was coming on in leaps and bounds and CDs, as they didn't deteriorate, would really help music live forever. That was our first 'comeback' single, and that was a mistake. It should have been "Solid Ball Of Rock" but I under-estimated the strength of that song. It's only recently that I came across the original demo of "Solid Ball Of Rock" that I did with Bram Tchaikovsky. What happened was, Bram wrote some songs and asked me to sing them for him so he could get a deal. I sang "Solid Ball Of Rock" and it was like a rock 'n' roll song about Jerry Lee Lewis and I thought, 'hey, we could do that.' So I arranged it for Saxon, taking the model off "Faith Healer" by Alex Harvey. The beginning of "Solid Ball Of Rock" is actually pretty much "Faith Healer". But I under-estimated how much airplay it would get, because it was getting tons and the single wasn't. As a song, "Requiem…" meant much more to me personally as Phil Lynott had died and he was a friend, and that song captured how I had felt at that time. But we made a mistake. We should have made a video for "Solid Ball Of Rock" because with the airplay that it got anyway, with a video it could have been huge.

Chapter Eighteen

I was worried about Graham Oliver. In my opinion, he no longer seemed to be himself. We could see we were slipping down quite badly through the late Eighties. We were still big, and we could still tour, but our profile in the press was lower than low. Our name was getting to be shit in the press because anything that went wrong appeared to be our fault. As this was happening, Graham was slipping more into a 'why aren't we big like them; we could have been this, we could have been that' way of thinking, and that's a very negative way to be. He was also falling back more and more into this Hendrix thing, making friends with Noel Redding and going to all these Hendrix conventions and getting up with bands and playing Hendrix songs with them. This all seemed to be becoming more and more important to him, this Hendrix obsession.

He was also really two-faced. People like that amass enemies against you. I found myself in an environment where he was smiling at me but behind my back was trying to turn people against me, and that wasn't a great place to be. Anybody that I met, even girlfriends, he would try and turn away from me by painting them his picture of me. He would also put down Paul all the time as well because he knew Paul was a genius and he didn't want his star to rise; he wanted to keep him down. But when you look at what Graham did – burning guitars or making love to them – it was just a cheap trick really. At least Hendrix was based on genius and flare. Maybe Graham was insecure; maybe inside it was eating him up that he wasn't really that good. I just don't know. He had had a couple of 'episodes', near-nervous breakdowns, and we had all tried to help him; I went to his house many, many times to talk to him to try to work through things with him. And, to be honest, I thought we were friends. So I think he must have been having a nervous breakdown. It's the only thing I can put his strange behaviour down to, because I don't know what else could have been happening to him.

One day Rainer Hänsel asked if any of us had heard about a live album that someone was trying to sell on the open market; we had »Dogs Of War« set for imminent release we didn't want somebody releasing an old live album at the same time because it would steal a lot of the new album's thunder. This album, we subsequently discovered, was the first ever Donington gig.

A couple of months went by and there was still somebody trying to flog this live album to record companies, although no-one knew who it was. I talked to our lawyer – can't remember who it was now but a big London hotshot – and asked if he knew or had heard anything about it. He said he didn't know anything at the time but would ask around. A little later he sent me a letter just saying, 'ask Graham Oliver.' Odd, I thought. So at the next band meeting I collared Graham in the lift and just between the two of us told him I'd had this letter from the lawyer saying to ask him about this live album, and asked him straight if he knew anything about it. He denied it to my face.

About a week after, a perfect stranger knocked on my door, a guy from a museum of pottery in Sheffield, saying, 'you don't know me but I'm a friend of Graham Oliver's.' So I invited him in for a cup of tea, as you do, and he said, 'did you know Graham's running around with a live album with a picture of you on the front as the next Saxon album?' I was absolutely gobsmacked. Obviously, this guy was more an ex-friend of Graham's, didn't like him and shopped him to me. I phoned Graham and confronted him about it.

'What live album?' he shouted back.

'Look, this guy has just come to see me...'

'How do you know him?' he cut me off.

'I don't know him,' I said. 'He just came down to talk to me. And he says you're the one trying to sell this live album.'

This went on for a while and although he still denied it we sacked him on grounds of betrayal. I wrote him a letter saying about all the times I'd helped him, and, having been in the band so long, how could he try to release an album behind our backs and then deny it. We just couldn't have it. 'You can do anything, really,' I wrote, 'but that was a betrayal,' and that was that. He wrote back some pathetic letter saying that he was trying to do it for the good of the band, but he wasn't. He was doing it for his own ends. And he had the fucking gall to put a picture of me on the front of it; not even a picture of him – it was me in front of the Donington audience. I sued him and got an injunction, so had it stopped. The injunction was on the grounds that firstly it was a bootleg, which it was: it was a cassette tape that he'd obtained from our old sound engineer which had then been recorded onto a two-and-a-quarter inch tape to make it look like an original – an act that could probably have landed them in jail had they followed it through. And secondly, they didn't have my performing rights, and had negotiated a contract without me being involved. Even then the guy that tried to release it came to me and asked if he could put it out. My response was something along the lines of, 'no, you can't. You've never talked to me, I don't know how much money you've been paid, I don't know what royalty rate I'm getting, and I've no idea what you've been doing. So if you want it released, you have to pay me.'

Eventually, they paid all costs and it was released, although at the end of the day though it's still just a bootleg. I suppose in one way it's a historical recording, so I can see why the fans wanted to buy it, and actually my performance on it is great. All you can hear is me because it's taken off the mixing desk: the only things that have been turned up on the desk are the drums and vocals. Little tip for you: you can always tell by the vocals if a live recording is taken from the desk because they'll be the loudest thing on there.

But that was Graham Oliver, and that's why we sacked him. What a lot of people don't know is that Rainer Hänsel got in an American guitarist to play his parts again which was a bit bizarre, we thought at the time. He didn't do everything, but a lot of the guitar parts, the solo work, is not Graham Oliver – well, the bulk of it's Paul Quinn anyway – but it's another guy, which is why the guitar playing on »Dogs Of War« is quite superb. I don't want to put Graham down too much but he was never a slick guitar player. He was more of a one-note bender, but he bent it well! I've heard all the recordings that have come to light in the early Eighties and the band were really cooking. So I don't want to knock too much his contribution because he did contribute a lot in those days – we all did – but he must have had a nervous breakdown or something because he went absolutely doodle-alley, so much so that we really couldn't work with him any more. You simply can't have band members releasing albums without the rest of the band knowing about it, and on the eve of releasing »Dogs Of War« as well. He knew »Dogs Of War« was coming up and we found out this other album was scheduled for release at the same time; maybe he was being manipulated and/or was being very naïve; or he was hoping to maximise the sales for the Donington album. But I really can't believe to this day that he was so jealous and greedy that he would have manipulated the release of another album at the same time as the release of »Dogs Of War«, I really can't believe that. I don't want to believe that. But the record company wasn't happy as you can imagine, and Rainer wasn't happy either; it costs a lot of money to release an album and if you lose ten thousand sales because something else takes the limelight, that's a big deal.

And to do something like that, to try and release an album behind everyone's back, your mates in your band, even if it hadn't been conflicting with the studio album, and not telling the singer of the band when it's his picture on the cover, it's highly controversial, highly confrontational, and I have never doubted in my mind that it was a sacking offence. In retrospect, with what's happened since, it was the right decision, because if he'd come clean, he may well have got his job back and I doubt that we would be where we are now with him still in the band. I think if he'd come round the table and talked things might have been different, but the first thing he did was serve us with a writ about accounting or something – which was impossible to sort out as our ex-manager Nigel Thomas had just died. He then hooked up with Steve Dawson and they went on and did the Son Of A Bitch thing which I thought was a pretty good idea, but it obviously wasn't enough for them; they wanted the name, and they couldn't have it.

Chapter Nineteen

T he »Dogs Of War« tour of Europe was massively successful, but now we had Doug Scarratt in the band. Doug was Nigel Glockler's mate; they used to play in this like splinter band called the Desperate Dan band until the comic – was it the Beano or the Dandy? – stopped them using the name so they called themselves the DD Band instead. With Graham gone, Nigel said that he knew a great guitar player who's a really nice guy, and we needed a nice guy after what had gone on because we were really fed up with the backstabbing and the bloody niggly-nagglings behind people's backs... It was like being in the CIA or something at that time; covert operations, you know? We never knew exactly what Graham was saying to whom. And we used to say that when Graham was happy, everyone else was miserable; and when everyone was happy, he was fucking miserable. He was like the rain man with storm clouds on the horizon – he used to walk around with a grey cloud over his head. Doug is so much the opposite. So we got Nigel to phone him and say, 'we've sacked Graham, are you interested?', and obviously he was.

This was about Christmas '94 or January '95. Nigel arranged a meeting for us – Nibbs wasn't there – and Doug had learned eight or nine songs. A very rich friend of his had this massive, massive house with a rehearsal room in it, and he was a huge Saxon fan. I think Doug said something to him like, 'how do you fancy meeting Biff and Paul and letting me audition at your house?' – well, house isn't the right word for this place, I think it was an old rectory or something. I don't remember this, but he claims that at the end of the rehearsal I said, 'well, I suppose I'll give you the job then. I'll probably fucking regret it though!'

Doug is a great guitarist, there's no doubt about that, but it's a personality thing you need in a touring rock band as well. It's different if you are session players and you just clock in. But you need somebody who's an individual and can bring a certain something to the band, and you need somebody who's not full of intrigue. You're stuck on a bus for days on end so you don't want intrigue – you don't want to be stuck in a James Bond movie not really knowing what's going on when you're touring. You need to be in a transcendental mood of peace and harmony or something: a mindset that you are on the road together to bring your music to the masses. I know that sounds bullshit, and it is difficult to describe, but that's kind of the state of mind you want to be in. You are on a mission, to play the best you can and be as entertaining as you can. If someone is destroying the vibe, it's very hard to leave it on the bus. You can't, in fact. It overspills onto the stage, and there's nothing you can do to stop it. All that stopped when Doug joined us. As I said, he's a great guy, a great guitarist, and he's actually a great songwriter as well. He's brought a lot of great riffs and a lot of great ideas into the band, and a more modern feel too, which we probably needed at that stage of our career.

We didn't audition anyone else; to be honest, we couldn't be arsed. Doug was great, and he fitted straight in. We had a lot of people suggested to us who were either in bands or had just left bands. The Manowar guitarist wanted the job with us and was quite good, but we wanted somebody English or at least British (but definitely English!) and Doug is a Southerner so it equalled up the north-south divide in the band. And he's a total musician: he spends all his money on guitars and bits and pieces and is totally absorbed in his music and – strange though this might sound – it's good when you get somebody in the band that just talks about guitars all the time. Paul gets on with him really well and they work well together which is obviously important. You can see there's a good chemistry onstage. They're not posey – they don't strike the poses – and I think that in itself is quite special. You'll never see Doug on the floor on his knees and Paul sticking his guitar in his face – the old blow-jobby guitar pose; they'll never do that, where some bands do it all the time. And you'll never really see them doing anything choreographed – they're just not into that, and they're far too experienced to be doing it. They're not typecast or stereotypical metal guitarists, and I quite like that. Some people might not; some people might want to see their guitarists in sequinned suits skipping about like sex gods, but I quite like them to be individuals. Not to say that they are not sex gods, though: if they want to be sex gods, that's up to them! (Poor Paul; a little while back Nigel and I were talking about sex in the Eighties and Paul chipped in with, 'I turned down a lot.'

'Sorry?'

'I said, I turned down a lot,' he repeated.

'What for?'

'No, I'm just saying, I turned down a lot.'

And Nigel said, 'and your point is?'

Paul does cop it in the neck all the time! He just makes these sweeping statements and we're all on him like a ton of bricks.)

But I digress... The point is, they have their thing and they do it very well. I think that when bands try to copy other bands, it can all start to look a bit silly. Individualism in music is very important; why clone someone else? Our sort of music in particular brings with it the need for the look of the band to be nearly as important as the music; dropping your guitar four inches and having a tattoo can make a big difference, you know. Paul and Doug didn't sell their souls for that. They are both true to their roots; they play guitar and they love guitars. They aren't kids that play guitars to make themselves look good; they are actually professional guitarists and they love what they do.

The »Dogs Of War« tour with the un-blooded Doug Scarratt... It was a life-changing experience for him. He really had no experience of touring on this scale, he must have been totally nervous; he must have been absolutely shit-scared in fact. As a session player, Doug was used to learning sets in a short space of time, but with written music, so he would write all the Saxon songs out. Also, he was used to being a hired guitar player so very much in the background. And then there was just one rehearsal. He'd been to Nibbs's house for a few days, went to Paul's house for a few days, and went through the songs endlessly on CD, but it's not the same as playing with the band. There was one day's rehearsal in Munich and the first gig of what was like a seven- or eight-week tour the next day. No pressure then! The first gig was in Kosice in Slovakia. He claims that the worst hangover he's ever had was the day of that rehearsal. The band arrived in Munich the night before and had been on the bus for a couple of days, drinking solidly. There was a party for someone else in this hangar where we were rehearsing, for whoever had been using it the night before us, and we were all invited, pigging out on bratwurst and German beer. Doug claims he thought he was going to die the next day. 'The slightest noise was like a fucking earthquake!' he moaned.

Welcome to Saxon!

After that, his first US gig was San Antonio in front of 29,000 people. And he hates flying, hadn't been on a plane for more than two hours in is life and now had an eleven-hour flight to Texas. He must have been absolutely petrified the whole time.

I said to him, 'you need a mask, you need to put something on metaphorically and turn into something or someone else otherwise you're going to blow it.' So we bought him a Stevie Ray Vaughan hat, not a cowboy hat but, I don't know, was it a Mexican one? Or is it Spanish? I don't know – a nice hat anyway. And a waistcoat with a skull on it and he put that on and he looked absolutely fucking fantastic. We started calling him Red Scarratt: 'ladies and gentlemen, please welcome Red Scarratt, the blues guitarist extraordinaire!'

He did that tour in that outfit and the pictures of him looked stunning. He's since ditched it, but that's how he got through the tour really. He got into a mindset of a character and that's how he did it. And he did well actually. We did some shows in the UK, but they were pretty miserable, I think, in terms of attendance; and I don't even think we did one in London (but as I've said, tours and shows do all blur into one after a few years). At this time, the mid-Nineties, I'm not sure Maiden were doing much in the UK either, nor Priest with Ripper Owens. It was a poor time musically in Britain back then though. Nobody was really interested in British metal music at that time, they were more interested in Bon Jovi, or U2, I suppose, or some of the newer bands like Limp Bizkit, and the nu-metal stuff. I think probably all the established bands weren't really that popular around then. I can't remember Maiden doing the massive tours they used to do. Obviously all of us had a following somewhere, and we just went where we were popular.

I often think that because the music of the Eighties was so strong, it must have resulted from a state of grace. I do believe that. From 1980 to 1984 British bands wrote some fantastic music. It must have been a golden age; I can't explain it any other way. I don't know why I wrote so many great lyrics in those days – they were just pouring out of my head. I just had to sing in the bath and I'd come out with a great lyric. Maybe because we were so excited and vibed and we had so much pent-up emotion and ideas were pouring out. I mean, we wrote »Wheels Of Steel« on a down time but that worked. Motörhead had a great time back then on the »Bomber« tour and the following album; I mean, you couldn't get much bigger than that. It was such a melting pot of talent really. I do feel really humble to be involved in that melting pot because it was so touch-and-go whether you would make it or not. Iron Maiden, in the Bruce days, wrote some great stuff, and the point I am trying to make is that the music was so strong, and so many people liked it, and it was such a magical time in the UK, that people now are mystified by it and want to know 'why?' – why Whitesnake were writing so many good songs. Why Judas Priest wrote "Living After Midnight". Why Saxon wrote "747". Why were we all writing all this great stuff. What happened? It's like, why did they build all the great cathedrals in, like, a hundred-year period? It must have been mass talent, mass hysteria, a golden age… I really don't know why.

But it was such a great period during which to be in a band. I don't see it as surreal, looking back, I just think it was maybe like the early Seventies when you had all the great bands like Zeppelin, Free, Sabbath, Purple. There was a lot of great music at that time as well. I mean, "Immigrant Song"; if somebody wrote that now, you'd probably say, 'are you nuts?' But at that time it was perfect; such a great riff, such a great song, and it's still such a great song today. And the same is true of some of the old Saxon songs. If we do "Princess Of The Night" in front of a young audience, even if they've never heard the song before, it's such a great guitar riff that they're simply blown away. We did a festival a while ago and Foreigner headlined. It's like, 'Foreigner? Gimme a break.' But then you listen to them and you realise their songs are fantastic – "Juke Box Hero", "Cold As Ice"… They're such great songs. They might not be heavy metal but they're great songs. Van Halen at that time were huge. It was a golden age for music, and I don't know why we were involved in it, but we were involved in it and that was fantastic. I think that now, when we write albums like »Dogs Of War«, we are trying to tap into that sort of feeling. In fact, I think we're trying to do that all the time, we're trying to tap into a period where everything seemed to be perfect. You can't deny that the early Eighties had a massive influence on people, musically; people are interested in it now, and they'll always be interested in it. I think we were very lucky to be a part of that, and we have to try and tap into it somehow, into that feeling of interest that there is for that time, to get people interested in the here and now. That's the secret.

So, the »Dogs Of War« tour was a good tour for us and really marked the start of our climb back to the higher level, specifically in Germany where, for whatever reason, the interest in Saxon has remained the strongest over the years. In December 1995 we recorded some dates there for what was to become »The Eagle Has Landed Part II«. We were on a package tour. It was Blind Guardian headlining, we were on second to them, just before us was Yngwie, I think, and there was some wacky American band whom I forget, and there was Sabbat. So it was a pretty good tour from an audience point of view, and we were happening and did a lot of damage to Blind Guardian. I like Blind

Guardian a lot, but they had to go on after us every night and boy, did they fucking grumble about it! I think they learned their lesson; never, ever, go on after Saxon. They're great guys though and I think they are probably my favourite German band, because a lot of their bands do tend to sound the same. There are obvious exceptions; Blind Guardian is one and I do quite like Edguy because Tobias Sammet is a good frontman, but I think a lot of the German stuff is quite precise – you know, almost the stereotypical military precision. We use a German producer, Charlie Bauerfeind, and I said to him when we were doing »Metalhead«, 'we're not building a Mercedes, we're building a Ferrari. There's a difference, right.' And that basically sums us up beautifully. We don't want it to be perfect, we want it to have some character. I think a lot of the German bands strive to make Mercedes albums, which is obviously better than making a Skoda album or a Vauxhall album. But I'm really into Ferrari albums: not perfect, but full of life!

From memory we recorded three shows at a time when the band was flexing its musical muscles a bit, and not just playing boogie-woogie twelve-bar stuff. We were a lot more, well, musical, and certainly a lot more adventurous. On that album there are guitar solos that can take your head off. We were much more confident; we were no longer relying on the hits or the pyrotechnics or shagging guitars. We were much more confident within ourselves. And it was less 'frantic'. If you listen to that album, we're in total control although the band is still learning to play together. Paul's playing brilliantly and Doug's really into the gig by this time, so it's a great snapshot of how we were at the end of 1995. We're playing the new songs, like "Dogs Of War" extremely well. And also we tried to feature Nibbs a bit on that album, because I told him I wanted him to do a bass guitar solo to show off what a fantastic all-round bass player he is. So on that album we are much more confident, and the band is much more complete. Listen to it and you'll see what I mean.

I think around the same time as »The Eagle Has Landed Part II« came out in 1996 came the Judas Priest tribute album. Götz Kühnemund at Rock Hard magazine in Germany was putting this album together and asked loads of bands like Helloween, UDO and Testament to appear on it. They had compiled a list of tracks and each band got to pick one. By the time we got the list a lot of the songs had been ticked off, although one that no-one else had chosen was "You've Got Another Thing Coming". They asked if we would like to do it, and it was like, 'are you nuts? It's a great song. Of course we'll do it!' So we covered "You've Got Another Thing Coming" for two reasons really. Firstly, there it was, one of Judas Priest's best songs that no-one had touched, and also, without us, there would not have been one British band on the entire CD; face facts, there should be an English band on a Priest tribute album. So we did it, and I think it's a great version.

There is a Saxon tribute album called »Eagleution«. There's nobody particularly famous on there; it's a lot of German death metal bands on it, but it's brilliant. A band called Dark Age do "Heavy Metal Thunder" but they slow it down. It's quite, 'whoa! What the hell is that?' Unlike the Priest album, a lot of the bands have done some quite interesting things with some of the songs. It's very different, it must be said.

Back in the UK, the first thing Graham Oliver did on being sacked from the band was start the Biff Byford Appreciation Society. He contacted everybody who'd had anything to do with the band and told them that I was an absolute arsehole and had said loads of derogatory things about them all. In doing so he basically brought quite a few people into his camp who hadn't been anti-me but soon were, like Pete Gill and Steve Dawson, and wound them up into a bit of a frenzy. I mean, some of the producers, business people, we'd worked with, he got them to turn as well. I don't know how he did it but he's quite manipulative.

One of the things that really got to him was 'why the fuck has he got the name? We should have it.' It soon became apparent that once he'd got his troops together he wanted to start the son of Saxon, which included Steve and Pete, and later Nigel Durham who you could say was ex-Saxon because he was in the band for a while, and Hadyn Conway who had nothing to do with Saxon whatsoever.

I think Graham wanted the Saxon name badly but the collaboration between Graham Oliver and Steve Dawson first appeared under the name Son Of A Bitch which I thought was quite clever really. It was our original name, after all, we'd had a lot of press in the early days and the fact that it was the name we'd changed from and that the album wasn't bad all added up to a smart move. They had a good singer in Ted Bullet, who was a nice guy, and a good friend of the band actually, but they obviously sold him a bill of goods that they were going to do a separate band, and Son Of A Bitch was it. But the Saxon thing started sneaking in more and more and they eventually ditched the Son Of A Bitch idea altogether and in favour of a take-over bid for Saxon.

I think they must have had some really dodgy legal advice. That's the only thing I can surmise. I think they were probably advised by friends of theirs and ours – two-faced friends, obviously – that they had as much right to the name as we had. And I think if you are talking on a purely emotional level, then I suppose they would think that. When you sack someone from a band you just want them to go away and most of the time they do. The problem for Graham and Steve is that the partnership went on without them. We as a band didn't stop. So in the eyes of the law a new partnership was made and it continued and prospered, and as such they could only claim to have been part of the old Saxon, which didn't give them any rights to the name. There have been many, many, many lawsuits and I don't think any ex-member of a band has ever won, ever, especially when the split is for a reason. If you just sack someone just because, I don't know, they're losing their hair, then they might have a case, but if you have a bona fide reason, like skulking around behind people's backs, trying to release an album without telling anybody in the band… Well, we thought that was a bona fide case. We didn't do it lightly, actually, and it wasn't just a matter of me sacking him. We had a couple of meetings of the band and talked through it and decided it wasn't worth going any further with him if this was the sort of thing he was going to do.

Graham and Steve registered the name Saxon without telling us. They had actually already registered it in England and were trying to register it in Europe as well before we found out. So we appealed against the registration and the registrar said, although obviously worded a lot better, 'too bad; first come first served.'

Fuck that! We took it to the High Court for a judicial enquiry and we won. The judge said that the registrar was wholly incorrect and that we had the right to the name; the case should never have been brought because the information that the registrar had given was erroneous. The High Court judge gave us leave to kick out their application and apply in our own right, which we did, and now I've got the trade mark. We did the same in Alicante, the European registration headquarters in Spain. We sent them the High Court Judgement and they revoked Graham and Steve's application and again, I got it. This might sound a bit egotistical, but I thought when all this happened that it was quite serious and that the name has to be kept safe by someone who actually cares about what's done with it. Graham and Steve would have run it into the ground. So I made a decision to register it once and for all with me. It's not so much a matter of not trusting other people, but I think that if the name, the trade mark, ends up with people you don't know, well, you don't know what might happen in the future. So it's safe now; it's with me, which I think is the safest place for the name to be. I think if we'd registered it for the whole current band, and one of them left, the whole thing could start up all over again and I can't risk that. So the name is safe. It was quite a difficult period for me personally, because of all I'd put into this band. Graham and Steve then went on to say that they had won the court cases, but they didn't – that was all a smokescreen. And to think it all started with that bloody Donington album that Graham had been hawking around.

The thing is, I let them use 'Oliver/Dawson Saxon' as a name. I probably shouldn't have agreed to it, but at the end of the day they do need to make a living, and if they do that without trading on us, or making people think it's us, then that was fine by me. But it turned out that there are other people who are making them out to be Saxon. In the original court order there were a lot of stipulations laid down regarding the Oliver/Dawson name and how it should be portrayed; for example, there have to be gaps between the name, it has to be in a certain script, they can't use the logo, the album covers mustn't look similar to ours – they did an album cover that came out that looked very similar to »Killing Ground« which was a repackage of the Donington tape so we went to court on that as well. Keeping the trademark safe costs us a lot of money and a lot of time; we can go a year or so without hearing anything and then all of a sudden it flairs up again. It's an ongoing thing, and I don't think that it's totally their fault all the time; let's just say that they are not working with people who are in the top ten of the business. They are always working with people that are a little bit backstreet, a little dodgy, and who are not averse to putting on posters 'Saxon – Eighties Show' with our logo. Of course, then we're straight on them like a ton of bricks. They can use 'ex-Saxon' and stuff like that, but nothing to imply that it's the real Saxon playing there. The stupid thing is, if they're not careful they'll ruin the very thing they're supposed to love, and of course the more successful we are, the more money they make through royalties off the back catalogue. We've recently gone through a massive surge in record sales so the royalty payments have gone up quite a lot, and they receive that so they're stupid if they do anything to rock the boat. The words 'goose' and 'golden egg' spring to mind. And they must be spending an absolute fortune on lawyers. Graham has obviously conned himself into thinking that he was sacked unfairly. He must really believe that; he must really think that he was innocent. Obviously, as they fail and we get more success it'll fizzle out anyway.

My bottom line is that I just don't understand where they are coming from. Maybe it's all about a re-union; maybe that's their endgame. I don't think anybody would give a shit though. Maybe in England people might be a bit curious, but it's not the same as a band splitting up totally and then coming back together a few years down the line. It's a bit like, well, would Iron Maiden be any bigger if the original drummer and guitarist joined again; would the band be better? Probably not. Would they pull more people? I don't think so. I don't really know if it would make any difference whatsoever because apart from the money, the only other reason to do it is for the fans, surely, and I really don't think they'd care if Graham and Steve were to rejoin the band. I mean, Nibbs has been in the band much longer than Steve was and Doug's been in now nearly as long as Graham. Graham claimed he was happy with this situation of the two bands co-existing, and actually said in his press release, 'let the audience decide'. Well, they have. It's just that Graham hasn't had the balls to tell everyone which way the decision went.

Besides, they've never actually appeared in front of the judge. They've always caved in on the steps of the court, and thereby lost by caving in. Everything has been done on the court steps before the case has been heard. On one occasion, they were up for a real hiding, but at the last minute I went a little bit soft on them; as I said, I don't want to deprive them of the means to make a living. Obviously, once you are in court, it doesn't cost you any more money to really go for the throat.

I can tell you though, it does sort the men out from the boys when you are waiting to go in, because they can send you straight to jail. No messing; this isn't Monopoly with a 'get-out-of-jail-free' card, it's serious hardball. I quite like it, to be honest. But there is always the chance that the judge will come down on their side, and that would be that. It's also strange to think that a barrister – one person – can put a case, and the way in which he presents it can completely affect the outcome. In the Donington album case their barrister just kept laughing. He kept trying to say 'Monsters of Rock' and he was obviously a highly educated guy, but in the court the clerk was a pretty-looking blonde and the two of them got the giggle fits 'My Lord, the Monsters of...' and he would burst out laughing. It was so funny to watch, and the judge wasn't with it at all. (They're not on this world are they, judges; they're not on the same planet as the rest of us.) All through this, though, aside from having to go to court and needlessly expend time and energy, we basically tried to ignore them, and carried on writing good albums. It's not been as important to us as people might think. Obviously, the issue over the trademark was quite serious, but generally the rest of the Oliver/Dawson pantomime hasn't been that big a deal, because we've just got on with our lives and our job, which is to make music. There wasn't really any bitterness from our side, and it didn't hit us at an emotional level either. It was purely a matter of legality.

Before all this kicked off, we've really never said much about Graham Oliver or Steve Dawson in the press. I was always happy to say they left the band and leave it at that, out of respect for them. But the truth is, they were both fucking sacked. End of story.

Chapter Twenty

I met my wife Sue around the time of »Forever Free« so she was there to support me through all the difficult times with Graham Oliver. Sometimes in life you find your soul mate; more often that not, you don't. I'm one of the fortunate ones in that respect. She's fantastic and she doesn't really have anything to do with the rock 'n' roll side of things. She did sell t-shirts for the band when I first met her, but now we have four children, Stephanie, Sebastian, and twins Thomas and Alexander, and she pretty much works full time looking after the family. She does support me and the band, and I have a fantastic life with her. We're very happy, which is quite rare in this business. People don't believe you when you say you've found your soul mate anyway, but I am happier now, with Sue and my children, having a stable base and a loving family, than I have ever been before. Back in the Eighties I used to think having sex every night with a different woman was happy, but actually it's not: it's a very shallow existence, living out of a suitcase and having a different girl every night. Having sampled both ways of life, I personally think it's much better to be settled down in a stable relationship; that's where real happiness comes from, if you are with your soul partner or whatever. Obviously, if you're not with the right person, you're not going to be completely happy. I've been with women and not been happy and been relieved when they've gone. And boy, have I been hurt too.

My greatest fear now – and there's a name for it but I forget what it is – is that when you're really happy, there's a fear of losing what you have. Sue is the living person I most admire. From a teenager she had a lot of adversity and was around a lot of people who really screwed her up. But she's come through it and I think I respect her more than anyone else because it can be difficult for women to survive in a situation where you are totally controlled; she was in that situation and she made it through to the other side.

Meanwhile, we had a new label and a new album to work on. »Unleash The Beast« was our first studio album for SPV, and Nigel's last album with us. We had a feeling that it was Nigel's swansong because the drumming on that album is fucking fantastic, and we thought he did it on purpose. When Nigel left, and we were auditioning drummers, the only song we auditioned them on was "Unleash The Beast" because if you can't play that then you can't play for us because it's so complex – it's all, like, cross-African rhythms and it's really difficult to pull off. It was so funny in auditions, hearing people's versions of what they thought he played; there were only two guys who could play it properly. "Unleash The Beast" laid most drummers flat because only the exceptional ones could play it.

»Unleash The Beast« is a much darker album. Parts of it are pure rock 'n' roll but "Unleash The Beast" itself is such a dark song where we're experimenting with harmonies and darker, lower voices and things – it was quite nice actually to be doing something different. I always thought in days when Graham Oliver was in the band that there was no emphasis put on the vocals. I never really had time to experiment because it was always taken up with guitars – Graham playing a thousand solos and then bouncing them all together to make one good one; hours and hours and hours would be taken up doing this, and then I had the last week to do all the vocals. And a week was considered a long time, even though it meant nailing two vocals a day. As a result, I didn't really have time to stretch my abilities or try out new things. In about 1994 or so I stopped smoking because my daughter Stephanie was born, so roundabout the »Unleash The Beast« period when my lungs started to open up again my voice came back from where it had been hiding for the last twenty-five years. I was able to stretch a lot more and experiment instead of singing and then collapsing in a heap, gasping for air! I found I was able to breathe and sing a lot more easily and have real power in my voice; before then I always thought it had been quite nasally-squeaky.

It was also Doug's first studio album, and he did bring a lot to the table. What Doug brought to the band that we didn't previously have – sounds like »Star Trek!« – was an ability to go places that we'd never been before. There were certain things we couldn't do – places we couldn't go – because Graham Oliver just couldn't play fast enough. That in no way demeans his guitar playing, but he just wasn't the guy who practiced and practiced and practiced every day. Yngwie Malmsteen to him was some sort of god who had some talent that other people couldn't attain, but actually, although he is a genius and a great guitarist, he's a man who practices twenty-four hours a day. When we toured with him, he plays guitar all the time. All the time. I love Yngwie's playing. He is a guitarist's guitarist's guitarist (three of 'em, because he's so good!). Before, we really only had Paul who could play fast; so when you hear all the fast guitar parts that Paul played, Graham's parts alongside these are all in half-time. "Heavy Metal Thunder" is a good example. Graham couldn't play it fast as he didn't have the plectrum technique, so played his parts in half-time. That was OK for us in the early days, but because Doug is very fast and more schooled in the arts of modern guitar playing it opened a lot of doors for us as a two-guitar band to be able to do more and obviously we leapt on that opportunity. We were able to flex a bit and play a lot more fast material as a piece of piss. And Paul likes that. He's a technician, as is Doug, so as a band we were able to put together some crazy guitar riffs, and Nigel was getting into all these complex rhythm patterns too to underpin them. Nigel had done some drum clinics with Terry Bozio and Simon Phillips and that feel stayed with him, so he was becoming more experimental as well. Nigel left the band on a musical high after »Unleash The Beast«, without a doubt.

Nigel had always been a really heavy prog rock fan and was always into keyboard parts. I think he's one of those guys who's great at one thing but really wanted to be something else. Well, it's like me: I'm a singer and a bass player who wanted to be a lead guitarist. And I think he's a drummer who wanted to be a keyboard player. Nigel came to keyboard playing quite late and did a solo album. After that, he went further down that keyboard road and was quite successful in that he got paid a lot for TV work where his music features quite regularly. But he really didn't have much success with Saxon fans because they wanted Nigel the drummer doing Saxon-type songs. If I was going to do a solo album it would be like Saxon but heavier; I wouldn't go off and do a Journey album. But he went off and did his thing and in all honesty he's never really been out of the band, he's always co-written with us and played with us from time to time. On »Metalhead« he played drums on the demos, so he's never been that far away from the band. But »Unleash The Beast« was definitely a great album to go on, because from a drumming point of view it was fantastic.

The album was dedicated to JJ – John Jones. JJ was my best mate. In the early days of our first album deal, we signed an agency deal with Rod McSween at ITB, a big agency, and he signed Def Leppard at the same time. Slade were doing a tour and basically we needed work so we did half the tour and Def Leppard did the other half. We met and got on well with their crew; their tour manager was called Swinn – Graham Swinnerton – and their guitar roadie and stage manager was JJ. I think that tour at that time was really Slade's last tour. It was a university circuit and it was a good tour, packed houses. Slade are typical Brummies, really sharp wit, fantastic guys; you'd turn up at the gig with your girlfriend and they'd say, 'oh, this is your girlfriend, because we thought the other one you were with last night was your girlfriend', stuff like that, and you're thinking, 'oh, fucking hell, pack it in, man.' So they were full on, in-your-face Brummie all the time, but I liked it, and I liked the tour. I think that the last show we did was a big disco someplace and some twat threw an ashtray at me so I walked off. Noddy Holder said, 'you're not bothered by an ashtray are you? We get a lot worse than that!'

When »Wheels Of Steel« went through the roof we'd got no crew – just mates helping us out. So there we were playing city halls with the cardboard eagle me and the roadie made from hardboard and little mirror squares stuck on; as you can see, we were well prepared for the album coming out. (There is a picture of it on the back of one of the albums. We cut out this eagle from hardboard and stuck these little square mirrors on it and this poor twat used to have to pull it up on a rope. We might bring it back for the next tour! The road crew on some of the later big tours remembered it from the pictures and they used to make eagles out of cigarette paper and tin foil and we'd be playing "Wheels of Steel" and they'd lower it down – an eagle about the size of my hand on a big rope. Seriously taking the piss.) But because we went so big so quickly, it was absolute chaos. So we nicked these two guys off Slade. Swinn was the tour manager, JJ was the road manager, and they basically whipped all our crew into shape and got it together for us. I think Swinn we lost along the way; I can't remember what happened but he didn't stay with us, I think he only did three or so years before he left, but JJ was a lovely guy and stayed with us right up to 1996 or 1997 when he died. He was totally loyal, although got us some terrible reputations because he really didn't give a shit. I mean, if our drum kit was on stage, it didn't move for anybody – he didn't give a toss who it was. He was the boss and that was that. When people tell tales about Saxon, putting them onstage before the doors opened and stuff like that, most of those stories are about JJ. I loved him like a brother. He was a really good guy and helped keep us together through all the bad times. I think Slade must have felt the same about him; he was in the Slade film »In Flames« and it was quite nice that they gave him the royalties from a couple of singles.

He had an embolism. Somebody 'phoned up and said they'd found him dead in the kitchen. He must have just gone, just like that. It's a strange thing about him because although he was an absolutely lovely guy, when he drank whiskey, especially Jack Daniels, it turned him a bit aggressive. And he could binge drink, believe me. I don't think his family and girlfriend knew how much he was drinking at the time he died. We flew to America and I think a couple of days before we flew he was working for »Disney On Ice« at the Birmingham NEC, working spotlight, and when they were packing away something fell out of the truss and hit him on the head. JJ being JJ he didn't give a shit – just had a plaster put on it or something – and then we went to America and he was binge drinking on the plane all the way there and all the next day. We played the gig but when we got there, instead of going to bed they went out on the piss and somebody slammed the car door on his hand. I wasn't there, so I didn't see exactly what happened, but he cut his hand really badly and he had this massive bandage on it.

It wasn't long after that it happened. To my mind, these events had to be connected somehow. Either the bang on the head or the car door slamming... It might not sound like it, but he was quite a healthy bloke. The only other thing was that, at that period of our career, it was quite stressful; there wasn't a lot of money floating around in the Nineties as we were still paying a lot of debts off. He did the job of tour manager, but I don't think he was up to it, really; his thing was stage manager, looking after the gig, looking after the band, and on the American tour that he was managing two roadies were driving this truck and turned it over on the freeway. JJ's credit card was securing the truck and instead of taking the £500 insurance limit we went for a cheaper option so basically they took the truck off his credit card. Our manager gave him a hard time, the bailiffs were sniffing around and there wasn't a lot of money in the kitty. I think his girlfriend believed that the stress of all this had killed him, but personally I can't believe that. He was as strong as an ox, you know. He was bigger than that. I mean, he was on the road in Slade's biggest period, and ours, and that didn't faze him.

Yes, he was worried about the truck – who wouldn't be – but it got paid eventually. I reckon the blood clot was the result of one of these bangs, probably the one on his head. I asked his family if they told the inquest about the blow to the head, and it was like, 'yeah, well, we mentioned it.' I guess we'll never know now. JJ had been a big part of our career, and I don't think really we could have done it without him.

Nigel had gone (again) and once again we were without a drummer. Before Fritz Randow joined we used a session drummer, a really nice guy called Trevor Thornton. After Nigel went we had a lot of work still to do so we were rehearsing people as I said and used "Unleash The Beast" at some point during the day. We tried all types of drummers – we tried established drummers, young kids... Some of them could play double bass like a blur, but couldn't play "Denim And Leather" to save their lives! It's very strange with drummers; it's very, very difficult to find a drummer that can play all our styles because some things have to have a real groove behind them and are full of beat and rhythm, and other things simply have to be played at a million miles an hour. Not to say that some of the drummers we auditioned weren't great; we took a couple of them on gigs, which was, well, all right, but nerves play a big part in any aspect of show business and especially rock music. It's so instant; it's a different audience every night and the travelling tends to screw you up a lot, so nerves play a big part and some of those guys... Some of the performances on those gigs... I still have nightmares even now. You can always tell when drummers are nervous because everything gets speeded up – 'let's just get through this as quick as we can and fuck off.' So we asked around a bit and people in the business all said, 'the guy you want is Trevor Thornton. Great drummer.'

We sent him a tape of the set, and he said he'd do it. Fantastic! We flew into New York to meet him and rehearsed with him there and he knew everything – he'd learned it all. And "Unleash The Beast", he sped through it. I think we would have asked him to join but his base was in America and he was a session player really. But he did a few tours with us – I think he's on the »Chronicles« DVD a couple of times. He was also a great exponent of the Alexander Technique; I didn't really understand it, I've got to be honest, but this Alexander guy wrote a book about the art of relaxation and repeating words and phrases to calm you, so Trevor was mega-relaxed the whole time. He never actually looked like he was even breaking a sweat, so it must be a fantastic technique. But he played well, and we had some good times with him. Although he was English, he was a typical American: a thousand pills every morning – vitamin C, garlic, bees' wings, seals' tits, all that sort of stuff. And he was also a total sex maniac. He was nuts really, but I like people like that. Another character. We had a good time with him, and he was the drummer that nobody really knew in Europe because most of his touring was in America. He did a few shows in Europe though – he did the Dynamo in Holland with us which was a really important show. We went on after Pantera and this was when Pantera were really up there. As they were finishing their set their singer Phil Anselmo said, 'fuck that, I'm off to see Saxon now' because we were playing in this huge tent. And then everyone came over with him; it was great, and we had a fantastic gig. Pantera really helped us out there. It's surprising how many fans we have in the music business really, people who you wouldn't think were into us. We were playing a festival in Holland and some guys burst in the dressing room saying, 'we've just driven all the way from Paris to see you guys,' and they were from The Undertones.

It's strange really. I think it's because a lot of bands, especially American bands, were quite young when we were 'in there' in America. As teenagers, they've later immersed themselves in the whole New Wave Of British Heavy Metal thing, even though they were too young to get it first time around, they've just remembered us, despite possibly going on to a completely different genre of music, So it is always strange when somebody pops out of another pigeonhole and says, 'whoa – we're big fans.' It's unexpected, and it proves a point that all forms of music have a connection really. Good music is good music.

We still needed a permanent drummer, and Fritz Randow came recommended. Fritz was, and is, quite a famous drummer in

Germany. He had played in a band called Victory and had been in the business for many years so seemed like an ideal replacement for Nigel. His drumming style was much closer to Nigel's than Nigel Durham's. I think he came from the same school – the John Bonham power, heavy hitting school, double bass drum as well – whereas Nigel Durham was a younger guy and he was more influenced by the younger generation, the likes of Mötley Crüe, Ratt, and bands like that. So he fitted straight in actually and although he had had quite a bad drink problem, he was on the wagon when he joined us.

I think through all our career, especially my career, we've tended to draw people to us like a magnet that need help. I don't know why that is. My second wife was an alcoholic, unbeknown to me at the time, but it soon became apparent that she was what I call a 'weekend alcoholic' which is the worst kind really, and my father was… Well, I don't know if you'd call him an alcoholic but he used to get drunk quite a lot: in his defence, he'd had a lot to cope with in his life, with my mother's death and him losing his arm, but I used to have to look after him and I used to have to carry him to bed because he would be collapsed behind the door, out of his head. So, all-in-all, I have a fair amount of experience of living with alcoholics.

So Fritz said he'd had a drink problem, and we just shrugged 'fair enough' and asked him to join us. He was at first a fantastic addition to the band, and he drummed beautifully on »Metalhead«, his first album with us. He was great live, and people in Germany really loved him. He'd been in and out of bands and had never really got the acclaim he deserved, and then when he joined us he was really up there. He did really well; he stayed sober for nearly a couple of years, right into »Killing Ground«. He did the »Metalhead« tour and the »Killing Ground« tour, but as with all people who have a drink problem and who are trying to keep it together, their biggest threat is their friends. If you are an alcoholic and your friends are encouraging you to have just one drink, you're finished; because once you have one, that's it. And I think he started slipping back into it. It started on one of the tours; it was pretty obvious he was pissed – it was quite funny in a way because he fell off the drum kit! Then it just got worse and worse.

We were rehearsing for »Lionheart« and he 'phoned up from the airport in Germany to say he couldn't be bothered to come over. Again, he was pissed. We gave him some slack but he did it again so we had to sack him. It's unfortunate because he was a great drummer and when he was sober he was a lovely guy; but, a bit like JJ, he was one of those guys who has a few drinks and gets totally aggressive, smashing things up, stuff like that. We're not the type of band that has people to look after us and take us to the toilet. We can't really baby-sit alcoholics or anyone else with problems. People have to get it together themselves. We couldn't force him not to drink: people like that have to say from inside themselves, 'I'm not going to drink, because I owe it to these guys,' or, 'these guys took a risk so I owe it to them not to drink.' Once he started drinking after a show, he'd drink until next morning and then he'd be fucking pissed for the next gig. And don't forget, drumming is a massive stamina job. As a drummer, even the fact that you're sweating does odd things to you when you are full of alcohol. You can't really do our job with a hangover. I know Nibbs has tried many times, but he can just about get away with it because he's the bass player!

The other thing about Fritz is that, again, he wasn't a songwriter. He was a great drummer and he played on two fantastic albums, but he didn't contribute to the songs at all. He just came in and said, 'I like that' and played it. Nigel was involved with »Metalhead« a bit; he helped out writing some of the riffs and wrote and performed the intro. But basically the album was written as a four piece, as was »Killing Ground«, with Nibbs playing drums and me on bass, Paul and Doug. We four became the Saxon song-writing unit, and that's the way it stayed.

Chapter Twenty-One

Our last album of the Twentieth Century was »Metalhead«. I love »Metalhead«. It's our biggest-selling album on SPV and still sells upwards of 5,000 copies a year in Germany. As I said, we wrote »Metalhead« (and both »Killing Ground« and »Lionheart«, come to that) as a four-piece, with Nigel popping up here and there. I think it's much more focussed because of that.

Again, it's a very dark album. I think the reason I like »Metalhead« so much is because it's the first album where I could both go for it vocally and really let my imagination go to the darker side of things. It's not something I've really allowed myself to do a lot; »Unleash The Beast« was a little in that vein, but »Metalhead« is for me a technically perfect album; a great piece of work. I think in a sense we were in that magical period again, that state of grace. Those that don't like it have criticised it for not being 'classic' Saxon; it's not classic rock. Maybe it was too early for its time. In the last few years it's become a bit of a cult album, a 'got-to-have album', which is why it's still selling, because I don't think »Forever Free«, for example, sells anything like that at all. It obviously must sell in some quantity or else they wouldn't stock it in the shops, but »Metalhead« is right in your face everywhere.

If you listen to the songs, and the lyrics, it is a great album. Some of my best lyrics, too, are on »Metalhead«. "Are We Travellers In Time" and that sort of thing. Recently, we've resurrected some of the »Metalhead« songs again, and we get asked to play "Metalhead" itself all the time (mainly from the younger section of the audience). »Metalhead« really was a turning point, both in our career and in our song-writing because we did it: we got to a point where we'd explored the darker side of our song-writing and came out again, so we can do it at any time and know it's not taboo. It used to be taboo to play semi-toned rock; it's not happy music, is it? But I don't think it's good to play happy music all the time, really. I think as a rock band, especially if you're trying to bring out the heavier side, the really metal side of your music, then it can't be happy all the time. If it is, you're selling yourself short.

We had a fantastic time making »Metalhead«. It was the first album we did with Charlie Bauerfeind and he was digital mad on that album – he wouldn't have anything analogue at all (and then on the next album he went totally the other way and didn't want anything digital). I always like to use the same microphone; I like to use this German microphone made in 1943. I think it's an AEG or something, but these people rent it to me and I've done quite a few albums with it now. I love the microphone and it loves me. If you're not a singer then it's hard to explain, but when you do an album your relationship with your microphone is quite intimate. Imagine it: when I sing in the studio, I sing in a very dark room, candle-lit, it's just me and the microphone, and it's a strange partnership. I've tried thousands of microphones and you have to have the microphone that suits your voice. I know people that have gold-plated microphones, microphones that their auntie's knitted for them or something, but I love this microphone. Other people have rented it because I've used it but have not got the same results from it. I've had a bank of microphones, singing into different ones, with engineers going 'not bad', 'OK', or whatever, and we always come back to the same microphone. This microphone obviously loves me, and I love this microphone because you can shout into it really loudly and it doesn't stop working (because I have been known to break microphones on a regular basis). On »Metalhead« we used this microphone so the vocals are quite 'in there'. You'll find that vocal performances on albums don't need a lot of echo and things, because they tend to cover things up. Obviously if the occasion calls for it, sometimes you might want some echo, but generally it should sound happening on the tape (or digital machine); it should be there, sparkling, clear as a bell, and »Metalhead« was the first time I'd used that microphone since »Dogs Of War«. And I'd missed it like an old friend so I was glad to have it back, and have used it ever since.

So, on »Metalhead« Charlie Bauerfeind didn't want anything analogue and this microphone has got a big transformer that's outside the microphone, it's got a big EQ unit and it looks like something from a German war radio station. Bloody great knob that goes on/off and it's all analogue and valves and he hated it! He kept turning up with these digital bits and bobs and saying, 'this'll do it; this'll do it,' so he had all these digital microphones and all this software that goes over it, hundreds of thousands of pounds of Pro-Tools but I had to use this analogue microphone because it was so soft, so he was stuck with it. Then, bizarrely, on the next album we did with him, it was, 'ah, now we have to use analogue' so we recorded everything on tape and then put it onto digital – totally the other way round. But »Metalhead« really does sound... Well, it's a Mercedes album, let's put it like that A dark one... »Metalhead« – the big, black Mercedes! The album with the dark side. It brings out really strong emotions, and it's all in there: Celtic stones, runes, things of the night, spooks and spirits and spiritualism – there's a lot of that in there, because it's something I've dabbled in at certain times in my life. So the Astral Plane and the Other Side, it's all there. And it's an album where the lyrics match the music perfectly, which is quite special; because when they don't match the results can be at best pointless and at worst fucking awful. It goes back to the

"Iron Wheels" song; I put the lyrics into the song, they didn't go together, and people didn't notice them, so I reworked them into a folky ballad and people paid attention. It's impossible to over-state that a lyricist really needs the right vehicle for the right words.

On the »Metalhead« tour we were supported by a German band called Freedom Call, who were managed by (or at least were involved somehow with) Rainer Hänsel. The singer, Chris Bay, had played keyboards on »Metalhead« and they're really nice guys, doing that sort of melodic, power metal stuff. They recorded an EP called »Tarragon« and they asked me to narrate the prologue for this »Lord Of The Rings« type concept piece called "Tale Of Tarragon" which was quite good fun.

In 2001 we headlined the first Bloodstock indoor festival in the UK. We were kind of connected to Bloodstock anyway, in that Paul Gregory does our artwork, but basically they needed a headliner and asked us to do it and we agreed. Like the first of anything, it wasn't that well attended, and I don't suppose it really did anything for our profile in England at that time – preaching to the converted, really – but it was quite a good gig, we liked it, and it's a nice venue to play. We did Wacken the same year, and filmed it for the »Chronicles« DVD. We've played there several times, in fact; one of the early festivals in 1992, when Twisted Sister pulled out in 1999, the one we filmed for the »Chronicles« DVD in 2001, then again in 2004. They used to have this slogan 'no headliners' and we used to think 'are they stupid? The band that goes on with the biggest light show and at the best time of the night's the headliner…'

That particular Wacken show in 2001 though was quite stressful for us because although we were cooking, we were in the middle of recording the »Killing Ground« album at the time and went straight from the studio to the festival, which is not a good idea. But we went down a storm, and for the audience, the re-appearance of the Eagle made it special. The Eagle had been in the warehouse for years and years and years; I think the last time we used it was Hammersmith 1989. The Wacken people said they'd pay for it to be fixed up if we'd use it, and they also asked

Motörhead who were on the next night about using the Bomber so it became known as the »Bombers And Eagles« festival. (There had been a »Bombers and Eagles« tour before Wacken, when Saxon and Motörhead had toured Germany together, although that was without either the Bomber or the Eagle. Great tour though.) So the Wacken festival was the first time anybody had seen the Eagle in Germany since 1986 or so, and consequently it was a big deal for the fans. It was a bit like when Beckham scores the goal from a free kick: when the Eagle started to descend there must have been 40,000 cameras flashing. It was an unbelievable sight to see it from the stage. We were stunned. Everybody whipped out their cameras and bang! The whole stage was lit up by camera flashes from the audience. A bit of a moment, like a religious thing... The same thing also happened at the Earthshaker festival too. It's such a big thing (in more ways than one), that Eagle, a bit like the Eddie thing with Iron Maiden.

It was at this time that Rainer Hänsel started having personal problems. It's hard to explain Rainer's relationship with the band. He told everybody he was our manager but he wasn't, because I was managing the band at this time. He was certainly our German representative, and he was our record company as well, so as I said, it was a bit of a strange relationship. And then he fell in love; seriously in love. Now there's nothing wrong with that, however...

I must point out that I had some fantastic times with Rainer. He is such a funny guy. He was, however, always taking the piss particularly out of me and Doug because we'd stopped womanising – well, Doug had never started – so there he was, off shagging everything in sight and putting us down because we were in fantastic relationships. I used to tell him, 'when you fall, mate, you're going to fall the farthest.' And he did. He became completely besotted; he was totally gone. When it all went wrong, he was an absolute wreck, crying all the time and wanting to kill himself. The problem was that we were trying to work at this time. He had so much to do with our 'comeback' and he was a great friend to all of the band; but he was also this big macho guy who never loved anybody that when he did fall in love and it all went wrong, he just went to pieces. This went on for a year or so and it was affecting us and what we were trying to do. Eventually, things got so bad that in the end we had to leave him and focus on the recording of »Killing Ground«.

I like »Killing Ground«, in particular because of "Court Of The Crimson King". It was my idea to give it a go. People were like, 'are you nuts?' and to me it was just a matter of, 'let's try it; it'll sound fucking brilliant, believe me.' I did the vocals slightly differently to Greg Lake's original: the King Crimson version is quite 'level', there's not really much emotion in it, which is how it was in those days; the emphasis was on the instrumentation. I think we did a great version of it, and I certainly think we did the song justice. I like doing that. I like doing songs that people don't expect us to do. We might do a Robin Trower track one day. I'd love to do "Bridge Of Sighs" because I really do like it. What I would like to do, in fact, after »Inner Sanctum« is a very mixed album, with a couple of completely unplugged songs, a couple of songs with full orchestral backing, a couple of re-recorded older Saxon songs, a couple of covers and three or four new songs. If that comes off we'll probably give "Bridge Of Sighs" a go; if it doesn't work it'll never see the light of day and no-one will ever be any the wiser.

I had to stop managing the band at this point, because, logistically, it was getting too much. If you think managing a band is an easy job, then think again.

We'd already split with Nigel Thomas by the time he died. We tried a bit of a re-union thing on the »Tenth Anniversary Tour« and he was involved a little, but then he sued us so it was all really bad at the end. But I was sad when he died. Although he probably wasn't the right guy for us, he did try really hard to break the band. I just don't think he ever really understood what we were about. He was just too old-school for a band like us.

I managed the band from 1990 up until the »Killing Ground« tour. We had an agent, Nick Peel, who was a very good agent for us, and a lot of people in the business helped us, but we obviously lost the contacts with the top ten people as our profile went down. It's hard work trying to manage yourselves. It's all right when you are at a certain level trying to go up the first time around, but it became apparent at the time of »Dogs Of War« that we were becoming popular again and I was doing more and more and more work. Ever tried booking an American tour and flights and accommodation? It's a fucking nightmare, believe me. OK, I was successful at it, and I did learn a lot more about how the business works. I don't know if that's a good thing or not though, because nobody likes a wise-ass. You learn all these things from trial and error and new people coming in have to learn it for themselves, and although you can tell somebody that getting American visas is a nightmare, everybody thinks, 'oh, it can't be that bad, can it?' Yes! It is, as a matter of fact! It's a fucking nightmare. You can lose a lot of money if you make a mess of co-ordinating flights and venues and hotels.

We did a tour with Thomas Jensen and ICS. They'd been staging Wacken and wanted to move into other things outside of promoting festivals so we decided we'd give it a try and let them manage us. It was a bit of a learning curve for Thomas and the rest of the organisation. When someone's been managing bands for years they've got a certain routine that they'll do for all their bands, whereas when we gave Thomas Jensen the job he was completely new to it. He'd never managed a band before. He'd managed big events but not a band, and they are two completely different things; but the fact that we're more successful now than we were before 2001 shows that the partnership definitely works.

I mean, in a perfect world, we'd still be headlining everywhere, with the Eagle as well, but in a perfect world they'd be a record company still giving us money for tour supports as well. That all ended years ago. The old way of doing things was to get the record company to spend as much money as possible so they'd have to promote the fuck out of the band to get it back. That's the Nigel Thomas way of doing things, and that's definitely the way it was back when we started. The record company have to pay for everything, and then at the end of the day they have to sell the albums to get their money back. You can tell when a record company has spent a lot of money on a band and the album's not really happening; I'm sure a couple of U2 albums weren't as good as the ones before but the record company really went to town on the promotion and the advertising and the touring anyway, really blitzing it. The same probably happened with some of the latter-day AC/DC albums. And besides, it does actually work sometimes. EMI in particular sank a lot of money into us over three years and three albums and basically had to write it off as a bad debt. Obviously we technically still owe it to them, but I don't think they ever seriously tried to get their money back. That's the business for you.

»Heavy Metal Thunder« was something I'd wanted to do. The original plan was to re-record some of the old classics and give it away with the »Killing Ground« album; it was done as a limited edition with the first so many thousand of the CD, and in theory that was that. The idea was there because I wanted to give it away so that younger fans could hear the older songs performed by this band; and besides, I think it's nice to give things away, even though that's not the done thing in this day and age. SPV though really liked the idea and decided that they wanted to release it as an album in its own right. So, not wanting to be an absolute arsehole, I said that we'd give eight tracks away, and that they could have thirteen for the full album. I think we gave away about 25,000 copies with »Killing Ground«, and the full album version sold about 40,000 copies at first so there's 65,000 copies out there and it's still selling really well today. The good thing about »Heavy Metal Thunder« from the band's point of view is that it's replaced a lot of our back catalogue in radio stations which means that our early songs sound really good on radio now. The idea I had for the artwork was one of my best album covers, with the guy on the horse with the helmet, although I've often wondered if I should have held onto it for a different album. I told the record company to find out what 'Saxon' is in Celtic and the overall effect looked brilliant. The original image and poster is better because it's a bit lighter; the CD cover is too dark in my opinion. But I finally got my chance to call an album »Heavy Metal Thunder«

which is what I'd wanted to call »Strong Arm Of The Law« twenty years previously. »Heavy Metal Thunder« would have been a much better title for that album. But I finally got my way, which was cool; anything with 'heavy metal' in the title is good by me.

I like »Heavy Metal Thunder«; I like the album cover, I like the songs, I like the production. We tried to mimic the Eighties sounds as much as we could and I think it sounds all the better for it. And I think it closed a chapter on the past once and for all, clearing the way for our next album, which was 2004's »Lionheart«. Despite the fact that Kerrang! hadn't really said a good word about us in almost twenty years, the magazine amazingly gave it a 4K thumbs-up – that's four-out-of-five! It should have been the full five, really, let's face it; they just held back because it would stick in their throat to give us top marks. 'We've been such wankers to them in the past, we can't give them five. That would really make us look stupid. So we'll give them four instead.' Classic Rock magazine also awarded »Lionheart« four-out-of-five. Writing almost twenty-five years – *twenty-five years*! – since he gave »Wheels Of Steel« that five-star review, Geoff Barton called it 'the best home-grown hard rock album of the year,' and noted that 'all the great Saxon qualities are here.' Shame he didn't give us five-out-of-five, really.

Before we could record it, we needed to find a new drummer – again – and Nigel recommended Jörg Michael. I knew Jörg – or knew of him anyway – because he'd played in a band that supported us a few years before called, I think, Headhunter. By this time he was the drummer of Stratovarius, and had been with them for ten years or so but things weren't going very well in their camp; I think the guitarist needed a break like I did back at the end of the Eighties. Jörg was kicking his heels a bit, killing time, and he was an absolutely massive Saxon fan – in fact, a massive fan of the Eighties music. Before he went on stage he played this tape of Eighties stuff – you see, we keep coming across this 'everything was great in the Eighties' thing. We got him in to jam with us, just to see if we got on, and it worked out really well. He wasn't really intended to be the drummer full-time; at first we just needed someone to do »Lionheart«, so he learned the songs and he drummed the album. I thought his style on »Lionheart« was great; he mixed up a classic drum style with a modern feel and then went back into an Eighties thing, so if you listen to »Lionheart« most of the songs have got two or three drum patterns going on. To be honest, I found it a little bit strange at first but if you listen to it, it sounds absolutely fabulous. So he did bring something to the album although he didn't write any of the songs, which just goes to show how someone's individual performance can enhance a song even though they didn't actually contribute to its writing.

Getting Jörg into the band worked out well and was a very good move for us. He was also a name fans knew. He is really well known around the world, possibly not so much in America, but definitely South America, Latin America and Europe because Stratovarius are a very big name. He did the »Lionheart« tour which was very long, and he did a great job for us. Then when the Stratovarius people were trying to put their band back together he returned to them. I think I'm right in saying that in Stratovarius he is a much more active member than he was with Saxon; I think he'd been in Stratovarius from fairly early on so he is more involved with the business side whereas with us, of course, all he really had to do was play the drums. It used to frustrate the hell out of him that he wasn't organising or doing something. He's quite an all-rounder and I think the tour manager side of him was itching to get out. After the first three or so weeks he settled down and began to enjoy himself, although he was totally mystified why we never really got that rattled about planes and trains and things that didn't happen on schedule. He'd start getting really hyper, and one of us would have to say, 'it's all right, Jörg; it'll take off when it takes off.' I think he wanted to fix everything all the time and we were more, 'well, it's not broke so it doesn't need fixing. It'll be all right in a minute.' We even ended up with a phrase about 'having a Jörg moment' if someone panics or gets into a flap unnecessarily. Once he settled down into a more relaxed state of mind, I think he really liked being a part of the band, and, as I said, he left his mark on a fantastic album.

»Lionheart« wasn't an easy album to write though. I can remember walking into the room and saying, 'right; I'm going to do a song called "Lionheart" so come up with some fucking riffs to match it.' And they were like, 'Richard The Lionheart? What?' None of them are singers or lyricists. They do help me out from time to time, but it's mostly just when I'm bouncing ideas around so they're not vocal orientated and consequently don't always get the idea behind what I'm trying to do. So, for example, when I tell them I've come up with an idea for a song called "Battering Ram" (which in actual fact I did, although it didn't make the final cut on »Inner Sanctum«) they immediately think, 'he's lost his fucking senses (again).'

I don't think many bands could get away with writing a song like "Lionheart", and "Lionheart" is a great song. I think that where we score heavily is that, because I work quite hard with the rest of the band on the music, all the songs have to be great pieces of music first, and then I add the vocals and the melodies which take them to another level altogether. But I particularly remember "Lionheart" as it took us eight months to write that song. I was never happy with it. I kept kicking out the choruses and then the verses, because it just wasn't working, the band weren't giving me what I wanted. It was purgatory for me because they were writing these really great riffs but when I tried to work with them it was like, 'Lionheart, Lion... Shit!' The riffs just refused to fit with what I had in my head.

One of the problems is that once you've written a great riff (and "Lionheart" is a great riff), whenever you try and write anything similar, you fail because the comparisons with the original are inevitable. We were working a while back and the riffs were coming somewhere between "Lionheart" and "Crusader"; I just told Paul and Doug that there's no way we'd ever get away with a song like that because it's just so reminiscent of them. You can imagine how that goes down, when you tell your guitarists to come up with something completely different. It's really hard for them. Doug wrote the riff for "Lionheart" I think (I might be wrong, but I think its his), but every time he writes something with a similar shape everybody says, 'nah; you can't do that; that's "Lionheart", mate.' Or Paul will start off slowly and it's, 'nah, that's fucking "Crusader", that is!' You can't write another "Princess Of The Night", can you? If you start a riff like that, people automatically assume it's going to be "Princess Of The Night". You start a song, 'duh-duh-dum, duh-duh-da-dum' and everyone's going to go 'that's "Smoke On The Water"!' So if you come up with something definitive, you shoot yourself right in the foot, because you can never, ever, come up with anything similar. The way around it is to write really ambiguous, straight-forward rock riffs, but if you do that, you'll never come up with a classic song that stands the test of time. This game isn't easy, you know.

»Lionheart« isn't a concept album as I've heard people say. It's just an album where, lyrically, I was quite focussed on English themes. The music took me to topics like the witch hunts, Nelson and the man 'o' war thing… Again, the common soldiers' (or sailors', in this case) lot. So we ended up with a set of quite patriotic songs, and that's the only real link through the album. Obviously it goes a bit vague in places but I think "Witchfinder General" is still totally English, even if witch hunts did take place elsewhere; Salem springs to mind, but it was probably English settlers anyway.

Also on »Lionheart« is "Man And Machine", about Donald Campbell and his jet boat Bluebird. In January 1967 he tried to break his own water-speed record and we watched him die on TV; I saw it happen, I remember it clearly and it stuck in my memory, his craft flipping over and disintegrating. Afterwards they couldn't find his body. And all the bad taste jokes that followed – 'they've just found him, he's come out of a tap in Huddersfield'. But you've got to respect the guy; he gave his life for a speed record, for something he believed in, and I wrote a song about him. I think that what he did is a part of our history, and deserves to be recognised as such.

So the »Lionheart« album turned out to be particularly English – total George Cross music really – although I don't think I planned it that way. It's simply the way it came out and once again, because there was nobody like Graham Oliver behind the scenes doing his CIA covert bit, saying to everyone in the band, 'these lyrics are a bit shit, aren't they?; what do you think?', I was able to go where I wanted; as a lyricist I had complete freedom, and it's great to be able to work that way, without any restrictions. And in this case, the result was an unashamedly English album. Only Iron Maiden go into that same territory, especially in the early days with the Spitfire thing and "Die With Your Boots On" – that's very much the same sort of thing really so I suppose lyrically I would think that Maiden and ourselves do fly the flag actually, and we're not scared of writing lyrics about those things and not scared of being British. I am quite patriotic, and it's something I've noticed more since I moved to France; it's bizarre really – I feel more English now I live abroad! That said, we've never been restricted in what we write about. I originally had some ideas for a song about the Twin Towers, but it eventually evolved into "Red Star Falling" about the demise of Communism. Maybe we'll go back to the Twin Towers theme one day; it depends if we can come up with something that does justice to the victims' memory. "Dallas 1pm" was a good effort to capture what it's like when something dramatic happens. Peter Gabriel had a song slightly after that about the shooting of Governor George Wallace in Alabama and he got a lot more press out of it than we ever did with "Dallas…", but I think ours is a better song. Obviously we used more of a rock medium to convey our message and weren't as radio friendly.

We really did spoil ourselves with »Lionheart« because we took a year to write that album; not totally, but we did keep coming back and back and back. It's all about quality control and it's all about crafting the song. "Lionheart" itself is very crafted. It's got some very nice parts in it, coming in and out of different tempos and different themes. The original version was just full-on, so it was nice to have the time to be able to sit back and change things around to make the song more interesting. With »Inner Sanctum«, we were much more up against it because our management had already booked the tour and dates stretched well into 2007. So we had a deadline, and we really were a bit to the wall with it, but that wasn't such a bad thing either as it kept us focussed on the task in hand. It's nice to have the luxury of time so that you can listen to the songs and do the 'through the wall' test (where you can sit in the living room with the music playing in the kitchen and if any of the songs seriously get on your tits after a week you change them or knock them off altogether) because when you're in the rehearsal room writing songs, your perception and your judgement can sometimes get a little skewed: everything sounds fresh and original and great. You really need to step back and have space. On »Inner Sanctum« we didn't have that luxury; but, like I said, we were focussed: when you're going at it full-on, it can be just as good a way of working because you know time is precious and you are so switched on that things just flow.

Besides, if we're ever recording a song and I don't like it, we'll kick it off the album anyway, or I'll just say that we need to rework it. Charlie Bauerfeind gets a couple of days off, and we go back to basics to see why the song's just not working. We didn't used to do that, which I regret, but I feel we have to now. The spotlight is on everything we do, and I often feel that there are people out there just waiting for us to screw up.

It's all about quality. As you get older you're supposed to get better, but at the same time I feel you do lose a certain edge. So you have to try and keep that edge which is why, for example, we opened »Lionheart« with "Witchfinder General". The natural way of doing it would have been to play on the whole epic thing and kick off with the title track, but I wanted to start the album with a 'fuck me!' opener, back in the tradition of "Heavy Metal Thunder" and "Motorcycle Man". I like to open albums that way. Sometimes the first track is lost; people don't really listen to it. They don't start paying attention till the second or third song. But to me that opening track is everything. If you haven't got the listeners in that first four-and-a-half minutes, you're screwed as far as I'm concerned. With that first track, I really believe you have to make a statement; and that statement, to my mind, should be, 'fucking hell!' Try it some time. It's really empowering.

Chapter Twenty-Two

*A*s I said, we never really lost touch with Nigel Glockler. He'd pop up every so often, and when we played London on the »Lionheart« tour in October 2004, he joined us onstage for "747 and "And The Bands Played On". And of course, once Jörg rejoined Stratovarius, we were minus a drummer. Again.

The idea to play a set of older songs originally came from Germany and the magazine Rock Hard which was involved with the Judas Priest tribute album. Saxon was on their first ever cover back in 1981 or so. They decided to do a sort of Eighties rock disco thing and thought it might be a good idea for us to do a tour, just once, featuring just songs of the Eighties. I mean, we've done a lot of albums since then and a lot of people want to hear the new songs; and when we've written a new album we obviously want to play the new songs. So this would give us a chance to play all the Eighties songs that we don't have time to play on our regular tours, and it seemed like a good idea. We started in Germany, playing material just off the first four albums, and it was really successful. Word got about and people started posting on the internet that they'd like to see it done in the UK so we decided to do one show – at the Astoria, in London – and then a few more shows were added as it started to snowball. Later on, of course, people started posting that they wanted to hear some »Lionheart« songs so you can't fucking win really!

As I said, we didn't have a drummer and we ideally wanted Nigel back, and because this »Nights Out With The Boys« tour was purely Eighties songs, we felt it was a good point for Nigel to rejoin. We didn't actually have it in mind that Nigel should rejoin the band again on a full-time basis, but we thought it would be a good idea for him to play the old songs really so that's what we asked him to do; join us for the Eighties tour and see what happens. It was the perfect tour for Nigel to do really because it was reliving what was a really good time for the band, there was no real production to the show, and he wouldn't have to learn any new songs. It was good fun, and it brought him back in at a good time. He 'ummed' and 'aahed' quite a lot about it but we worked on his girlfriend and he finally agreed to do it, which also meant we didn't have to audition anybody else.

The original plan for the tour was early in 2005, but the dates had to be shelved when our house in France burned down. From the off, although it was a tragedy for us, it's worth pointing out – because there's been so many rumours doing the rounds – that it was not arson, and none of my family was injured. The only casualty was our son Sebastian's hamster, which was upsetting for Sebastian (and pretty upsetting for the hamster as well).

Sue and I went to bed as normal and I woke up about 4am or so – honest to God, someone shouted 'wake up!' in my sleep – to find the room filling with smoke. We got the kids up, got down the stairs, and bundled them, the dogs, the guinea pigs and the unfortunate hamster into the car. The fire had started in the attic, and as it was an old timber-framed farmhouse, flames were dropping through the ceiling onto the old circular stairwell. A couple of minutes more and that would have gone, and then we would have been in serious trouble.

It had been pissing down all week, but that night a strong wind kept the rain off and fanned the flames beautifully. As we tried to drive off the car sank in the lawn so Sue and I had to get everyone out and into the other car, and then we set off to some neighbours, another English family who'd only recently moved in, and knocked them up.

Sue's attempts to alert the fire brigade in pidgin French while panicking appeared to be successful, until they called back about ten minutes later to ask in broken English exactly what the problem was.

'OUR FUCKING HOUSE IS ON FIRE!'

Once we'd got over the language barrier, the fire brigade were great. They're all volunteers, and they did everything they could, retrieving as much as they could from the ground floor when the upper stories burned. I went back and watched, watched them working as our house burned down. It's not a pleasant thing to see, and I just kept consoling myself with the thought that things could have been so much worse. It started to snow that night as well, which added to the feeling of disconnection, the feeling that none of this was real.

The ruins kept re-igniting for a while, but when I went back two or three days later there was a smoke alarm, lying there in the ash, still bleeping. It's funny what you remember of things like this.

We moved into a gîte for a while, and were told it would probably take the best part of a year to sort out the insurance. As the kids were getting older, we'd been looking at getting a bigger place, and were quite interested in a place we'd seen which was now owned by an architect who was living in Australia. I 'phoned him up to say that because it would take so long to sort out the insurance, we were withdrawing our interest in the property, but he said he had a better idea. 'Why don't I take it off the market, you move in now, and then buy it when the insurance is sorted out.' Just like that. So we took him up on his offer, and lived there for about a year, paying no more than a token rent, before we finally bought it. It's great when people come through for you like that.

I lost a lot of personal stuff in the fire; I suppose the photo albums and things of sentimental value from my parents were the worst, because they're the things you can't replace. It was very sad, but at least we're still alive to tell the tale. The fire brigade concluded that it was either an electrical fire or a spark from the chimney – what they call a 'sinistre'; a calamity or disaster. These days we've got fire escape ladders and smoke alarms all over the place; we're so safety conscious I almost walk around with one on my back! But the twins still freak out if a smoke alarm battery starts to run down and bleeps a warning.

The tour finally took place later in 2005 and, as it was so successful, in 2006 we came back to the UK for a second set of Eighties shows, playing six dates (well, including one in Dublin). The tour was billed as »Dayz In April 2006« and was probably the last time we will ever play a set consisting entirely of older songs. We can't keep on repeating it. I mean, it's great that people still want to hear the old songs, but we literally just don't have time to play them. You can't play everything, we'd be there all night otherwise. There's some old favourites we obviously play regularly, like "747" and "Wheels Of Steel", but we don't normally play things like "Backs To The Wall", "See The Light Shining", "Suzie Hold On" (which is another big song of ours that people seem to like) and "Stallions Of The Highway" off the first album. We've sold a lot of copies of the first album now yet we very rarely get chance to play anything from it so it was great to be able to do three or four off that as well. As for how we chose the songs, I pretty much went through my head to work out what we hadn't played for a long, long time, and there's a couple of songs we've never played live. I've got a few cassettes from the Eighties, and of course on, say, the »Wheels Of Steel« tour we were only playing stuff of the first album and »Wheels Of Steel«. To make things more interesting, we widened the scope to include songs off »Power And The Glory« and »Crusader«, and as the tour kicked off in London on April 23rd 2006, we also dropped in "Lionheart": what better place is there to play "Lionheart" than London on St Georges Day (besides, I thought we'd better do it before some do-gooder banned St Georges Day on the grounds of political correctness). So as far as we're concerned, we've done it now; time to move on. Our star is definitely rising again. We've been working really hard for the last ten years or so to really go for it. And it's worked. We've been bringing back more and more older fans to the fold and we've brought in a lot of new fans too. And I think this is because the last four albums have been of a really high quality. People like that: they realise that we still care about what we do. I mean, realistically, we could release any old shit and still get our advance, but it's important to us to release class material. And I really believe that we do; even now, even after all these years, we really do care about what we do.

After those dates a summer of European festivals stretched out in front of us, from Italy to Spain to Bulgaria. We'd been invited to play a festival in

Dubai and that would have been really cool; we've never been there before so we were all looking forward to it. Then an Arabic newspaper decided that the lyrics to "Crusader" were against the Arab Muslims and the invitation was pulled. They missed the point that "Crusader" is just an historic song, written from the point of view of a young Englishman seeing the knights go on crusade and wanting to join them. That's all it is. It's pretty much like the American Civil War – you know, young men running off to fight for the South or the North – or the First World War; young men going off (or being encouraged to go off) to fight for their country, and thinking that it's all a big adventure until they find out that the thought of war is much better than the reality. As far as the Crusades went, I think it was all very even anyway. It swept backwards and forwards, backwards and forwards, and I think Saladin probably had the upper hand in the end, but to be honest, does it really matter? It's just a song about what I think it would have been like almost a thousand years ago. I guess I half expected it to happen. It's a sign of the times, and the same thing happened about ten years ago when we were going to play in Turkey. It's very easy to pick a song and take the lyrics out of context, and their translation of the lyrics into Arabic was pretty awful anyway. The lyrics were taken out of a musical context and put in a political context. It wasn't written as a political statement, and saying that we're racist because of the lyrics is just plain silly. We could just have easily written a song about Saladin and the Saracens, but we're an English band and I write historical lyrics and from an English perspective. The only really political songs we ever write were anti-establishment songs, anti-being fucked with. Our historical songs don't have anything to do with that. Religion comes into it in some ways, I suppose, but that's because history, conflict and religion are all interwoven. Fucking good job they didn't hear "Lionheart" really.

The summer of 2006 saw the release of the long-awaited »The Eagle Has Landed III« – like the title? I thought of it all by myself! – live album. We had thirteen shows' worth of material to choose from, and in keeping with the 2005 and 2006 Eighties gigs, divided the album into a CD of earlier songs, and a CD of later material. Before the year was out, it was joined in the record shop racks by a re-issue of the original »The Eagle Has Landed«. This was the first time EMI had approached me about any of our back catalogue re-issues, and they made a nice job of topping the original album up to CD length with some additional tracks, purportedly from Hammersmith shows in either 1981 or 1982. I still maintain that there were no out-takes from the original album because of the way the tapes were cut, and some of the bonus songs were originally included on the »Wheels Of Steel«/»Strong Arm Of The Law« re-issue, but it's still quite a nice package all the same.

That summer also saw us getting involved, rather bizarrely, in a TV programme for Channel 4 television in the UK. We had an email from the production company owned by Bob Geldof about a series of programmes in which famed promoter Harvey Goldsmith takes a look at one act each programme and tells them what they're doing wrong. The pitch for us was to look at why Saxon aren't so big in the UK any more, when we are massively popular everywhere else in the world (aside from Dubai). It's not reality TV but fly-on-the-wall stuff in which he comes along to see what's wrong and then fixes it. Goldsmith came out to see one of the summer festivals, and then the TV company put on a free secret gig in a club in Lincolnshire – 'Harvey Goldsmith presents a mystery band' – in front of a fairly young audience. A lot of fans found out about the gig afterwards and weren't too happy that we hadn't publicised a UK show, but we'd signed a contract saying we'd keep it secret. Anyway, we came on, opened with "Witchfinder General" and the place erupted: two hundred kids pogo-ing up and down. It was absolutely fantastic.

Next up, they asked us to send three new songs to be worked up by two hotshot producers as a single. The one they chose, "If I Was You And You Were Me" (a song about gun and knife crime), wasn't really representative of the album, so we went to London to record it with them. The whole thing was tied into a big PR operation, and culminated in a gig in January 2007 at Sheffield City Hall (promoted by the big man himself) and the airing of the TV programme.

We just rolled with it. The way I saw it, we had nothing to lose (apart, maybe, from some dignity). Besides, all our UK fans tell us we should be bigger in our home country than we are, so who knows; maybe in the long run this will raise our profile in the UK once more. I don't mind looking a bit foolish if that's the outcome.

Chapter Twenty-Three

O ver the years, there have been great times, and there have been fucking struggles. But it's all been worth it, in the long run. I'm very content with the way things are, which actually is not a good thing for a singer writing lyrics. I've said to the rest of the band on a number of occasions, 'you're a right bunch of miserable happy bastards, you lot. You're not giving me anything to work with!' I was so deeply involved with Rainer Hänsel and his stormy relationship, I was so close to it that a lot of great songs came out of it like "You Don't Know What You've Got" and "Prisoner"; "Yesterday's Gone" off »Dogs Of War«, all those kind of songs are taken from my experiences and the experiences of other people around me. So I tell the band that they need to have some really bad problems because then I can write about them. They're going to have to tell me they're innermost fears, to be immortalised in some Saxon lyrics. I tend to write more songs about war and things when I'm happy; to write a good, personal, song you have to be really pissed off yourself or able to capture somebody else's fears, sorrows and anxieties, so it's no good to me if everyone's bloody happy-clappy around me.

Are there things on reflection that I would have done differently? Of course there are. Certainly I wouldn't have agreed to having my balls gaffa taped in when my spandex split just before we went on stage. The show must go on, but getting the spandex off afterwards was fucking agony. But yes, looking back now, with the benefit of hindsight, I'd say, if pushed, that my greatest regret in a musical sense would be signing with Carrere Records and not holding out for a better deal. But life is so interwoven with different paths and one thing fires off another thing which fires off another thing, and maybe we wouldn't have written »Wheels Of Steel« if we'd signed to Warner Bros or EMI or any other bigger company. You meet people along the way who influence what you do and what you say, and if you change one thing in the past you can well end up changing everything, and I'm quite happy with things as they are. I certainly regret working with some of the producers we've been saddled with in the past, and I certainly regret having to do everything too quickly in the Eighties. At the time I didn't like it, the way we were rushed into writing albums because we thought that if we sold 200,000 to half-a-million albums then at least we should be OK for a year and could have a rest, sit back and enjoy ourselves. But it was work, work, work, and I regret not being stronger in the Eighties and saying to the management, 'fuck you! We're not doing that. We need a break.'

Has my life changed me? Yes, I suppose it has. Back in the Seventies, I was just a typical 'Yorkshire lad' – a cheeky bastard, really. A long-haired kid wanting to be a professional musician. Up to that point we were pretending to be professional, although the fact was that we were on the dole, playing some gigs and thieving things along the way, with an aspiration to write songs; great songs, ones that would stand the test of time. And of course I had no responsibility, because I had nothing. As you acquire things you acquire responsibility, you know, like houses, and furniture and cars. Back then I was just with the rest of the guys living a gypsy lifestyle, sleeping in the back of the van with no responsibility. Some of the guys were married, don't forget, so obviously they had their own problems with that lifestyle, but I wasn't so I was completely footloose and fancy free, trying to write memorable songs and get laid. The highlight of those early days was the sex probably; we went from like trying really hard on Friday and Saturday nights to get laid to not really having to try too hard at all to get laid all the time. That's the biggest bonus of being successful. The low point was not getting laid on Friday and Saturday nights! We were young guys, and that's all we were interested in. Sex, fast cars, playing rock 'n' roll... What else is there? I mean we were quite happy with that.

The biggest difference now though is that I can see through the bullshit because I've now been in the business over twenty-five years. I know that, for some people, that's nothing. Some have been in the business fifty years, or longer. I hate to think what people like Frank Sinatra had in their heads after being in the business for what, sixty years or whatever. It must be mind-boggling. God knows how many tales Ian Gillan must have to tell. And steering through the early part of your career, it's just so hap-hazard really, bumping into this and banging into that, and doing this and doing that just to get to a point where you are able to do what you actually want to do musically.

The thing is with music, it's really not age-related. I know in the UK they try to make it an age thing, but in fact music is actually timeless, ageless; it's the people like me that perform it that get older! I mean, "Wheels Of Steel" is just as relevant a song now as it was in 1980 to some people. But the difference in me is that I was a naïve young man back then and I thought that everybody was my friend, there to help me out. And I guess in some respects that's still the same. I don't think you ever lose that naivety; either you are born without it or you're stuck with it. I still think that I am quite naïve in some respects, and, to be honest, I quite like that.

But you have to become much harder. You build up walls that you didn't have or didn't think you needed when you were younger. I had to become more private than I was naturally. I think that in the early days everyone knew everything about us, but now I want to hold some of that back. In the Eighties, even though I was quite a known person, I never felt I needed a security fence around the house, things like that; but we had no privacy, none at all: especially me. We were massive, we were on TV all the time, and I was a celebrity (whatever one of those is) so I do know what it's like for people who want privacy and can't get it. That sort of thing does affect you, having people climbing up your drainpipes and looking through your curtains and stuff like that. If I wanted to do anything that involved other people, I couldn't really, because I was recognised immediately. I couldn't even go shopping. I'm not saying that it wasn't great, because it was – let's be honest! – but if I wanted some privacy, if I wanted to have a shag on the sofa, I had to make sure that there wasn't anybody peeking through the window first. It was all a bit surreal, that whole Eighties period really. It was almost like we were blasted into another world, and being the singer I was blasted further into it, because that's the way of the singer. It goes with the territory, and I was always willing to take that on. So it was a great time, but that's a difference in me, a change from being a naïve guy friendly with everybody to somebody who wants some privacy, some intimate moments that aren't being shared with everybody else. And that's a big change. Also, technically, I'm more experienced now and in the last few years in particular I've become a better performer, particularly in the studio where I've learned to focus my voice more, rather than just screaming my bollocks off.

But having said all that, maybe I'm the same person that I always was with just a different perspective, because this life-style definitely changes your perspective. My passion for music certainly hasn't changed, though. I'm going to keep on going and going and going now, as long as anyone's interested, and as long as the old machine keeps going. I mean, you have to stay quite fit and on top of things. As for my epitaph… I don't know; I'd have to leave that with other people. Not Paul though, who once suggested, 'he went out on a high note.'

I don't really want to write my own epitaph, to tell you the truth. I don't even think I need a gravestone – I'll just let them feed me to the dog. I don't even know whether I want to be burned like a Viking or buried, or what. I haven't decided yet. There's something to be said for both – whether to be eaten by worms and maggots or burned and have your bones crushed in a grinder. I still think they should let you burn yourself in the garden. You know, you're feeling a bit ill, so you build a pyre, and as soon as you snuff it they chuck you on top and burn you. Or send you out into the river in a boat with all your worldly goods to be sent to the bottom of the lake. Or cryogenically frozen: buy a chest freezer and stick me in there. I guess that's the trouble with death – none of the options are particularly fantastic. I do believe though that there is something there, something beyond this life. I suppose I am a bit of a spiritualist if truth be known: a Church of England Methodist spiritualist. There: I've got all bases covered!

The most important lesson life has taught me is the power of positive thought. I once met somebody in America who gave me my birth stone, which is some purple thing which I still have, and who said to me, 'if you imagine things to happen that are good, then they will happen.'

Fair enough. Whatever. But I started to try it in various different things, and I think it does work. Not in all circumstances, admittedly, but in some situations it does work. That's positive thought, and I'm actually a big believer in it. I think you can use it to turn your life around. I think that's what life's taught me; always the glass is half full, and when something bad happens, there's always something good that can come from it. I'm a strong believer in that. I've been through a lot of bad situations, and come through. I think it's like a power that permeates through everybody. If people are negative, it can ruin their lives, but if somebody is positive, it can really help you though. Put two negative people together and the results are fucking horrendous. If you get one negative and one positive person together, they can kind of balance each other out. I know I sound a bit like a wacko, but that's what I believe.

Humour is a big part of being in this band. We do spend hours laughing our heads off on the tour bus or wherever so comedy plays a big role. It helps with the fuck-ups and the waiting too, because in this game you spend your whole life waiting: waiting to go on stage, waiting to go on a plane, waiting to get off, waiting to get to your hotel; so one of the in-jokes is, 'looks like someone's booked some waiting time for us.' And on the surface you can maintain this 'nothing fazes you' mood but inside you are actually seething because you've wasted so much time. That side of the business is fucking awful. Occasionally, one of my neighbours (none of them really has a clue what I actually do) will ask something really innocent like, 'what did you do at the weekend?'

'I went to Brazil.'

'Really?'

'Yeah, I went to Brazil on Friday and came back Saturday.'

'Were you working there?'

'Yeah, we played for thirty minutes and came straight back.'

There's no other job in the world where you'd fly to Brazil, play at a festival for half-an-hour and fly all the way back. I mean, why would you do that? But after a while you get totally blasé about it. And doing two gigs in one day – we played at a festival in Milan and then had to get to Germany to headline another one, with a horrendous journey between the two, and then the next day you're back at home watching the TV. A lot of people think it's so glamorous, but you go to Brazil, and people ask, 'did you see the jungle?'

'Yeah, I saw it from 40,000 feet. It looked really great as we flew over it!'

Yes, you do get time to sightsee, but me and Paul in particular have seen it all before so a lot of the time now we just stay in the hotel or meet some fans. It is fantastic to travel the world and we are so lucky to have been able to go to all these countries. But it's not glamorous, and no band will ever tell you it is. It's the most tedious thing, driving everywhere on a fucking bus with sixteen people farting and snoring, or hanging around waiting to fly. Someone should write a book on all the things you can do while waiting. All airports are geared for waiting. They get you there early just so you can shop. You never get on the plane till the last minute anyway.

I've never been excited about travelling. I hate it actually. When you are a seasoned traveller, all you want to do is get on the plane, get some sleep or listen to some music, or have a little chat, and get to the other end. I really am jealous of people who can get on a plane and just fall asleep. Thomas, our manager, as soon as we get on a plane he goes straight to sleep. We used to put a paper bag on his head and draw silly faces on it and he doesn't notice at all; he's completely out of it. (In fact, he's fallen asleep in the car while I've been talking to him. He just goes, just like that.) There I am on a plane with sleeping tablets, headphones on and towels wrapped around my head, lying down and praying for sleep, and he's there 'zzzzzzz'! I just can't sleep on planes at all. Then when everybody gets off, they're all, 'yeah, fucking-go-for-it!' and I just want to go to the hotel. And it's like, 'what's up with Biff? Is he upset?'

'No! I'M FUCKING TIRED! I'VE BEEN ON A PLANE FOR FOURTEEN HOURS WITH NO FUCKING SLEEP WHATSOEVER!' But people don't expect that. What they expect is for you to be buzzing – 'yeah! Fucking metal!' – but sometimes I just don't feel like that. I've been on a plane all that time and not slept at all, and before that I've been hanging around in an airport for four hours before the fucking thing even took off, being herded around like sheep. Is it any wonder I hate flying! And then what happens? I get whisked off to do an interview, and I'm sat there, totally relaxed, and I nod off.

I can't see how anyone over the age of ten can get excited about flying. Even the pilot must hate it! He's probably thinking, 'oh fuck; not again! Fucking thing flies itself anyway; why am I here?' On a number of occasions we've flown to America and have slept in the same hotel as the flight crew and I've been with a few stewardesses – naughty girls, stewardesses! The pilots used to tell us that before they handed the plane to the next crew they'd hide the porno mags which they used to pass the time. And the pilots would party like crazy all night and have a flight the next morning so they must have been all over the sky, completely pissed up and hung-over.

The other thing on the road, which a lot of people don't realise, is that you have to make sure you have a life, because sometimes with sixteen people on a bus it's inevitable that they're going to clash. There's only so much space on a bus, and so the bunk is the inner sanctum. It's your sanctuary. You sleep in there, you wank in there, you listen to music in there; that's your space. There's a place for partying and a place for quiet. It's quite difficult for people to live together like that and sometimes the choice of a new band member comes down to how well you can all live together, rather than how good they are on any particular instrument; if people don't have respect for other people's space it will cause big problems. There are a lot of different things that come into the equation of being in a rock band; everybody has to get on, and sometimes that's quite hard.

And sometimes it's fucking impossible!

But everything just revolves around those two hours on stage… It's like winding a clock. All through the day you're winding the spring up, all through the day, and then when it gets to nine o'clock you pull the pin and it goes bang! for the next two hours. And then the next day you start winding that spring again. That time you are on stage, it's so frenetic, such an explosion of energy, that you can't be like that twenty-four hours a day – unless you're either touring with or a member of Mötley Crüe! And after the gig it can be quite wild for a while because there's still a bit of power left in the spring, and that has to wind itself down before you can start all over again.

Normal people, those not fucked up by music, just don't get it. But believe me, when all's said and done, it is a fantastic job.

It's definitely better than working.

Saxon
Discography

1979 »Saxon« LP

1979 »Big Teaser/Stallions Of The Highway« 7"

1979 »Backs To The Wall/Militia Guard« 7"

1980 »Big Teaser/Rainbow Theme/Frozen Rainbow« 7"
Re-issued as part of the 'Heavy Metal' box series

1980 »Backs To The Wall/Militia Guard« 7"
Re-issued as part of the 'Heavy Metal' box series

1980 »Wheels Of Steel/Stand Up And Be Counted« 7"
limited edition with free badge

1980 »Wheels Of Steel/Motorcycle Man« 7"
German 7" single in different sleeve

1980 »Motorcycle Man/See The Light Shining« 7"
Japanese 7" single

1980 »Wheels Of Steel« LP

1980 »747 (Strangers In The Night)/See The Light Shining« 7" (12" adds "Stallions Of The Highway" live)

1980 »Suzy Hold On/Judgement Day (live)« 7"/12"
A-side mis-spelt on 7" version, and cover picture printed back to front

1980 »Monsters Of Rock« LP

live album from Castle Donington
Saxon contribute "Backs To The Wall" on LP; cassette adds "Freeway Mad"

1980 »Strong Arm Of The Law« LP
Originally issued in gatefold sleeve
US version in black sleeve
New Zealand version on red vinyl

1980 »Strong Arm Of The Law/Taking Your Chances« 7"/12"

1980 »Heavy Metal Thunder« 7"
Japanese 7"

1981 »And The Bands Played On/Hungry Years/Heavy Metal Thunder«
7" and 7"picture disc

1981 »Never Surrender/20,000 Feet« 7" (plus free single »Bap Shoo Ap live/Street Fighting Gang«)

1981 »Denim And Leather« LP (also released on blue vinyl)
New Zealand version on red vinyl

1981 »Princess Of The Night/Fire In The Sky« 7"

1982 »The Eagle Has Landed« LP (also released as a picture disc)

1983 »Power And The Glory« LP (also released as a picture disc)

1983 »Power And The Glory/See The Light Shining

(live)« 7", 7" poster bag and 7" picture disc (12" adds "Denim And Leather" live)

1983 »Warrior« 7"
Spanish 7"

1983 »Nightmare/Midas Touch« 7" & 7" picture disc (12" adds "747 (Strangers In The Night)")

1984 »Sailing To America/A Little Bit Of What You Fancy« 7"/12"

1984 »Crusader« LP (also released as a picture disc)

1984 »Do It All For You/Just Let Me Rock« 7"/12"

1984 »Do It All For You/Just Let Me Rock«
French 7" in different sleeve

1984 »Rock City« 7"
Spanish 7"

1984 »Bad Boys« 12"
Italian 12"

1984 »Greatest Hits – Strong Arm Metal« LP
The first of many Saxon cash-in compilations; German version with different sleeve

1985 »Back On The Streets/Live Fast Die Young« 7" & shaped picture disc

1985 »Back On The Streets« 12" extended version/"Live Fast Die Young" & "Back On The Streets" 7" version

1985 »Innocence Is No Excuse« LP

(also released as a picture disc)

1986 »Rock 'N' Roll Gypsy/Krakatoa« 7" (poster sleeve) and 7" picture disc (12" adds "Heavy Metal Thunder Medley")

1986 »Broken Heroes/Give It Everything You Got« 7"/12"

1986 »Waiting For The Night/Chase The Fade« 7"

1986 »Waiting For The Night« 12" extended version/"Chase The Fade" & "Waiting For The Night" 7" version

1986 »Rock The Nations« LP

1986 »Rock The Nations/747 (Strangers In The Night)« 7" & shaped picture disc (12" adds "Waiting For The Night" live; also available in clear vinyl)

1987 »Northern Lady/Everybody Up (live)« 7" (12" adds "Dallas 1pm" live)

1988 »Ride Like The Wind/Red Alert« 7" & shaped picture disc (12" adds "Back On The Streets" live)

1988 »Destiny« LP/CD (first Saxon album to appear simultaneously on CD)

1988 »I Can't Wait Anymore/Broken Heroes (live)« 7", 7" pouch pack with poster and discography & shaped picture disc

(12" adds "Gonna Shout" live)

1989 »Rock 'N' Roll Gypsies« LP/CD

1990 »Greatest Hits Live!« LP/CD

1991 »Solid Ball Of Rock« LP/CD

1991 »Requiem (We Will Remember)/Altar Of The Gods« 7" & shaped picture disc (12" and CD-s adds "Reeperbahn Stomp")

1993 »Iron Wheels/Forever Free« 12"/CD-s

1993 »Forever Free« LP/CD UK version on Warhammer with different sleeve

1995 »Dogs Of War« LP/CD

1996 »The Eagle Has Landed Vol II« CD

1996 »Donnington – The Live Tracks« CD First issue of much-disputed live album from 1980 Monsters Of Rock festival; Donnington mis-spelt

1996 »Legends Of Metal« (Judas Priest tribute album) Saxon contribute "You've Got Another Thing Comin'"

1997 »Unleash The Beast« CD

1998 »BBC Sessions/Live At Reading« CD BBC sessions from 1980 and 1982, and edited live set from Reading 1986

1999 »Metalhead« CD

2000 »Diamonds And Nuggets« CD A collection of early demos and out-takes

2000 »Live… In The Raw« CD

2001 »Killing Ground« CD

2002 »Live In Nottingham« CD Part of a series of gigs by various artists recorded for TV

2002 »Heavy Metal Thunder« CD & picture disc LP

2004 »Lionheart« CD

2006 »The Eagle Has Landed III« CD

Odd Items Of Interest

1980 »Wheels Of Steel« LP Japanese promo with different sleeve

1983 »Savage Return« live bootleg LP

1983 »Red Line« live bootleg LP

1984 »Heavy Metal Thunder« live bootleg LP

1986 »Rocking Again« 7" single free with Sounds music paper

1986 »Interview« bootleg LP

2005 »Eagleution – A Tribute To SAXON« CD

Note that making, selling and trading bootlegs is illegal – but they are fun to collect!